INTIMATE ENEMIES

Moral Panics in Contemporary Great Britain

INTIMATE ENEMIES

Moral Panics in Contemporary Great Britain

Philip Jenkins

ALDINE DE GRUYTER

NEW YORK

About the Author

Philip Jenkins is Professor of Criminal Justice at Pennsylvania State University. His major research interests focus on the means by which social problems are constructed and presented in politics and the media. Specifically, this has meant exploring such issues as terrorism, serial murder, organized crime, child abuse and satanic or "ritual" crimes.

ALDINE DE GRUYTER
A division of Walter de Gruyter, Inc.
200 Saw Mill River Road
Hawthorne, New York 10532

The paper used in this publication meets the minimum requirements of American National Standard for Information Sciences—Permanence of Paper Printed Library Materials, ANSI Z39.48-1984. ∞

Library of Congress Cataloging-in-Publication Data

Jenkins, Philip, 1952–
    Intimate enemies : moral panics in contemporary Great Britain / by Philip Jenkins.
        p.   cm. — (Social problems and social issues)
    Includes bibliographical references and index.
    ISBN 0-202-30435-3. — ISBN 0-202-30436-1 (pbk.)
    1. England—Moral conditions—Public opinion. 2. Crime—England—Public opinion. 3. Cults—England—Public opinion. 4. Sex customs—England—Public opinion. 5. Child abuse—England—Public opinion. 6. Public opinion—England. I. Title. II. Series.
HN400.M6J46   1992
306'.0941—dc20   92-7171
                                                       CIP

Manufactured in the United States of America

10 9 8 7 6 5 4 3 2 1

Was it a friend or foe that spread these lies?
Nay, who but infants question in such wise?
'Twas one of my most intimate enemies.

Dante Gabriel Rossetti, *Fragment*

Contents

3   *Sex Beasts and Serial Killers*

4   *Preying on Children:*
    Pedophilia and Child Murder

Preface

The idea for this study can be traced to 1986, when the British news media were carrying almost daily headlines of violence, sexual abuse, and assault directed against children and, to a lesser extent, adult women. It was, of course, possible that there had been a genuine upsurge of such criminal attacks, but it also seemed likely that the reporting represented a sudden discovery and exaggeration of phenomena that had long been in existence. In other words, the affair offered a classic case study of what in sociological theory had come to be known as a moral panic.

Over the following years, there emerged a number of very threatening stereotypes, which culminated in the 1990 stories of the pedophile murder ring, the bogus social workers who stalked and abducted children, and the satanic rings that were said to abuse or even kill children in a ritual context. These stereotypes (the satanist, the serial killer, and so on) had been the focus of my research and teaching interests for many years, and the British events offered a unique opportunity both to explore the roots of such panics and to understand American conditions from a comparative perspective. In addition, the concatenation of events in particular years, like 1986, suggested that these apparently new problems were somehow linked in ways that have not often been addressed in the literature. This book represents my attempt to explain the construction of the particular problems and the crucial interdependence between them.

I would like to acknowledge the generous assistance of several individuals who have provided information or sources, or who have suggested directions for the study. Prominent among these have been Stefan Fabian-Marks, Gita Faux, Dan Maier-Katkin, and that excellent scholar, Bill Thompson. I owe particular thanks to Joel Best, and in fact it is difficult to imagine that the book could have appeared without his assistance.

As always, I owe my greatest debt to my wife, Liz Jenkins.

Approaching Social
Problems

— 1 —

SOCIAL PROBLEMS

In the last three decades, sociologists have paid much attention to the nature and construction of social problems, and there is a continuing debate about the objective reality of perceived threats. There are essentially two very different approaches. The first, more familiar view can be termed *objectivist*. This accepts that a particular phenomenon exists and constitutes a problem by virtue of causing harm or disturbance to a significant section of the society. The role of the social scientist might be to quantify that problem, to explore its roots, and perhaps to investigate possible solutions by which the problem could be removed or ameliorated.

The second view may or may not accept that the phenomenon exists or, if it does, whether it is indeed harmful; but such questions are subsidiary to the more fundamental issue of how and why the condition or event comes to be viewed as a problem. Following recent practice, this approach will be termed *constructionist*. For a constructionist, "our sense of what is or what is not a social problem is a product, something that has been produced or constructed through social activities" (Best 1989:xviii). From this perspective,

A social problem is a condition which is defined by a considerable number of persons as a deviation from some social norm which they cherish. Every social problem thus consists of an *objective condition* and a *subjective definition*. The objective condition is a verifiable situation which can be checked as to existence and magnitude (proportions) by impartial and trained observers. The subjective definition is the awareness of certain individuals that the condition is a threat to certain cherished values. (emphasis in original; Fuller and Myers 1941:320)

1

For a constructionist, this subjective definition is critical. To take a current example, for an objectivist, there *is* a drug problem because many thousands of people suffer from the effects of illegal drugs, which cause untold harm to the society and economy. For a constructionist, the drug problem is very complex. There are social reasons why certain substances rather than others are designated illegal drugs, and the degree of harm to the individual is only one criterion among many. Other factors include the symbolic value of the substances for various social and ethnic groups, the needs and agendas of bureaucratic agencies, and the electoral usefulness of wars on crime. It is also difficult to know the actual prevalence of the use of drugs, and many of the figures quoted are unsubstantiated and probably exaggerated. These uncertainties become all the greater when they are extrapolated to assess the degree of harm to the nation as a whole. The problem is a matter of public perceptions, and it is socially constructed.

For a constructionist, it is impossible to define a problem in an objective or value-free way, as to name a problem or crisis ipso facto implies that there is a solution: that is, that change of some kind is necessary or desirable. For example, in the nineteenth and early twentieth centuries, much was written about a "Jewish problem" or "Jewish question," and many contributors to the debate asserted their well-intentioned sympathy to the interests of the Jewish people. However, by presenting their arguments within these terms of reference, they were implicitly accepting the agenda of their overtly antisemitic opponents. It was similarly difficult to address the "drink problem" without accepting in some measure the Prohibitionist agenda. As many so-called primitive peoples have long realized, the act of naming a thing gives a person symbolic control over it.

Within the general area of constructionism, there are important questions of degree (Spector and Kitsuse 1987; Schneider and Kitsuse 1984). For a strict constructionist, it is unnecessary and perhaps impossible to know the objective reality behind a problem:

> The strict constructionist is not interested in assessing or judging the truth, accuracy, credibility, or reasonableness of what members say and do. . . . the theoretical task is to study how members define, lodge and press claims; how they publicize their concerns, redefine the issue in question in the face of political obstacles, indifference or opposition; how they enter into alliances with other claims-makers. (Kitsuse and Schneider 1989:xii–xiii)

A contextual constructionist holds what is perhaps a more moderate position, and seeks first to examine the plausibility and factual basis of the claims made in order to support the reality of a problem. However, there is then the same concern about the processes by which the problem is constructed, brought into the arena of public debate, and used to shape matters of policy.

Debates over the nature of social problems often take the form of case studies, which customarily address "new" problems. These may take the form of a sudden upsurge of public and media concern about an issue like drug abuse, drunk driving, or the sexual exploitation of children. An objectivist scholar may well believe that a genuinely new situation has arisen: Either a new form of aberrant behavior has emerged, or else an existing form of deviance has become more common or more extreme in its manifestations. Any objectivist researcher would therefore seek to understand the reasons for this increase in deviant behavior.

In contrast, a constructionist would argue that social problems are rarely a novel as they sometimes appear (Best 1989, 1990). Behaviors like the use of violence against children or the elderly are endemic in society, until they come to be perceived and defined as new problems with a name such as "child abuse" or "elder abuse." The task of the sociologist is to determine the social, political, and bureaucratic forces that lead to this new recognition and definition. These forces should be understood not as a response to a genuine problem, but as a symbolic campaign that may reflect the interests of particular movements and pressure groups, regardless of the objectives basis of the alleged danger. The three key areas of research involve the *interests* that particular groups have in promoting a problem, the *resources* available to them, and the *ownership* that they eventually secure over the issue, or the degree to which their analysis is accepted as authoritative (Best 1990:11–13; Gusfield 1981).

The distinction between objective and subjective views is not absolute, in that it is virtually impossible to be a complete objectivist: No scholar is likely to accept the reality of each and every problem as popularly defined in every society. To take an obvious example, there are few contemporary academics who would examine the roots of a "witchcraft problem" in the seventeenth century, except in terms of public reaction to a largely imaginary menace. To some extent, we are all constructionists.

EXPLAINING WITCHES

On the other hand, there are many possible explanations for the manufacture of a particular problem, and one critical question concerns the definition of *interests*. There is a distinction in the literature between those who see a new problem or panic as useful for society as a whole, or some substantial part of it; and those who stress the role of some smaller unit—a group or even an individual. This latter view draws on the conflict tradition in sociological theory: It emphasizes that some groups have far more power than others, and consequently have much greater ability to impose their views through legislation.

To take the case of witchcraft once more, the classic study by Erikson (1966) offered a social perspective on the generation of a panic. This suggested that the Salem witch trials resulted from a profound crisis within New England society, which was riven by social and political conflict. Following Durkheim, this analysis proposed that the witchcraft menace was effectively created by the community in order to provide an outside enemy against whom "normal" society could untie. "The deviant individual violates rules of conduct which the rest of the community holds in high respect; when these people come together to express their outrage over the offense and to bear witness against the offender, they develop a tighter bond of solidarity than existed earlier" (Erikson 1966:4). Since the 1970s, the emphasis in studying "witchcraft problems" has shifted largely toward a feminist analysis, but the panic is still seen in terms of generalized fears and anxieties of a large part of the population (Karlsen 1987).

Others, however, took the same evidence to focus on the role of much narrower interest groups. Chambliss, following the Marxist tradition, agreed that the new witch problem was artificially generated, but not by "the community" at large. Instead, he stressed the usefulness of witchcraft in a class-polarized society, where traditional elite groups were under political threat. It was these groups, especially the Puritan clergy, who generated the panic to promote their immediate interests and their broader ideological position. Erikson thus neglected "the important role crime plays . . . by enabling the ruling stratum to maintain its privileged position" (Chambliss and Mankoff 1976:15–16). Scholars were attempting in various ways to deduce the interests underlying the making of claims.

Both the Durkheimian and Marxist traditions came to be applied in understanding other problems and panics. Chambliss's emphasis on the role of elites has, for example, been followed by Moore (1987). In *The Formation of a Persecuting Society*, an examination of the phenomenon in early medieval Europe, he showed how powerful interest groups could over a few decades generate a terrifying series of threatening stereotypes, including not only witches but also Jews, heretics, and lepers.

Such historical case studies were much employed in the 1960s and 1970s, in part to provide a historical foundation for contemporary debates over issues like drug legislation. Among the most important works was Joseph Gusfield's *Symbolic Crusade* (1963), which sought to explain the temperance movement in nineteenth-century America in terms of the Weberian concept of "status defense." In this view, once-prominent ethnic and social groups found their position increasingly challenged, and supported temperance as a symbolic issue that would allow them to reassert their power and their values through legislation: "Status issues function as vehicles through which a non-economic group has deference conferred upon it or degradation imposed upon it. Victory in issues of status is the symbolic conferral of respect upon the norms of the victor and disrespect upon the norms of the vanquished" (Gusfield 1963:174).

Gusfield's view has been influential on some contemporary studies of present-day pressure groups who agitate, for example, against drugs, abortion, or pornography (Zurcher and Kirkpatrick 1976). On the other hand, the idea has been challenged. Other current scholars see less need to go beyond the ostensible moral justications provided by participants in such movements: "There is no reason to believe that an increasing disparity between the standards of morality and behavior which one has grown up to believe were true and right and those displayed and legitimated in the surrounding society can not *of itself* provide the ground for the commitment to a movement of moral reform" (emphasis in original. Wallis 1977:197).

THE ROLE OF INTEREST GROUPS

Gusfield's approach echoes Erikson's to the extent that he located the cause of the movement in broad issues of social structure and community tension. Other scholars argue that more attention should be paid to the specific individuals or relatively small groups that generate particular problems, and the appropriate legal or bureaucratic responses. In this view, some problems at least are defined "from above," and might be strongly political or partisan in their origins. This position *can* shade into conspiracy theory, but it is often valuable. When Gerassi (1968) explored a homosexuality panic in an American city, his explanations did not involve ill-defined anxieties or unease requiring the reassertion of moral boundaries, or the defense of social status. Instead, he placed the events firmly in the context of local factional conflicts, and cynical attempts to stigmatize enemies by exposing their personal sexual lives.

A classic definition of this position comes from Becker, who emphasized the role of one particular individual in the formulation of American narcotics policy on the 1930s:

Wherever rules are created and applied we should be alive to the possible presence of an enterprising individual or group. Their activities can properly be called "moral enterprise" for what they are enterprising about is the creation of a new fragment of the moral constitution of society, its code of right and wrong. (Becker 1963:145)

This is usually known as *moral entrepreneur* theory. A related view of interest group politics emphasizes the role of bureaucratic agencies, seeking to expand their influence and resources by focusing public attention on perceived problems that fall within their scope of activity.

MORAL PANICS

In the early 1970s, the British sociological profession was becoming increasingly radicalized, and ideas like labeling, interactionism, and deviancy theory were often giving way to New Left and Marxist ideas. There was great interest in matters like the making of law and the changing definition of crime and deviancy, and the recent American literature on scares, problems, and symbolic crusades was avidly read and applied to British conditions.

The concept of *moral panic* was defined by Stanley Cohen (1972) in his study of juvenile movements in Britain in the early 1960s. After seaside fights between gangs of teenage "mods" and "rockers," British media and politicians had reacted with a massive outpouring of concern and indignation. For Cohen, this was a not uncommon pattern:

Societies appear to be subject, every now and then, to periods of moral panic. A condition, episode, person or group of persons emerges to become defined as a threat to societal values and interests; its nature is presented in a stylized and stereotypical fashion by the mass media; the moral barricades are manned by editors, bishops, politicians and other right thinking people; socially accredited experts pronounce their diagnoses and solutions; ways of coping are evolved or (more often) resorted to; the condition then disappears, submerges or deteriorates and becomes more visible. Sometimes the object of the panic is quite novel, and at other times it is something which has been in existence long enough, but suddenly appears in the limelight. Sometimes the panic is passed over and is forgotten except in folklore and collective memory; at other times it has more serious and long

lasting repercussions and might produce such changes as those in
legal and social policy or even in the way society conceives itself.
(Cohen 1972:28)

For Cohen, like Durkheim and Erikson, panics served to reassert the
dominance of an established value system at a time of perceived anxiety
and crisis, and folk-devils provided a necessary external threat (compare
Pearson 1983).

Again, we find in Britain a similar dichotomy between explanations
based on social anxiety and on more specific interest group politics. The
latter view was represented in the work of Hall et al. (1978), in their
classic study of the creation of a British "mugging" problem in the early
1970s. They shared Cohen's basic definition:

> When the official reaction to a person, groups of persons or series
> of events is *out of all proportion* to the actual threat offered, when
> "experts," in the form of police chiefs, the judiciary, politicians and
> editors *perceive* the threat in all but identical terms, and appear to
> talk "with one voice" of rates, diagnoses, prognoses and solutions,
> when the media representations universally stress "sudden and
> dramatic" increases (in numbers involved or events) and "nov-
> elty," above and beyond that which a sober, realistic appraisal
> could sustain, then we believe it is appropriate to speak of the
> beginnings of a *moral panic* (emphases in original).

In this more explicitly Marxist perspective, however, the moral panic
had to be understood in its political context. Mugging arose in 1972 at a
time of severe economic crisis and soaring unemployment. Increased
social fears thus helped justify police actions against the "reserve army
of the unemployed," against the young, poor, and black; while barely
veiled racist rhetoric served to divert the working class from united
action. This moral panic at least had many tactical uses for the political
elite.

Moral panic theory has been extremely influential in Great Britain. It
has been applied more recently to concern over "baby-battering" or
child physical abuse (Parton 1979, 1981, 1985a), to AIDS (Vass 1986;
Porter 1986), to British "dole scroungers" or welfare cheats (Golding and
Middleton 1982), and to the domestic heroin "crisis" of the early 1980s
(Pearson et al. 1987). Pornography campaigns and censorship have been
fruitful sources of material in this area, notably the attempt in the early
1980s to close sex shops and to ban violent "video nasties" (Barker 1984;
Taylor 1987; Thompson 1989, 1990). Cohen's theories of social anxiety

and boundary reaffirmation also influence British studies of urban legends, which have become a flourishing genre (White 1979, 1982).

However, the moral panic concept has been criticized in several ways. For instance, the key work of Hall et al. (1978) was attacked over the issue of the concern being "out of all proportion" to the actual threat, the "objective condition." It has been argued that rates of violent crime, including the ill-defined offense of mugging, were in fact rising sharply as the claims-makers argued, and thus the problem was not as subjective as initially claimed. Also, the term *moral panic* was used in a polemical and ideologically selective way: "It seems virtually inconceivable that concern expressed about racial attacks, rape or police misconduct would be described as a moral panic" (Waddington 1986:258). Moral panic "has become a form of sociological shorthand or insult to throw at societal reactions to everything from soccer hooligans to welfare scroungers" (Thompson 1990:1).

There has also been movement away from the more Marxist analyses of the 1970s. Ben-Yehuda (1985, 1990) has been significant in taking moral panic theory in the direction of American interest group theories, which draw on both Gusfield and Becker. Thompson, for example, emphasizes the growing pluralism of European societies, and the increasing potential for value conflicts between social groups. These trends are reflected in a proliferation of moral panics:

> As an overt claim to the superiority of one lifestyle over another is unlikely to be tolerated by people who prefer another, social groups turn to moral enterprise to enhance their life-styles against other groups. They can do this because styles of life are not exclusive: there are numerous common facets: Consequently, all that needs to be done is to identify a threat common to a majority of life-styles and beliefs. (Thompson 1989:3)

There is also more concern with understanding the ways in which a panic is generated or perceived, such as the rhetoric employed to promote ideas, and the use and abuse of statistics and examples to support claims. Also crucial are the means by which claims come to be expressed through the media, and the wider relationship between the media and the making of policy. These factors all contribute to the process of typification, the decision to view a problem in one way rather than another: for example, classifying drug abuse as a criminal justice issue rather than a medical one, with all that implies for possible solutions.

BRITISH PANICS OF THE 1980s

Studying a moral panic may well have intrinsic interest, but it also illuminates the values, fears, and conflicts of the community, which apparently needs to imagine such an external threat. Observing the construction of conspiracies and problems therefore provides a powerful tool for social analysis. If, in fact, a society can be understood in terms of its fears and folk-devils, then Great Britain in the last decade offers a rich mine for social scientists.[1] There have since the late 1970s been repeated scandals and public panics focusing on different types of sexual predators, who targeted women and especially children. The image of the male predator had several facets—the rapist, the serial killer, the child molester, the ritual or satanic child abuser, and the child murderer—but as the 1980s progressed, the different stereotypes became increasingly intertwined.

Moreover, the threats appeared to grow more serious in various ways. The alleged number of perpetrators steadily increased; molesters and killers were more likely to be found within the family circle, as opposed to solitary outsiders; the harm purportedly inflicted on victims was conceived in ever more harrowing terms. The emphasis generally shifted from the lone criminal to the organized group of offenders, perhaps with prestigious connections in politics or law enforcement.

The phenomena themselves were scarcely new. Child abuse and serial murder have been familiar throughout the present century, while satanism has been spasmodically denounced by the mass media since at least the time of Aleister Crowley ("wickedest man in the world") in the 1920s. It can be argued that Britain was one of the first societies to experience a very modern scare about extreme violence, with the panic over the Ratcliffe Highway murders of 1811 (James and Critchley 1987); while London in 1888 was the scene of the Jack the Ripper case. What has been different about the last decade is the sheer scale of media coverage concerning the alleged events, and the extent to which the offenses were believed to represent a very widespread threat that could affect almost any family. In turn dangers attracted attention from legislators and law enforcement agencies, who advocated draconian solutions that undermined traditional concepts of due process justice. The intensity of public concern was more than sufficient to justify the term *panic*.

The goal of this book is to describe and explain these various perceptions of social menace, and to understand why they arose at the time they did. It will be argued that the British experience offers strong support for the constructionist theory in general, and affirms the value of the methods characteristic of that approach. In each case, we find a number of influential claims-makers, each with a set of interest or a political agenda. There is evidence for the role of all types of moral entrepreneurs and interest groups: individuals, pressure groups, and bureaucratic agencies, with a complex and often shifting pattern of alliances between them.

The work of Cohen drew attention to the underlying fears and social anxiety said to have give rise to the panic over the mods and rockers. The present study will place more emphasis on the role of interest groups, but deeper social factors provided the essential context for their work. The examples in this book thus tend to support interest group interpretations of moral panics and social crusades, though some evidence will be offered for the role of the politics of anxiety. As might be expected, the observed reality is rather more complex than might be suggested by any single theory.

SYMBOLIC POLITICS

Most of the panics described here were concerned with threats to children, an emphasis that can be explained in terms of the recurring issue of symbolic politics. Claims-makers often drew attention to a specific problem in part because it symbolized another issue, which for one reason or another could not be attacked directly: what might be described as the "politics of substitution." There were in the 1970s groups who wished to denounce and stigmatize moral offenses such as homosexuality or the sale of pornography, or religious deviations such as satanism. They could achieve little support for these views in the prevailing moral climate, which emphasized the freedom of consenting adults to determine their private moral conduct.

However, shifting the focus to children's involvement fundamentally changed the moral and legal environment, as by definition children could not legally give informed consent to sexual activities. Adding children to the picture made it impossible to claim that actions were "moral," "victimless," or "consensual" offenses. In the 1980s, therefore, we find morality campaigns directed not against homosexuality, but pedophilia; not so much against pornography in general, but child pornography; not against satanism, but against ritual child abuse. In each case, the claims-makers raised the stakes by arguing, first, that real physical harm resulted from these offenses, and second, that the crimes were the work of organized groups. Children were not only ritually abused, they were sacrificed; they were not only photographed nude, or molested by pedophiles, they were murdered. And in each case, the perpetrators were tightly-knit conspiratorial gangs, child sex rings, or devil-worshipping covens.

This process of escalation was discussed in the work of Hall et al. (1978), who see it as part of a "signification spiral, . . . [a] *self-amplifying sequence within the area of signification*: the activity or event with which the signification deals is *escalated*—made to seem more threatening—within the course of the signification itself" (emphases in original; p. 223). The authors postulated the existence of "certain thresholds which mark out symbolically the limits of social tolerance" (p. 225). These proceeded from the lowest level, of mere "permissiveness," to the higher thresholds of legality, and ultimately of violence. In this view, deviant acts are likely to be signified as involving a high threshold in order to permit official sanctions, so that a permissive act like tolerating pornography will be depicted as leading to acts of illegality and violence:

> The higher an event can be placed in the hierarchy of thresholds, the greater is its threat to the social order, and the tougher and more automatic is the coercive response. . . . One kind of threat or challenge to society seems larger, more menacing, if it can be mapped together with other apparently similar phenomena— especially if by connecting one relatively harmless activity with a more threatening one, the scale of the danger implicit is made to appear more widespread and diffused. . . . As issues and groups are projected across the thresholds, it becomes easier to mount legitimate campaigns of control against them. (pp. 225–226)

The focus on children meant that deviant behavior automatically crossed a higher threshold of victimization than would have been possible if adults alone had been involved.

A number or rhetorical devices are involved in this process, but one of the most frequently used is what the authors call "convergence":

> Convergence occurs when two or more activities are linked in the process of signification as to implicitly or explicitly draw parallels between them. Thus the image of "student hooliganism" links student protest to the separate problem of hooliganism—whose stereotypical characteristics are already part of socially available knowledge. . . . In both cases, the net effect is amplification, not in the real events being described but in their threat potential for society. (p. 223)

THE INTERDEPENDENCE OF PANICS

Problems and panics were closely connected to each other, so that it is essential to understand them as an interlinked complex rather than as single incidents. Hall et al. (1978) discuss this process as part of what they perceive as an inexorable movement toward the authoritarian state required to defend a capitalist order in terminal crisis. In the early 1960s, there were "discrete moral panics" addressing social or moral issues, often "the result of local organizing and moral entrepreneurship" (pp. 221–222). These led in a few years to "crusading—mapping together discrete moral panics to produce a speeded up sequence", in which we find "an increasingly amplified general threat to society". Finally, there was a "general panic about law and order" by the early 1970s, in which minor forms of dissent were characterized as components of the wider threat.

This scheme has been criticized as overly teleological. It also under-values the various social and moral movements by depicting them as concealed or unwitting elements of the "real" political dynamic. How-ever, it is important in emphasizing the linkage between panics within a broad historical framework; and this provides an impressive contrast to some case studies that treat the origins of a particular scare or problem in isolation. The present study finds no support for the political processes suggested in the earlier Marxist account; but it provides strong confirmation for viewing panics as interdependent. Problems come "not single spies, but in battalions."

The issue of interdependence is not frequently discussed in the social problem literature, though it is a powerful theme in Best's *Threatened Children* (1990). This similarly studies a complex of phenomena, includ-ing child sexual abuse, missing children, child murders, and Halloween sadism; and in each case, a similar cast of claims-makers was at work. Taken together with the various British case studies, this American account suggests a number of reasons why panics should appear to emerge in groups rather than singly. These can be summarized under three broad headings: the continuity of personnel in the claims-making process, the heightened awareness of generalized dangers in the after-math of a successful panic, and the cumulative nature of problem construction.

The issue of claims-makers requires little explanation, as very few political or moralist campaigners are interested in only one cause or topic. There is a natural tendency for activists who have been successful in exploiting one fruitful issue to employ similar rhetoric and examples in related causes. Also, they bring to the new campaigns the enhanced prestige and public visibility acquired through earlier movements. It is not therefore surprising to find the same individuals or groups active in leadership roles in several movements more or less linked by themes such as children's issues or decency. In the United States during the 1980s, we find John Walsh as a prominent leader in the causes of missing children, child murder, child pornography, and victims' rights; in Great Britain, Geoffrey Dickens emerged in the same years as a crusader in precisely the same range of areas, in addition to denouncing satanism and ritual abuse.

Meanwhile, the success of one campaign might predispose the public to accept claims put forward in a like area, while popular fears and anxieties are enhanced. This is important because it helps to explain how several intense panics appear to strike a community within a very short time. In the United States, the period from mid-1983 to early 1985 witnessed the height of public and media concern about loosely linked menaces such as serial murder, child sex rings, child abduction, and ritualized child abuse. In Great Britain similarly, panics appear to have been grouped together in particular years and even months, with 1986 the year par excellence of perceived dangers from sexual killers and child abusers. (This pattern may be observed in the rough chronology of major events appended to this chapter.) This synchronicity can often be explained in terms of a few highly sensational incidents that are interpreted as parts of a generalized social menace. Subsequent events or scandals are often linked to this broader trend, however tenuously, and their significance is amplified through the connection.

Problems may appear to be defined and publicized in a remarkably short time, and they become especially visible during what are often perceived as periods of crisis. However, tracing the formation of such problems usually requires a much longer perspective, and it is essential to take account of the influence of other issues and movements during this time of gestation. Problem construction is a cumulative or incremental process, in which each issue is to some extent built upon its predecessors, in the context of a steadily developing fund of "socially available knowledge." As Best remarks,

> As an acknowledged subject for concern, a well established social problem becomes a resource, a foundation upon which other claims may be built. Rather than struggling to bring recognition to a new problem, claimants may find it easier to expand an existing problem's domain. These new claims take the form [new problem] X is really a type of [established problem] Y. (1990:65–66)

To take one instance in this book, it would be impossible to understand the British ritual abuse panic of 1989–1991 without tracing its roots in at least three originally separate scares of earlier years. These acted as essential precursors, though at the time they appeared to have little connection with each other. At a minimum, a comprehensive account would need to consider the concern over child sexual abuse within the family (1985–1987), the issue of pedophile sex rings (1987–1989), and the alleged wave of child murder cases (1986–1990). We would also need to appreciate the lateral dimension, that is, panics that were under way more or less simultaneously and that helped form popular thinking on menaces to children during 1990. These would include the bogus social workers case, and the panic over child sex "snuff" films, believed to record the actual murders of children, perhaps following sexual acts.

None of these incidents should be seen in isolation from the others, and the later panics would not have had the force they did if they had not built upon earlier memories and preconceptions. Each, moreover, grew out of other issues and problems over the previous decade. In other words, the British experience indicates the necessity of an approach to social problems that is at once holistic and historical in nature.

THE BOOK

It will be argued that the panics of the 1980s must be understood in their broader social and economic context. Chapter 2 will sketch major changes in British society in the last two decades, which have had a profound impact on the organization of the traditional family. Many more women now live independently of men, and far fewer children live at home in traditional nuclear families. Tentatively, many possible consequences might be proposed. Women living alone are more likely to be concerned about the threat of sexual violence, and more sensitive to the existence of pornographic material that may enhance the likelihood of sexual assault. There is therefore a larger and more receptive constituency for both feminist and moralist claims in this area.

Attitudes to children are likely to be affected, in that women might suffer conflicting expectations between traditional roles and contemporary realities. Guilt about leaving children unattended or in day care might be reflected in increased concern about threats to the young, and an urge to offer whatever protection was possible. In this—and many other areas—the claims-makers had a good deal of preexisting anxiety on which to build their case.

This chapter will also describe the politics of morality in contemporary Britain, and the role the local and national party politics in creating the panics of the 1980s. Party conflict in this decade had been deeply affected by matters of gender and sexual identity: To stigmatize the evils of homosexuality and to denounce "man-hating feminists" was in effect to attack the Labor party in its urban strongholds like London. This identification was at its height during 1986, which may go far to explaining why this was such a year of panics. The political context further encouraged the largely conservative British press in its campaigning zeal against homosexuals, pedophiles, and other associated evils. In Best's terms, large sections of the media were willing to offer the resources necessary for claims-makers to present their views.

Social and moral issues have been central to political debate in contemporary Britain, reinforcing the familiar feminist statement that "the personal is political." However, this had many consequences for the ways in which problems were presented and interpreted, and these issues will repeatedly be encountered in the following pages. Many of the interactions and conflicts that became central to controversy occurred in an intimate or family setting, and by definition were not readily susceptible to observation or quantitative study. Statistics could be obtained, for example, by survey evidence, but there were many pitfalls in interpreting this type of material. In addition, policy reactions required interventions in personal or family life, actions that might easily be regarded as intrusive or oppressive in nature. The problems of this era were especially vulnerable to weakly substantiated claims of prevalence, while official responses were likely to be profoundly controversial.

Chapter 3 will examine the success of feminist attempts to typify rape and serial murder as components of a general threat of sexual violence (see the appendix for a chronology of events and claims) The term *sexual violence* was expanded to include all forms of sexual assault, which were linked in an unbroken chain that led ultimately to the multiple homicides of the Yorkshire Ripper. This campaign was at its height between about 1978 and 1982, and it succeeded in large measure in securing the ownership of these issues for feminist experts and authorities. Also, typification implies solutions, or at least the directions in which solutions might be sought; and the new classification implied that the problem of extreme violence could only be cured by fundamental reforms in social and sexual attitudes, by economic reform, and by a general acceptance of the feminist political agenda.

However, the problem had other dimensions and other active interest groups. The development of the serial murder issue was also assisted by the desire of police agencies to create national structures and large computerized databases at a time of controversy over police powers and civil liberties.

The focus on serial murder and serial rape enhanced public awareness of possible linkages between apparently unrelated crimes. This perception would be central to the new concepts of pedophilia that emerged during the decade, which are discussed in Chapter 4. A series of incidents and investigations encouraged the typification of pedophilia as a criminal threat rather than a medical problem, and promoted the idea of organized pedophile conspiracies.

The turning point here was a harrowing incident in Brighton in 1983 in which a group of men raped a small boy, providing a notorious example cited for years by claims-makers. Investigations into possible serial child murders changed the image of pedophilia into a still more threatening stereotype, of the child sex ring, which killed its victims after exploiting them sexually. The theme of child pornography recurred throughout this panic, culminating in a 1990 case said to involve the making of snuff films and videos.

But even the most lethal predatory strangers were perhaps less frightening than the image of the abuser within the home. Chapter 5 examines the changing ideas of child abuse from the 1960s onwards, and especially the shift of definition from 1980 toward an emphasis on sexual rather than physical abuse. This will be explained in several ways: in terms of the influence of feminist theorists and pressure groups; of charities and interest groups, above all, the National Society for the Prevention of Cruelty to Children (NSPCC); and of the bureaucratic needs of social service agencies.

Assisted by the much-misunderstood evidence of opinion surveys about the prevalence of abuse within the family, a panic was under way from 1985–1986 onwards. One consequence was the creation of agencies and units with a full-time responsibility for detecting and combating child abuse. This naturally tended to increase abuse statistics, which further raised public consciousness of a threat. Extensive legal changes soon revolutionized the position of children in the courtroom.

Sexual abuse appeared to be uniformly distributed regardless of region and class. This was ideologically significant for feminist claims-makers, as it confirmed their basic tenet about gender rather than class being the major determinant in sexual exploitation, which could not thus be seen as a product of family dysfunction. This view was supported by new pediatric theories about the diagnosis of sexual abuse. If accepted, these appeared to give objective scientific validation for suggestions about the ubiquity of sexual abuse, and of the most harmful nature. As with sexual violence, the typification of sexual abuse lent support to the feminist political platform.

Chapter 6 will describe what may have been the logical consequence of earlier trends, when one region claimed to find evidence of mass intrafamilial abuse, and began the extensive removal of children from their families "for their own good." This Cleveland affair of 1987 created vigorous and acrimonious debate about the nature of child abuse and the reality of the current panic.

Opinion became polarized, and two stereotypes emerged. For supporters of the idea of widespread child abuse, the problem was symbolized by the incestuous father, effectively protected from retribution by the skepticism of "patriarchal" police agencies, media, and politicians, all refusing to believe children's testimony. For critics, the chief folk-devil was the interfering social worker, probably a rabid left-wing feminist, determined to shatter the family unit.

These stereotypes culminated in the ritual abuse affair, the origins of which are discussed in Chapter 7. This emerged partly out of the emphasis on organized abuse (the pedophile sex ring) and partly from concern over mass abuse within the family. The idea were combined in the form of groups of adults forming rings to exploit their children, with a ritual or satanic setting added either from genuine belief or else to make children's reports sound ludicrous. The issue of belief was central here. Before the 1960s, nobody had suspected widespread child physical abuse, but a series of harrowing cases seemed to prove its prevalence. Extensive sexual abuse had been unsuspected before the 1980s, but now its existence was an article of faith for many. Ritual abuse represented a third stage in what was almost an evolutionary process, and to question the charges (to exhibit "denial") was to betray children.

Ritual abuse offered a rich opportunity for religious and fundamentalist groups, anxious to promote their beliefs by an assault on satanism. The theories originated in fundamentalist circles, but by 1989 social workers were disseminating these ideas through their professional journals; so the resources available to religious claims-makers expanded significantly. Satanism ceased being typified as a religious or moral problem, and because a social work and criminal justice issue: It thereby moved into the realm where legal intervention became possible.

Chapter 8 describes what occurred when social service agencies began action upon these frightening new theories, and started to uncover what they believed were satanic child sex rings. The charges were discredited in several courts, and by 1991 the whole structure of accusations had collapsed. The press once more denounced the social worker as at the same time an incompetent and a credulous fanatic. Atrocity tales abounded of disrupted families and children seized from their homes by heartless officialdom.

The various panics involved a complex interplay of beliefs and interests. Chapter 9 explores the different interest groups active in these years, and the means by which they presented their ideas to the public. The rhetoric of the various claims is analyzed, and the factors required for the generation of a "successful" and influential panic are described.

Comparative studies in the construction of social problems have not been abundant: In a recent collection (Best 1989), only one of thirteen essays addressed comparative or international issues. A concentration on American conditions and problems can lead to the neglect of the very similar phenomena that were occurring at the same time in other countries, and this can tend to exaggerate the distinctiveness of American conditions. One might attempt to explain the creation of a problem by domestic or local conditions and political realities; but such an explanation would be seriously weakened if similar events were happening simultaneously and independently in another country.

Chapter 10 considers the parallels between the British and American panics of these years, and considers the powerful influence of American moral entrepreneurs and interest groups. The chapter also compares the mobilization of opinion on such issues in Britain and the United States, and suggests some reasons why panics evolve differently in the two political settings. The chapter will therefore be addressing, in however meager and tentative a form, questions that have played so important a role in modern approaches to comparative sociology.

THE MASS MEDIA

Describing the problems of the 1980s will inevitably rely to a large extent on the evidence of newspapers and broadcasting, and it is necessary to describe briefly the structure of the British media. Specifically, we must address the question of whether changes in the press coverage of issues during the decade illustrated authentic developments in popular beliefs and sentiments, or whether they merely reflected new patterns in the ownership or commercial outlook of the media (From the lively literature on the contemporary state of the media, see, for example, Seymour-Ure 1991; Soothill and Walby 1991; Chippindale and Horrie 1990; Philo et al. 1982; Whitaker 1981; Cohen and Young 1973.)

Undertaking research in Britain is facilitated by the strong tradition of national news coverage, which results in large part from the unquestioned dominance of London over "the provinces" (that is, the rest of the country). There are provincial and regional papers of some distinction, like the *Yorkshire Post, Western Mail,* and *The Scotsman;* but most local stories of any interest or significance whatever will soon be picked up by one of the national daily or Sunday papers. In this sense, it is very difficult to speak of "local" stories in a British context, as the concerns of Cleveland or Cardiff, Exeter or Rochdale, so rapidly find themselves projected on the national stage. This tendency is reinforced by the broadcast media, where there are effectively four national television networks.

Traditionally, national daily newspapers covered a broad spectrum of journalistic traditions, from the tabloid or yellow press approach of the *Daily Mirror*, the Sunday *People*, or *News of the World*, to highly conservative and meticulous reporting in quality dailies like the *Times*, *Guardian*, and *Daily Telegraph*. The *Times* stood at an extreme here, and was so conservative that it resisted placing major news stories on the front page until the mid-1960s. In the middle stood the *Daily Mail* and *Daily Express*, which were popular mass readership papers but eschewed the sensationalism of the tabloid papers like the *Mirror*.

However, the whole world of the print media was transformed during the 1970s. Rupert Murdoch's new daily newspaper the *Sun* enjoyed enormous success by adopting an aggressively down-market style of presentation, including material that in the United States might have been thought more appropriate for supermarket tabloids like the *National Enquirer* ("Werewolf Seized in Southend" was an actual front-page headline from the *Sun*). The *Sun* presented a heavy diet of sex, scandal, violence, and right-wing populism, with a cavalier attitude to older standards of journalistic accuracy and ethics (Seymour-Ure 1991; Soothill and Walby 1991; Chippindale and Horrie 1990). This approach forced other papers to pursue similar tactics. Several adopted a tabloid format, while the *Daily Mirror* imitated the *Sun* device of portraying nude or topless models under the title of "page three girls."

Both papers enjoyed enormous success. By 1990, the *Sun* had a daily circulation of 3.7 million, with annual profits of some $100 million. The major Murdoch Sunday newspaper was the *News of the World*, with a circulation of 4.8 million; and the two Murdoch tabloids probably reached some 12 to 15 million readers. Murdoch's major rival was the international media empire of Robert Maxwell, which operated the *Daily Mirror* (3 million circulation), *Sunday Mirror* (2.8 million). and *People* (2.4 million). The Murdoch approach also influenced traditionally more sober papers like the *Mail* and *Express*.

The impact of the Murdoch revolution is suggested by assessing the actual readership of the individual papers, as opposed to sales (*Social Trends* 1991), as shown in Table 1.1.

While many mass circulation papers recorded steep drops in readership, tabloids like the *Sun*, *Daily Star*, and *News of the World* flourished.

The drift to sensationalism also had an impact on the "qualities," above all from the late 1970s when the Murdoch conglomerate came to

Table 1.1. British Newspaper Readership

	Readership (millions)		
	1971	1989	Change (%)
Daily newspapers			
Sun	8.5	10.8	+27
Daily Mirror	13.8	8.8	−36
Daily Mail	4.8	4.3	−10
Daily Express	9.7	3.9	−60
Daily Star	×	2.7	new
Daily Telegraph	3.6	2.5	−30
Guardian	1.1	2.3	+109
Today	×	1.8	new
Times	1.1	1.1	unchanged
Independent	×	1.2	new
Financial Times	0.7	0.7	unchanged
Sunday Newspapers			
News of the World	15.8	13.0	−18
Sunday Mirror	13.5	9.2	−31
People	14.4	7.5	−48
Sunday Express	10.4	5.2	−50
Mail on Sunday	×	5.5	new
Sunday Times	3.7	3.6	−3
Sunday Telegraph	2.1	2.0	−5
Observer	2.4	2.2	−8

include the *Times* itself. The once staid daily became more popular and sensationalistic in its choice of stories and its manner of reporting. Largely in reaction to this, the 1980s saw the creation in the *Independent* of a new quality that regained some of the ground abandoned by the *Times* (Seymour-Ure 1991).

THE MEDIA AND SOCIAL PROBLEMS

These changes are important in forming our perceptions of British social problems, which must to some extent depend on media sources.

First, there is a problem with the obvious "newspaper of record." The *Times* is the British paper most commonly held on microfilm in libraries around the world, and it is well indexed. It is the natural source for a researcher seeking to analyze the treatment of a topic in the British media, a close parallel to *The New York Times* in the United States. It is therefore likely that any survey of media treatment based on the *Times* and its index will suggest a surge of interest in topics like child abuse and serial murder, though this need not in itself imply a genuine growth of concern in society at large. This is not entirely a negative phenomenon, as the *Times* came to be more representative of the tone of most of the British press; but care must be exercised in using this paper alone to remark on long-term trends.

Second, we must recognize that a change in media coverage did not necessarily reflect new public concerns that had not been present before the 1970s. There was now a larger number of newspaper prepared to explore issues that would once have been viewed as unsuitable, and to cover them in explicit detail. Material that would once have been deemed fit only for the *News of the World* might now gain publicity in eight or ten daily papers, even if that constituted prurient and grossly improbable allegations about snuff films or human sacrifices.

Internal changes in the newspapers go some way to accounting for the new wave of perceived social problems, and in turn, they offered fertile new fields for claims-makers. The resources available to claims-makers thus increased, especially for groups or individuals traditionally far removed from access to government and public opinion. Naturally, this had its impact in the real world: Media-induced panics continued to play a role in affecting public policy, for example, by creating pressure on politicians and bureaucracies, and helping to determine the priorities of law enforcement agencies. If the press is part of an "arena" of public opinion in which "the collective definition of social problems occurs." then the size and ground rules of that arena have changed rapidly in modern Britain (quoted in Best 1990:16).

On the other hand, it would be inaccurate to see the panics of the decade as solely a result of media activism. General press hostility to the Labour party is a long-established phenomenon, which did not prevent the election of several Labour governments over the years. Perhaps the media's most uniformly vilified figure during the 1980s was London Labour leader Ken Livingstone ("Red Ken"), who managed to retain considerable public popularity and won election to a number of positions including member of Parliament. Also, it is dubious if the media could create and sustain a campaign to demonize a group or individual if there was not already a constituency prepared to accept such a view: a point explored at greater length in Chapter 9.

The question then arises why, with so many options available, the media choose to focus their attention on one villain rather than another. This is illustrated in the ritual abuse affair of 1989–1991, when the media initially publicized bizarre and sensational stories about satanic worship and sex rituals. However, when the police and social service agencies began acting to root out these alleged rings, the media with few exceptions denounced the social workers who falsely accused innocent people of nonexistent crimes. The suggestion is surely that the hostile stereotype of the social worker provides a better accepted and more substantial folk-devil than the altogether more speculative satanic ring. In summary, the post-Murdoch media may have amplified stereotypes, but they rarely created them de novo.

NOTE

1.   The study will concern itself with England, Wales, and Scotland, but will omit conditions in Northern Ireland. This area has had numerous moral panics and mythologies in recent decades, including cases (real and imaginary) of satanic rituals, serial murder, and organized pedophilia (see, for example, Foot 1989; Dillon 1989). However, the political context is totally different from that found in the rest of the United Kingdom, and Ulster is better treated as a separate entity.

APPENDIX: CHRONOLOGIES

Sexual Violence

1974–1975   Cambridge Rapist case, first known incident of serial rape in modern Britain

1975–1976   Feminist antirape campaign; emergence of feminist campaigns against sexual violence, including a national network of Rape Crisis Centers.

1976   Law on rape reformed in directions favored by feminist campaigners

1977–1980   Yorkshire Ripper investigation at its height

1978–1980   Sexual violence campaign; extensive feminist activism attempts to link phenomena of rape, sexual homicide, and pornography as part of a generalized phenomenon of sexual violence

1980   Radical Labour factions take power in many urban local authorities throughout Britain, and act as focus of feminist issues and concerns

1981–1982   Feminist antipornography campaign achieves several successes, including legal restrictions on indecent advertising, and parliamentary campaign to close or regulate sex shops; Women Against Violence Against Women movement; series of attacks on pornography shops.

1982   Television documentary focuses attention on unsympathetic police treatment of rape victims
Celebrated court cases suggest necessity to change unsympathetic judicial attitudes toward victims of sexual assault

1983   Serial murder case of Dennis Nilsen

1984–1985   National Miners' Strike promotes movement toward national co-ordination of policing

1984–1986   several serial rape investigations reported in national news media
Police forces develop specialized units to deal with complaints of rape and sexual assault

1986   Disappearances of Anne Lock and Suzy Lamplugh lead to major serial murder investigations; appearance of references to a "serial murder problem"
Serial murder cases of Michele Lupo and Kenneth Erskine
National police computer system HOLMES becomes operative

1988   Marie Wilks case suggests randomness of the threat of lethal sexual violence

1991   News media suggest sharp growth in incidence of sexual homicide against women
Rape within marriage made a criminal offense in England and Wales

(continues on following page)

23

Pedophilia

1974   Formation of Paedophile Information Exchange (PIE)
1977–1988   Campaign against child pornography and PIE
              The term paedophile enters British parlance; national denunciation
              of PIE
              News media express intense concern about danger and prevalence
              of child pornography
              Legislative campaign results in prohibition of sale and manufacture
              of child pornography
1981   PIE leaders convicted of conspiracy to corrupt public morals
              Exposure of PIE activities of diplomat Sir Peter Hayman; Parlia-
              mentary campaign of M.P. Geoffrey Dickens against pedophilia
              and child pornography
1983   Brighton sex attack focuses attention on group pedophile activity,
              and violent assault against children
1984   Spurious charges of pedophile activity against home secretary
              New prosecution against PIE leadership
1985   Murders of Jason Swift and Barry Lewis by London-based pedo-
              phile ring
              Widespread reporting of cases of missing and murdered children
              New publicity about possibility of additional murders in the Moors
              murders series of the 1960s
1986   Sarah Harper murder leads to announcement of Operation
              Stranger investigation; media and police speculate about possible
              links between numerous child murders across Britain
1986–1987   Prosecution of Conservative M.P. Harvey Proctor in rent boy case
1987   Operation Hedgerow investigation of large pedophile network
              based in London: new public focus on organized abuse and six
              rings
              Charges pressed in Jason Swift murder investigation
1989   Metropolitan Police form specialized Child Pornography Squad
              Convictions in Operation Hedgerow case
              Convictions of members of London pedophile ring in murder of
              Jason Swift
              Operation Spanner prosecution of homosexual sadomasochistic
              ring
1990   Operation Orchid: investigation of murders attributed to London
              pedophile ring; search for possible grave sites in London area
              Height of rumors about snuff videos recording some of the alleged
              deaths in the Operation Orchid case
              Bogus social workers case suggest national network of pedophiles
              seeking victims by posing as authority figures
1991   Convictions of member of London pedophile ring in murder of
              Barry Lewis

Child Abuse

1973–1974   Inquiry into death of Maria Colwell leads to widespread publicity about prevalence of physical abuse and battering of children

1976–1978   Extensive media and official concern about extent of baby battering

1978   Founding of Incest Crisis Line as offshoot of existing antirape campaigns

1978–1979   Work of C. Henry Kempe disseminates American theories about prevalence of child sexual abuse

1980–1982   Feminist campaigns against sexual violence place major focus on child victims of incest and sexual abuse

1981   Sexual abuse becomes a separate category for reporting maltreatment on child protection registers

1981–1984   Great Ormond Street Hospital becomes a national center for diagnosis and treatment of sexually abused children
Formation of national group of interest experts including Arnon Bentovim and others

1984   NSPCC centenary is marked by a campaign to raise funds and spread awareness of child abuse
Bexley Project: Home Office establishes pilot project in London Borough of Bexley to promote cooperation between police and social workers
National opinion poll by MORI organization is believed to show that one child in ten is the victim of sexual abuse
Conference at Teesside Polytechnic on American work in the area of child sexual abuse

1984–1986   Inquiries into violent deaths of Jasmine Beckford, Tyra Henry, and other children lead to criticism of failure of child protection agencies to react with sufficient speed and determination
Extensive media criticism of social work profession
Growth of publishing industry of books seeking to advise children about protecting themselves from abuse and molestation

1986   Esther Rantzen television special and founding of telephone service ChildLine suggest the existence of a massive and underreported population of abuse victims
"The Leeds Discovery": Leeds pediatricians report evidence of extensive anal abuse of children, often by other family members
Debates in Parliament and the legal profession about problems encountered by children giving testimony in abuse cases; experimental use of video links to create an environment more favorable to child witnesses

1987   Several jurisdictions report finding extensive evidence of serious sexual abuse within the family, often involving anal or vaginal asault; Cleveland Affair: in the county of Cleveland, the issue

(*continued on following page*)

achieves national celebrity as many children are taken into care and removed from their families; the national press and political activists suggest that the case arises from overreaction by local social service agencies and pediatricians

1988   Conclusion of Butler-Sloss investigation into Cleveland affair renew controversy between believers in mass intrafamilial abuse, and critics of alleged social worker overreaction

1989   Children's Act seeks to resolve problems raised by Cleveland cases

1991   Children's Act implemented
            Criminal Justice Act provides extensive changes in the rules governing the presentation of testimony by children in the courtroom

Satanism and Ritual Abuse

1986   Trial of Derry Knight indicates that wealthy Charismatic and fundamentalist Christians believe in the danger posed by satanic beliefs and practices among the political elite

1987   Sexual abuse case in Nottingham involves charges of multiple assaults by several members of a family

1988   Growing concern about satanism among fundamentalist and Charismatic Christians; investigative committee established by the Evangelical Alliance
            American experts on ritual abuse become influential in Britain; British newspapers publish interviews with American exponents of the reality of ritual abuse of children
            Charges of ritualistic or cult activity raised in Nottingham case

1989   Convictions in Nottingham case
            Series of conferences and seminars disseminates ritual abuse theories among social service and child protection agencies; also several articles on the topic in social work journals like *Community Care* and *Social Work Today*

1990   NSPCC publicizes allegations about widespread ritual abuse throughout Britain, and holds meetings with Social Services Inspectorate and other interested bodies
            Ritual abuse cases emerge in Manchester, London, Rochdale, Strathclyde, Derbyshire, and Merseyside
            Court verdicts overturn Manchester abuse case
            Books and articles on alleged satanic danger published by Evangelicals such as Russ Parker and Kevin Logan

1991   Ritual abuse case emerges in Orkney Islands
            Courts overturn care orders and reject ritual charges in most cases, including major incidents in Rochdale and Orkneys
            Official inquiry into Orkney Islands case

This chapter describes the social, economic, and political setting of Britain in the 1980s, with an emphasis on those factors of strain and conflict that gave rise to new perceptions of social problems. It will be argued that many of the problems considered in this book must be understood in the context of local and national politics, so it is useful to describe some of the major parties and interest groups that were active in defining the issues of the 1980s. Broader trends in social and economic structure will be sketched, with a particular emphasis on changes that affected the workings and attitudes of the police and social services, though of necessity this discussion is very selective in nature.

POLITICS AND GOVERNMENT

British political parties are much more ideologically homogeneous than their American counterparts. Since 1945, British politics have been dominated by two major parties, Labour on the left, and the Conservatives (Tories) on the right. There are other parties, notably the centrist Liberals or Liberal Democrats, but the working of the parliamentary system makes it difficult for a party with widely diffused support to gain national strength. In 1983, for example, the Liberal Alliance obtained almost as many votes nationally as Labour, but received only 23 seats in Parliament compared to Labour's 209 (Derbyshire 1988; Kingdom 1991).

Labour controlled the national government from 1945 to 1951 and 1964 to 1970, the Conservatives from 1951 to 1964 and 1970 to 1974. Politics became sharply polarized during the Labour government of 1974–1979, with the growth of extremist groups on the left and right, and an upsurge of political violence and terrorism. In 1975, the Conservative party chose as its leader the strongly right-wing figure of Margaret Thatcher, who was elected prime minister in 1979. She led her party to reelection with massive parliamentary majorities in 1983 (144 seats) and

1987 (102). The landslide victories were in part a result of the vagaries of the electoral system, and the Conservatives never received over 44 percent of the votes in a general election. However, divisions in the opposition were enough to ensure that Thatcher remained the longest serving prime minister in the last century and a half. She finally resigned in 1990.

The 1979 election is commonly seen as a turning point in modern British politics. The Thatcher government reasserted government authority in matters like censorship, individual rights, and police power; and it undertook radically right-wing policies in matters like privatizing state-run economic enterprises (Skidelsky 1990). The economic impact of the new regime was enormous. Interest rates rose, public spending was cut, and Britain entered a deep recession. Manufacturing output fell by some 19 percent between 1979 and 1983, and unemployment rose from 1.2 million to over 3.2 million in the same period. The damage was worse in the north and west of the country, including Scotland and Wales, the traditional core of heavy industry; and polarization continued through the relatively improved conditions of the late 1980s. A prosperous and European-oriented southeast confronted a greatly weakened north and west. The inner cities similarly suffered while the suburbs flourished.

One consequence of the recession was a substantial growth in the numbers receiving some form of welfare payments or unemployment benefit (Field 1989). Three million received supplementary benefit in 1979, 4.5 million in 1982, while some 6 million received some form of means-tested benefit. Between 1978–1979 and 1986–1987, central government spending on social security rose from £31 to £43 billion, largely in response to the swelling ranks of the unemployed. This represented an increase from 25 to 32 percent of total government expenditure (Derbyshire 1988). For the purposes of studying child abuse, the growth of a welfare population from 1979 onwards meant that a larger section of the community was likely to come into contact with social services agencies in one form or another.

Strikes and industrial conflict declined under Thatcher. One turning point of her rule came in 1984 and 1985, when the powerful National Union of Mineworkers launched a national strike of the sort that had brought down the previous Conservative government in 1974. On this occasion, decisive (and controversial) police tactics ensured the defeat of the strike (Coulter et al. 1984; Hillyard and Percy-Smith 1988).

This would be a critical event for the Left (Kingdom 1991). Since the 1960s, a radical left-wing movement had gained strength in Britain, partly through the Labour party, partly through smaller left-wing groups like the Socialist Workers party and the Communist party. Each had some strength in the union movement, which had been so powerful in the 1970s. One Trotskyist group, the Militant Tendency, is said to have penetrated many Labour constituency parties. Whatever the reason, sections of Labour were strongly left-wing in tone by the early 1980s, more radical than many European Communist parties. The successes of the Thatcher government resulted in a widespread decline for the Left, while radical groups within the Labour party and most unions lost power.

The 1970s and 1980s were years of intense partisan conflict, and there were rumors of imminent military coups between 1974 and 1976 (Foot 1989; Leigh 1988; Hain 1987). These conflicts contributed to the growth of a powerful tradition of conspiracy politics in Britain, on both left and right. For the right, this involved elaborate theories of political subversion inspired by international communism, but extensively aided by the machinations of domestic dissidents and cultural radicals (Pincher 1981, 1984, 1988). It was Margaret Thatcher who described the striking miners as "the enemy within." For the Left, theories involved conspiracies by government, intelligence, and law enforcement agencies (Foot 1989; Hain 1987; Hain et al. 1980; Aubrey1981). Both types of theory enjoyed much support during the decade, and helped disseminate ideas about official cover-ups and upperworld malfeasance that would permeate the debate over threats to children.

RACE AND NATIONAL IDENTITY

Britain since the 1940s has experienced two major changes in its national identity, both of which remain at the center of national politics. One transformation concerned the controversial reduction of British political sovereignty due to membership in the European Community since 1973. A majority of the electorate see European ties as the only possible economic direction for Britain, and surveys repeatedly show younger people as less insular than their elders; but there is residual hostility, and Germany still plays a distinctly ambiguous role in the British media. On the one hand, it is portrayed as an enviable success story, an economically dominant partner in Europe; on the other, it remains the eternal enemy in endless fictional depictions of the two world wars. It was largely her reluctance to commit Britain still further to a supranational European state that cost Margaret Thatcher her position as prime minister in 1990.

This ambiguity will often be depicted in the British conception of social problems such as serial murder, pedophilia, and child pornography, which can be seen as dangerous foreign importations. The growth of Britain's European role added the sense of exposure to foreign menaces that had hitherto been excluded, a point neatly symbolized by periodic panics over the threatened introduction of rabies from France or Belgium. Fear of losing control over national frontiers also gave added fervor to the drugs issue in the early 1980s, when Britain was said to offer an "open house to heroin" (*Sunday Times,* October 2, 1983; Picardie and Wade 1985).

The other major change involved the mass immigration of people from the old empire, with the result that Britain has become a multi racial society. Ethnic definitions are malleable, but most estimates place the non white population around 2.6 million, or 5 percent of the whole. During the 1980s, about 7 percent of all live births in Britain involved mothers born in the "New Commonwealth and Pakistan," the common euphemism for the main sources of nonwhite immigration in South Asia, the Caribbean, and Africa (Castles et al. 1984; *Social Trends* 1991). Racial issues have played a controversial role in British politics, and have caused special strain on the police and the criminal justice system. Margaret Thatcher won support by her apparent opposition to further immigration that would "swamp" British society.

Race has often served as a scapegoat for other long-term problems in British society, with which it is not necessarily connected. Since the 1950s, British economic performance has steadily declined relative to most other leading countries, and one consequence has been a growth of poverty and urban decay (Field 1989). As the country has become more diverse socially and ethnically, it has also become a poorer and more violent place, with a great deal more crime, more violent offenses, and a greater use of firearms. In marked contrast to the 1950s, Britain in the 1980s was a land of inner-city poverty, hard drug use, and high criminality. Blacks and Asians, who are often the primary victims of economic and social decline, can readily be portrayed as its culprits. As in the United States, law and order politics contain a veiled racial agenda, which is manifested in the rhetoric surrounding an offense like mugging (Hall et al. 1978; Gordon 1983; Brake and Hale 1992).

CRIME AND DISORDER

Yet even without a racial context, it can hardly be denied that Britain in the last three decades has become a more violent and crime-prone society, and crime is crucial to political debate. The murder rate was much quoted in the mass media to assert that British society was becoming more lawless. Conservatives blamed the trend on the "soft" policies of various governments, and especially the 1967 abolition of capital punishment by the Labour administration of Harold Wilson.

Traditionally, England and Wales had one of the lowest murder rates in the industrialized countries, with about 150 cases a year in the first quarter of the century. A large proportion of murders involved domestic disputes, and between 10 and 20 percent of offenses were followed by the suicide of the perpetrator. By the 1960s, the number of murders had risen to an annual average of 300 or 350, but this still gave an overall rate of under one per hundred thousand population, compared to a U.S. rate eight or ten times greater. British figures are still low by American standards, but the number of homicides has grown substantially. By the mid-1980s, there were between six and seven hundred murders annually, and the number of stranger homicides had risen substantially, to perhaps two hundred each year. During the 1980s alone, the proportion of stranger homicides rose from 20 to 30 percent of the total. This was important for public attitudes and fears, in that it was easier to speculate on the existence of random or "motiveless" killers, possibly roaming the country to commit their crimes.

In the United States, offenses are measured in the Justice Department's Uniform Crime Reports; the British equivalent involves "notifiable crimes known to the police." There were 2.5 million such offenses in 1979, 3.6 million in 1985, 4.5 million by 1990. London and the six major urban areas accounted for over half of all offenses. Most disturbing was the increase in serious offenses, equivalent to the American "index crimes": murder, rape, robbery, burglary, and motor vehicle theft. These increased by 71 percent between 1975 and 1985.

Between 1975 and 1985, recorded murders rose from 515 to 616; rapes from 1,040 to 1,842; robberies from 11,311 to 27,463 (Rose 1990, 1991; *Criminal Statistics* (1985). The figures were even more disturbing when expressed as rates related to overall population. In England and Wales, the annual number of such crimes per hundred thousand population ran at about five hundred during the 1930s, over one thousand through the 1950s. By the early 1970s, the rate reached three thousand; by 1985, it exceeded seven thousand.

There are many factors that can affect recorded crime rates, including changes in recording practices and a substantial growth in the number of police officers since 1979. On the other hand, it is often argued that the offense of robbery provides one of the most reliable indices of the changing rate of violent crime in a particular society. By this criterion, the deterioration of public order in Britain in recent years is very marked. Taking England and Wales as a whole, there were 227 recorded robberies in 1939, compared to 1,900 in 1959. The dramatic increase has come since the mid-1970s, with an explosive growth during and following 1981, which was linked by many observers to the breakdown of police authority in the rioting of that year. There were 12,482 recorded robberies in 1979, 27,463 by 1985.

In London alone, it was only in the early 1960s that the annual number of recorded robberies reached one thousand. There were nearly 7,000 incidents by 1977, 13,570 by 1984; and this was not only a metropolitan phenomenon. Bristol recorded just one robbery in 1939, 303 in 1982 (compare "Thieving in the City," *Guardian*, November 20, 1990). It is becoming hard to believe that such changes could solely be a result of changes in reporting or police practice: Serious criminal behavior appears to be far more common that it was twenty years ago (J. Jenkins 1991).

Drugs were commonly believed to be linked with growing violence. Concern about heroin use reached a peak between about 1982 and 1985, and there is no question that the addiction figures cited in those years were wildly inflated; but hard drug use of this sort was novel in Britain. Heroin was rare before the 1970s, and even in the early part of that decade, police seldom seized more than five or ten kilos each year. By 1983, the figure was almost two hundred kilos; three hundred kilos by 1984. Cocaine seizures rose from one hundred kilos in 1986 to four hundred in 1987. The impact of drug abuse was especially marked in certain major cities, such as London, Liverpool, and Edinburgh (Mac-Gregor, 1989; Pearson et al. 1987; Picardie and Wade 1985).

The image of growing violence was enhanced by the increase in the criminal use of firearms. By American standards, this activity remained limited and Britain is still one of the countries in which it is most difficult for civilians to obtain guns; but the statistics were disquieting. In 1975, police in England and Wales recorded 3,850 incidents in which firearms were used; by 1985, the figure was 9,742. In London between 1945 and 1963, there were about 40 robberies each year involving firearms; between 1981 and 1985, the annual average was about 1,500. Even the police were increasingly likely to use firearms, remarkable in a British context, and there were an increasing number of incidents where officers shot either civilians or unarmed criminals (Waddington 1991).

Gun use was widely publicized by the novel phenomenon of apparently "crazed loners" undertaking mass murder rampages. The most notorious occurred in the village of Hungerford in August 1987, when Michael Ryan used an assault rifle to kill sixteen people before finally shooting himself (Seabrook 1987b; Marriner 1991). In October that year, Kevin Weaver killed four in Bristol; in 1989, another man shot sixteen people in northeastern England, though only one victim died on this occasion.

PUBLIC ORDER

There was a widespread perception that growing violence and unrest were related to a decline of public order, and an increase of violent demonstrations and riots. As a long-term historical view, this is questionable, as Britain has a lengthy record of violent urban rioting and industrial conflict, dating back several centuries. On the other hand, such incidents were not common at midcentury, and this gave plausibility to the notion that events of the 1970s and 1980s were novel or unparalleled. Riots in these years were a not uncommon occurrence, from the antifascist outbursts of the late 1970s through the poll tax rioting of 1990, and there was frequently a strong racial element in the disturbances.

This reached a height in the summer riots of 1981, when twenty towns and cities were affected (Kettle and Hodges 1982; Gordon 1983). The conflicts in London and Liverpool were savage, and two died in the latter city. In 1985, a police officer was killed in rioting by (mainly) black youths in the Tottenham area of London. Such incidents suggested a decay of traditional civility and social restraint, a pattern that was used by both major parties to blame the policies of their opponents. However, the police certainly did not escape criticism, and academic and journalistic investigations approached charges of brutality and corruption with a frankness that would have seemed unthinkable before the 1970s (Holdaway ed., 1979, Holdaway 1983; Young 1991; Waddington 1991). In the common phrase of political debate, the social fabric appeared to be unraveling (Brake and Hale 1992).

RECONSTRUCTING THE FAMILY

The nature and status of the family institution changed substantially during the Thatcher years, and this was regarded by conservatives as a sign of fragmentation and decay quite as serious as the urban rioting. (Others might naturally regard the same changes as liberating in nature.) During the 1970s and 1980s, Great Britain had moved toward a mature postindustrial economy, with a substantial growth in the service sector. The proportion of workers employed in the service sector rose from 59 percent in 1971 to 75 percent in 1989. Among other things, this opened a large number of jobs to women, and the proportion of women in the labor force rose in the same period from 38 to 47 percent.

By 1989, 66 percent of all women of working age were employed either part-time or full-time, including an unprecedented number of women with small dependent children, five years old or younger (*Social Trends* 1991). The proportion of all children five or younger in schools or day care was 15 percent in 1966, 49 percent in 1989. Day care places grew from 128,000 in 1966 to 783,000 in 1989. Economic emancipation coincided with a decline in family size, due partly to new contraceptive technologies. The number of children aged sixteen or under was 26 percent of the British population in 1971, and then fell steadily to reach a trough of 20 percent by 1989 (*Social Trends* 1991).

Changes in the family created new expectations about women's roles, which contributed to a rapid growth in the divorce rate. The number of persons divorcing per thousand married people was 2.1 in 1961, 6.0 in 1971, 11.9 in 1981, and 12.8 by 1988—what Lawrence Stone has termed the "divorce revolution." Britain now has the second highest divorce rate in Europe. The number of divorce petitions filed in England and Wales rose from 32,000 in 1961 to 111,000 in 1971, 180,000 by 1986. The proportion of the total filed by the wife grew from 56 percent in 1971 to a steady 72 percent through the 1980s. In the United Kingdom as a whole, the proportion of all marriages where one or both partners had previously been divorced stood at 9 percent in 1961, 33 percent in 1986. The proportion of single-parent families in the United Kingdom roughly doubled between 1971 and 1987.

Changing standards and expectations are suggested by the British abortion rate, which is very high by European standards. The number of legal terminations performed was 101,000 in 1971, and rose to 139,000 in 1981, 181,000 by 1989. In 1971, 12 percent of conceptions ended in abortion; in 1988, 20 percent. By 1987, the British Social Attitudes Survey suggested that almost half of those questioned favored a right to abortion for a wide variety of social and economic reasons, and a vast majority supported abortion where the issue was the health of the mother or gross deformity of the fetus (compare Heald and Wybrow 1986:272–273; Wybrow 1989; Jacobs and Worcester 1990:77–92).

By many different types of measure, women in the 1980s were more likely to be independent, or at least to have a life that did not entirely revolve around husband and children (Llewelyn and Osborne 1990; Beechey and Whitelegg 1986). The changing status was reflected in new political aspirations. The number of women members of Parliament in 1990 was forty-three, or 6.6 percent of the total. This may seem unimpressive, but rarely before the late 1980s had the figure even approached thirty at any given time.

FEMINISM

From the mid-1970s on, there evolved in Britain a strong feminist movement, which has had an enormous impact on many aspects of society and politics. The movement had its critics, and it might be argued that its early dynamism was manifested in statements that appeared extreme, but its achievements are beyond question. The new feminism perhaps represented the most significant leap forward in the extension of democracy and popular involvement in politics since the widening of the franchise a century earlier.

American influences initially played a major role in shaping the new feminism, which grew out of the radical New Left (Rowbotham 1989; Coote and Campbell 1987; Ashworth and Bonnerjea 1985). As in America, the movement rapidly developed a network of institutions such as consciousness-raising groups, medical self-help groups, and Women's Aid centers to advise and protect raped or battered women (Rowbotham et al. 1981). The first refuge for battered women opened in 1971; two hundred more followed during the decade (Edwards 1989). Europe's pioneer Rape Crisis Center opened in London in 1976, and there were thirty such centers in Great Britain by 1985 (C. Roberts 1989). The *Women's Health Handbook* also appeared in 1976, as an imitation of the celebrated American text *Our Bodies Ourselves*. Feminist slogans and buttons were much in evidence by 1973–1974. Feminist political campaigns mobilized around many issues, but especially on the platform of resisting changes to the 1967 abortion law: The National Abortion Campaign thus became another focus of activism.

There were also many bookshops, and feminist publishers like Virago, Pandora, Onlywomen, and the Women's Press. The magazine *Spare Rib* became the major voice of the movement, with *Feminist Review* and *Trouble and Strife* also influential. Feminist ideas soon prevailed in radical and left-wing journals like the *Leveller*, and were commonly expressed in liberal newspapers like the *Guardian*, and in left/liberal periodicals like *New Society* and *New Statesman* (and in the *New Statesman and Society*, which resulted from their 1988 merger).

British feminists were often far more thoroughgoing in their critique of sexism and patriarchy than most American counterparts (Snitow et al. 1984; Cartledge and Ryan 1983; Edwards 1981). By the late 1970s, there were strong separatist and political Lesbian wings within feminism (Rowbotham 1989). During the European antinuclear movement of the early 1980s, one celebrated British contribution was a separatist women-only peace camp established at the site of U.S. military installations like Greenham Common.

THE POLITICS OF GENDER

Gender issues also played a role through the strong homosexual movement that emerged in the early 1970s, which was generally allied to the political left (Weeks 1977, 1985, 1986; Galloway 1983; Porter and Weeks 1991). The widespread Marxist and New Left movements of the 1970s had increasingly adopted feminist and gay rights campaigns as fundamental; and these were now projected into national politics through the influence of the New Left on the Labour party (Cant and Hemmings 1988).

A notable example of his new political culture was provided by the radical Labour movement, which took control of the Greater London Council (GLC) in 1981. Under its chair, Ken Livingstone, the council supported strongly left-wing policies in international and defense matters, while favoring affirmative action, women's rights, and gay rights platforms within London itself. It carried its policies into action through a new network of women's equality units, race advisers, police monitoring groups, and gay/lesbian officers. Some London boroughs pioneered women-only bus services, to protect women from male assault, an idea imitated in other conurbations during the decade. By the mid-1980s, fifty local authorities had women's committees (*New Statesman and Society*, March 24, 1989). The cities were seen by the Left as the foundation for resistance to the Thatcherite national government.

Livingstone's faction even viewed Irish Republican aspirations with sympathy, an extremely daring attitude in view of the thorough demonization of the IRA and its allies in the British media [hostile stereotypes and myths of the Irish are among the most powerful and enduring in British culture (Campaign for Free Speech on Ireland 1979)]. In contemporary American terms, the Labour-controlled GLC carried political correctness to an extreme. Despite this (or perhaps because of it) the council was remarkably popular among broad sections of the London electorate, and it was removed only by a controversial law that abolished both the council itself, and the elected authorities of other large cities (1986).

Local authorities like that in London presided over a substantial growth in the social services, which were often seen by critics as vehicles for radical and feminist ideas. In 1981, there were 250,900 people employed in "personal social services" in the United Kingdom, which rose to 293,900 by 1989. Of the latter, 34,600 were social work staff, 32,900 "management, administrative, and ancillary," and 226,300 miscellaneous others. This represented an increase in overall employment of 17 percent at a time of widespread decline in other parts of the public sector: Employment in the National Health Service fell by 3 percent during the same years (*Social Trends* 1991).

The social work profession had become radicalized since the 1960s, perhaps inevitably when women comprised so large a proportion of its employees. Many of those newly recruited in the 1970s and 1980s had been influenced as students by New Left and feminist ideas, while the growth of social work departments in universities had influenced the radical agenda of the profession. By 1988, the Central Council for Education and Training in Social Work (CCETSW) presented a "statement of minimum requirements" for the qualifying professional, asserting that a primary goal of social work was the promotion of equal opportunity. This included among other things the ability of social workers to "identify and challenge structural disadvantage, discrimination or prejudice on grounds of . . . sexual preference" in addition to race, sex, and class (*Community Care*, July 7, 1988). The 1980s was a period of many difficulties for the British Left, but it survived through its footholds in such institutions. As a *New Statesman and Society* columnist observed: "Where the Left has embedded itself in institutions— parliament, universities and polytechnics, Channel Four, social work—it survives and may even flourish" (Benton 1991).

THE CONSERVATIVE REACTION

Labour and the Left were strong in London, but the association of Labour with sexually unorthodox life-styles proved controversial in the rest of the country, where a "London factor" was blamed for several Labour electoral defeats. In the conservative press, the activities of the far left in the early 1980s were portrayed as malicious silliness, dogmatic support of terrorists, homosexuals, feminist separatists, racial minorities, and the disabled, all to the exclusion of the "normal" population. The term *loony left* became common shorthand for the militants in London and elsewhere. Right-wing political activists could now assert that political conservatism was intimately bound up with traditional morality, the family, and even heterosexuality.

The radical demands of the activists opened them to caricature, and the right-wing satirical magazine *Private Eye* featured stories of extreme feminist abuses in the regular column "Wimmin," named for those dogmatic feminists who wished to describe themselves without having to spell *men*. More substantially, *Private Eye* recounted scandals surrounding the radical councils in London and other major cities, and often ran columns under titles such as "Rotten Boroughs," "Murkeyside" (i.e., Merseyside), and "London Calling." These reported corruption and the abuse of patronage, which seemed to show the hypocrisy of the dominant left in power.

Similar stories were the common fare of conservative magazines like the *Spectator*, of daily papers like the *Telegraph* and *Express*, and the more popular tabloids like the *Sun* and *Star*. In 1987, for example, there were repeated stories about the mismanagement of an old people's home in the London borough of Southwark, the Nye Bevan Lodge, said to have been the scene of repeated brutality against and neglect of the residents, as well as financial and sexual irregularities. Local Labour councillors and union officials had allegedly attempted a cover-up of the emerging scandal (*Private Eye* 643,669). This was particularly relished because Nye Bevan had been a hero of radical socialism in the 1950s.

Education became a controversial issue from the late 1970s, when local councils were accused of using schools to propagate extreme left-wing views. The militants of the GLC were committed to encouraging progressive educational practices, in matters like the promotion of antisexist, anti-imperialist, pacifist, and antiracist views. All were contentious, but perhaps the most sensitive issue was the use of materials that attacked "pernicious heterosexism," and portrayed homosexual life-styles with sympathy. This was characterized by enemies of the GLC as advocating homosexuality, or carrying out propaganda among impressionable children and instilling in them values contrary to those of their parents. In 1986, there was vigorous parliamentary debate over proposed amendments to a current education bill that would allow parents to withdraw children from sex education classes (Lumsden and Campbell 1986).

The government also responded with a measure to prohibit the advocacy of homosexuality by local authorities, "Clause 28," which specifically forbade the use of public money in any activity that promoted homosexuality. This was a controversial device that troubled many Conservatives by its erosion of local autonomy (Skidelsky, 1990; Kingdom 1991). It also gave rise to charges of a new persecution of homosexuals, and an acrimonious controversy ensued. It was especially during 1986 that the twin issues of sexual identity and control over children's morality occupied a central position in British political debate; and this was also the year that rumors and fears about sexual predators reached an unprecedented height (see Chapters 3–5).

For the purposes of the present study, these political and ideological divisions would be extremely significant. The agenda of British feminism was in large measure defined by the concerns and fears discussed in this book—issues such as rape and sexual violence, family violence, and child abuse. These concerns could be projected into the wider society in a number of ways, but crucial was the power of the radicals in the local authorities. These controlled the social service agencies and educational authorities, which we will so often find as the voices of concern about family violence, sexual exploitation, and child abuse.

In turn, the activists could be stigmatized for their apparent extremism. These debates occurred at an unusual point in British history, when the views of local authorities enjoyed a rare prominence in national politics. Attacks on feminists or homosexuals could thus indirectly undermine the Labour party and especially its activist wing. Moralism became a powerful weapon in the campaign for a restoration of "Victorian values" in state, society, and economy, a Thatcherite moral revolution (Skidelsky 1990). Both as activists and as symbolic enemies, feminists and homosexuals would play a central role in shaping the moral issues of the decade.

MORALITY AND PERMISSIVENESS

But moralist campaigns were by no means a simple or cynical electoral tactic. They reflected older and deeper underlying concerns, mobilized as effectively by Margaret Thatcher in Britain as by Ronald Reagan in the United States (Skidelsky 1990; Kingdom 1991). One fundamental idea was the notion of the "permissive society," a phrase originally used in an approving sense by Labour home secretary Roy Jenkins in the 1960s. Jenkins's policies had resulted in the liberalization of the laws on divorce, abortion, and homosexuality, and the abolition of capital punishment, while his tenure in office coincided with a substantial relaxation in the censorship of written and visual material. As with the Warren Supreme Court in the United States, the Jenkins era defined the agenda of the right wing for a generation.

For the Right, permissiveness was an ill to be combated and reversed, and the term was itself almost invariably used by critics of perceived moral degeneracy. Frequently, the panics that will be described in this book were used as weapons to attack the permissive attitudes that so pervasively infected British society. Among the major groups advocating moral traditionalism were the National Festival of Light, the Evangelical antiobscenity movement of the early 1970s, and the "Responsible Society." Especially active was the National Viewers and Listeners Association (NVALA), founded by Mary Whitehouse in the 1960s to combat media permissiveness. This group supported Margaret Thatcher's calls for a return to Victorianism; and in 1978, the NVALA conference was addressed by Conservative deputy party leader, William Whitelaw (Tracey and Morrison 1978; Wallis 1976).

As in the United States, one important vehicle for conservative activism was the antiabortion movement. In Britain, there were repeated efforts through the 1970s to repeal the liberal 1967 act, or at least to restrict the term at which abortion was legal (repeated opinion surveys showed little support for a ban on abortion as such). Several unsuccessful bills were introduced, and there were attempts to tack abortion restriction proposals on bills limiting research on fetal tissue. Parliamentary activism was unsuccessful, but the campaign permitted the emergence of grassroots movements like *Life* and the Society for the Protection of the Unborn Child (SPUC), (Clarke 1987). In 1989, a contingent from the American Operation Rescue campaign arrived to spread tactics of "sidewalk counseling" and blockading clinics. The leadership and activists of the antiabortion movements frequently overlapped with those of antiobscenity and children's rights groups, and there were tactical alliances against permissiveness.

Moralist reaction was also evident in the case of Victoria Gillick, a Catholic prolife campaigner, who in 1985 brought a celebrated court action to prohibit National Health Service doctors from prescribing contraceptives to girls under sixteen without parental consent. The ensuing public furor raised the issue of a family's rights over the morality of its children, in the same way that the teaching of homosexuality in the schools would be so controversial the following year.

Struggles over morality legislation often depended on the individual views of an official or politician in a particular locality. From his appointment in 1976, one of the best instances of a crusading police chief was James Anderton of Manchester, an aggressive opponent of pornography, feminism, and gay rights. Authoritarian in his attitudes to public order and individual rights, Anderton saw the police's role primarily as moral enforcement against "social nonconformists, malingerers, idlers, parasites, spongers, frauds, cheats and unrepentant criminals." He denounced those who "openly hanker after total debauchery and lewdness," and massively increased the number of obscenity raids in the Manchester area. In 1986, he gave a well-publicized speech in which he denounced the "moral cesspool" inhabited by AIDS sufferers, by which he meant homosexuals and drug users (Lumsden 1987).

His campaigns brought him into direct conflict with Manchester's left-wing Labour-dominated council and police committee, which found that it lacked the power to control his activities. Moral conflicts once more formed the battleground for struggles over democratic rights and constitutional powers; and in the Thatcher era, the conservative and centralist causes won on all fronts.

THE PORNOGRAPHY ISSUE

Moralist campaigns frequently focused on the issue of pornography, where surprisingly large coalitions were possible. In the late 1970s, child pornography provided an invaluable rallying point, while in the 1980s the main focus of activism shifted to adult material, especially that available on video. From 1981, throughout the country there were demonstrations and pickets against sex shops and cinemas, often under the auspices of local Community Standards Associations (Thompson 1989, 1990).

Legislative activity continued steadily from the late 1970s onwards, under the auspices of moralist M.P.s like Timothy Sainsbury and Geoffrey Dickens (Tomlinson 1982:146–156). In 1978, the Child Protection Act prohibited the manufacture and sale of child pornography; in 1981, Sainsbury's Indecent Displays (Control) Act forbade public advertising of explicit material; in 1982, a clause of the Local Government Act permitted the closure of hundreds of sex shops (Thompson et al. 1989; Thompson 1989, 1990). Sex cinemas were attacked by Cinematographic Acts in 1982 and 1985. In 1986, M.P. Winston Churchill launched an unsuccessful campaign to prohibit the broadcast of indecent and homoerotic material on television (Lumsden 1986).

There were also recurring campaigns from 1981 onwards against violent and sadomasochistic video materials, or "video nasties," films with titles like *SS Experiment Camp, Driller Killer*, or *Cannibal Apocalypse*. Banning such materials became a plank in the 1983 Conservative party platform and was strongly supported by papers such as the *Daily Mail* and the *Sun* (Barker 1984). A common theme in the debate was that these materials were readily available to small children (the *Sun* headlined "Six Year Old Addicts of Video Nasties"). In 1984, the Video Recordings Act introduced precensorship for video materials and a licensing system similar to that prevailing in the cinema (Thompson 1989, 1990; Taylor 1987).

Supporters of censorship enjoyed great success in spreading their views in this area, and the British Social Attitudes Survey shows a steady decline in public tolerance of pornography (Harding 1988; Jowell and Airey 1984; Jowell et al. 1991). In 1983, 52 percent of those surveyed supported the availability of pornography in special adult shops, with 33 percent wanting total prohibition. By 1987, only 42 percent favored specialized adult stores, while 38 percent supported prohibition. Women were significantly less likely than men to favor libertarian attitudes in this area (Heald and Wybrow 1986:273–274).

Morality campaigns often had a party political agenda, and antiobscenity groups like the Festival of Light were strongly conservative or Evangelical in nature. A leading force in the nasties activism was the Parliamentary Video Group, which produced some of the most damning evidence of the impact of the material on small children. The group is an offshoot of the Organization of Christian Unity, which simultaneously struggled against the evils of abortion and divorce (Harris 1984).

But the pornography issue was complex, and moralist conservatives were likely to find staunch allies among feminists and the radical left, who frequently believed that pornography contributed to violence against women (Chester and Dickey 1988; Benn 1987; Rhodes and McNeill 1985). There had since the late 1970s been "Reclaim the Night" demonstrations against areas of adult bookstores and cinemas, and one 1978 protest in Soho led to a major confrontation with police (Feminist Anthology Collective 1981:221–222). By 1987, films and slides prepared by American antipornography campaigners were being used to create a national Campaign Against Pornography among British feminists (Benn 1987); and American Andrea Dworkin spoke at a number of meetings and rallies. The *New Statesman* was sympathetic: "What we are seeing is a form of woman hatred—if not an organized male conspiracy, then certainly an exhibition of male power at its worst."

Feminist activists in radical local authorities supported antipornography campaigns, with targets by no means confined to overt erotica. Among the films most often denounced were mainstream productions such as *The Shining*, and *Dressed to Kill*. The Brighton Women's Committee even imposed a local ban against a serious film like *9-½ Weeks* (Miles 1986). From 1987, women M.P.s like Clare Short and Jo Richardson waged a lengthy parliamentary campaign to prohibit the soft-core photographs of topless models in daily papers like the *Sun*.

RELIGION

In the United States, recent debates over morality and permissiveness owe a great deal to religious attitudes, especially those of fundamentalist groups. Britain is a more secular society, in which religious groups have played a far less significant role in debates over public morality, at least in modern times. However, matters have changed substantially in the last ten or fifteen years.

The Church of England is an established state church, which for centuries was supposed by law to comprise all citizens of England and Wales (a quite distinct Presbyterian church is established by law in Scotland). In practice, this had long been recognized as a fiction, and

Anglicans have for centuries had to compete with rival religious groups, either Roman Catholic or Protestant Nonconformist. During the twentieth century, the established church has declined steadily in membership. This dilution of strength has also affected other maintstream religious bodies, especially those which, like the Anglicans, have adopted more liberal theological views. Table 2.1 suggests the extent of the change (*Social Trends* 1991).

Table 2.1. Religious Practice in Great Britain

	Adult Members (millions)		Change (percent)
	1975	1990	
Trinitarian churches			
Anglican	2.27	1.82	−20
Presbyterian	1.65	1.29	−22
Methodist	0.61	0.61	unchanged
Baptist	0.27	0.24	−11
Other protestant	0.53	0.65	+23
Roman Catholic	2.53	1.95	−23
Orthodox	0.2	0.23	+15
Total	8.06	6.7	−17
Nontrinitarian churches			
Mormons	0.1	0.15	+50
Jehovah's Witnesses	0.08	0.11	+38
Spirtualist	0.06	0.05	−17
Other nontrinitarian	0.09	0.13	+44
Total	0.33	0.44	+33
Other Religions			
Muslim	0.4	1.0	+150
Sikh	0.12	0.22	+83
Hindu	0.1	0.17	+70
Jews	0.11	0.11	unchanged
Other	0.08	0.24	+200
Total	0.81	1.74	+115

Anglicans are not even the largest religious group, while the most dramatic growth has occurred outside Christianity altogether, among the British Muslim population. This group scarcely existed in 1950, but now exceeds one million. However, the weakness of the established church is less remarkable than the pronounced secularism of British society. Between 1975 and 1990, the total adult membership in trinitarian churches fell by 17 percent, while the membership of such churches represented a mere 14 percent of the overall population. Even by European standards, this was a low figure, compared with a West European norm of between 20 and 30 percent. Between 1971 and 1988, the proportion of British marriages conducted according to civil ceremonies rose from 40 to 48 percent of the whole. In the mid-1980s, opinion polls found only 8 percent of British respondents characterizing themselves as very religious, compared to 34 percent who said they were not religious (Heald and Wybrow 1986:227; Jacobs and Worcester 1990:77–84).

In this hostile environment, religious groups have attempted a number of different responses to change. Sections of the established church itself have sought to adapt to the modern world by abandoning a great deal of what appears old-fashioned in theology (Welsby 1984). To many observers, this has seemed a wholesale rejection of what is basic and essential to Christianity. Since the 1970s, there have been a number of highly publicized controversies about issues such as the Virgin Birth, the bodily Resurrection, and the divinity of Jesus Christ, with skeptics like Bishop Jenkins of Durham and Dr. Don Cupitt of Cambridge University as frequently quoted authorities (compare Hornsby-Smith 1991).

There was a furor in 1977 when a group of theologians, mainly Anglican clergy, published a book entitled *The Myth of God Incarnate*, which argued against the divinity of Christ, and consequently sought to demolish the whole trinitarian structure. The authors affected surprise at the shock caused by their use of the word *myth*, but the resulting controversy was far-reaching, and rallied Evangelicals both within and outside the established church. Other controversies have concerned the ordination of women and practicing homosexuals, and the degree of overt liberal politicization in the church.

THE NEW FUNDAMENTALISTS

These controversies have weakened the church, but there have been areas of growth that are relevant to our present subject. Fundamentalist and Charismatic or Pentecostalist churches on the familiar American model have spring up alongside the declining mainstream groups. Churches following the new piety emphasize the work of the Holy Spirit in everyday life, and the central importance of a personal "born-again" conversion experience. They practice speaking in tongues and prayer healing, in addition to espousing a strict theology that encompasses traditional ideas like the Virgin Birth, Resurrection, and Trinity, as well as Hell and a literal devil (Thompson 1989, 1990). By 1979, the Charismatic House Church Movement had some fifty thousand members drawn from various denominations, including Catholics (Welsby 1984:245). Between 1979 and 1989, membership of independent fundamentalist churches grew from 44,000 to 128,000 in England and Wales, and this does not count the growth in parishes of the established church.

The Church of England has for over a century been divided between Evangelical and Anglo-Catholic wings, disrespectfully known as "low and lazy" as opposed to "high and crazy." The low wing has flourished in recent decades, and formed many alliances with Evangelical and charismatic groups in other denominations. Despite its nominally hierarchical nature, the Church of England allows considerable de facto independence to the individual clergyman; and the main Charismatic organization, the Fountain Trust, was founded by Anglican clergy (Welsby 1984:241–245). In 1991, a cleric sympathetic to the new Evangelical trend became head of the Church of England, when George Carey became Archbishop of Canterbury. Religious life in Britain has become polarized between the liberal and Evangelical movements.

Evangelical groups have also been active in the political arena, where local churches and groupings have cooperated to fight pornography, gay rights, and abortion (Wallis 1979; Wallis and Bland 1979; Thompson 1989, 1990). Such movements drew Catholic activists in large numbers, despite the traditional pro-Labour loyalties of Britain's large Irish population (analogies with the American Democratic party will be apparent).

The year 1977 marked an important turning point in political activism by religious groups. There was another failed abortion bill that year, while Evangelical sentiment was deeply stirred over the issue of blasphemy. The newspaper *Gay News* had published a poem by James Kirkup, which implied promiscuous homosexual relationships between Jesus and the apostles (Weeks 1981; Welsby 1984:203–207). Mary Whitehouse undertook a private prosecution on the grounds of blasphemous libel, an offense that most thought extinct. It is difficult to say whether gay activists or religious groups were more galvanized by the newspaper's conviction in July, but the decision had lasting consequences. Later that year, Mary Whitehouse and her triumphant allies began a successful movement to prohibit child pornography (see Chapter 4). The two weeks of the *Gay News* trial coincided exactly with the height of the controversy over *The Myth of God Incarnate*, which was depicted as an equally gross blasphemy, and Evangelicals often linked the two phenomena.

The success of the various decency and prolife coalitions has sporadically encouraged hopes of a British equivalent to the American Moral Majority. One recent attempt at a permanent coalition involved a national Movement for Christian Democracy, under M.P.s David Alton (a prolife veteran) and Kenneth Hargreaves. Also important is the International Congress for the Family, which coordinates antiabortion and antifeminist groups. It held its first meeting on British soil in Brighton, in 1990 (*New Statesman and Society*, July 20, 1990).

For fundamentalists, the most important national group remains the Evangelical Alliance, an umbrella that includes congregations both within and outside the established church. There are also organizations like Christian Action Research and Education (CARE), with some eighty thousand members. Other informal means of national organization include a network of bookstores, radio shows, and publishers like Kingsway, Monarch, and Word; and occasional meetings and revivals that owe much to the American tent meeting tradition.

Like many European countries, British society in the last two decades has become more oriented to the politics of interest groups than to traditional notions of class, and issues of race, ethnicity, and gender have become pivotal. British politics in the 1960s and 1970s were dominated by issues with a powerful and overt class content: union power, regulation of strikes and industrial conflict, nationalization of industry. In the 1980s, the emphasis shifted to interest group politics and social issues such as censorship, feminism, gay rights, education, and public morality (which is not to say that a class agenda may not underlie many or most of these issues). In all of these areas, debate would be conditioned by moral panics, by sterotypes of sexual violence and threatening sexual predators.

Sex Beasts and
Serial Killers

— 3 —

In 1988, British television broadcast a film entitled *Sweet As You Are*, in which a woman finds that her husband has contracted AIDS through an extramarital affair. Traumatized, and awaiting her own test results, she begins obsessively collecting newspaper cuttings with headlines like "Barmaid Raped in Pub Raid," "Child Pornography Doctor Jailed," and "Woman Raped Outside Church during Mass." When her husband asks for an explanation, she replies, "One newspaper, one day. There's a lot of it about." "A lot of what?" he asked. "Male damage—men visiting prostitutes, men buying pornography, men who rape."

Perceptions of social menaces in Britain during the 1980s often focused on threats to children, and these fears are the main subject of this book. However, the new views of dangers to the young must be understood in a broader context of "male damage," a topic that indeed came to preoccupy so much of the news media. Since the mid-1970s, there has been intense concern about sexual violence, the harm caused by predatory men, usually in the quest of selfish sexual fulfillment. Under the influence of several celebrated cases, most notoriously the Yorkshire Ripper, there was a rapid growth in the influence of feminist ideas about the dangers posed by serial killers and predatory sexual offenders to innocent women and children. Within a few years, media and law enforcement had become familiarized with the whole new vocabulary of concepts and terms about these threats. These ideas helped shape thinking about threats to children, who were seen as particularly vulnerable to sexual predators and murderers.

The ideas and beliefs that became popular in the mid-1970s can be summarized as follows;

- Rape is a common crime, far more so than official figures would suggest.

47

- Rape and sexual assault are experiences common to a large number of girls and women, possibly a majority.
- Rape and sexual assault often occur within a family setting.
- The criminal justice system should be reformed in the interests of the women and children who are the victims of rape and sexual assault.
- Sexual violence includes a spectrum of related behaviors, which includes rape and sexual homicide among its most extreme manifestations.
- Serial murder is a form of sexual homicide, and it is a rapidly growing social problem.

SERIAL MURDER IN BRITAIN

During the 1980s, serial murder was widely defined in the British media as representing a new and particularly frightening social menace. During 1986 especially, there was a spate of media reports and articles about a perceived wave of such cases, perpetrated by "maniacs who kill for pleasure" (Deer 1986). The change was believed to be both quantitative and qualitative: There were far more serial killers, they claimed many more victims than hitherto, and they formed a particular threat to women and children.

These concepts would have considerable value in ideological debate, but they are not necessarily based on fact. It we examine the history of the offense over the last century or so, then it becomes apparent that serial murder on the model found in the 1980s is by no means a new phenomenon. The issue then is to explain why concern grew so sharply in the last decade, and why particular types of multiple murder began to receive so much attention [Jenkins 1988 (and sources listed therein), 1991 b; Wilson and Seaman 1983].

There are obvious problems in writing a "history" of serial murder in any society. We cannot know about murders that were never discovered or identified as crimes, or about murders that were not recognized as forming part of a series. In addition, the precise number of victims attributed to a particular offender may never be known. On the other hand, Britain offers perhaps the richest potential for constructing a relatively full account of known cases. The relative rarity of murder in this country makes it likely that recognized cases of serial murder can be retrieved and tabulated.

British murders have traditionally had a high rate of clearance by police, so an unsolved series of killings is likely to attract intense attention and investigation. The British police have always been far more centralized than their American counterparts, so that killings in separate jurisdictions would probably be connected by the authorities: Since the latter years of the nineteenth century, a major unsolved crime in the provinces would probably lead to "calling in Scotland Yard," drawing on the specialized homicide investigation skills of the Metropolitan Police. Once a crime was committed, it was likely to be reported by a national mass press with a long-established interest in sensationalism. The British media were national rather than local or regional, so that local events were unlikely to be ignored in the metropolis.

In summary, British records in this area are full and accessible; so it can be claimed with some confidence that the list of serial murder cases cited here is a fairly accurate account of the incidents known and recognized as such. For present purposes, serial murder will be defined as the killing of four or more victims over a period greater than seventy-two hours, where the primary motive does not appear to be connected with political ideology or professional crime. By these standards, we find perhaps twenty-five known serial murder cases between 1880 and 1990, as enumerated in Table 3.1. The inclusion of some of these names might be regarded as inappropriate in the strict terms of the definition: Jamieson and Neilson were operating in large measure as professional robbers, while it is questionable whether the seven cases marked with asterisks involved as many as four victims. However, Table 3.1 provides a maximum figure of known cases.[1]

These twenty-five cases in England and Wales compare to an absolute minimum of six or seven hundred in the United States in the same period (Jenkins, forthcoming). Moreover, the scale of this British activity is in contrast to conditions in other advanced countries like Germany, where serial murder cases were common between about 1919 and the 1940s. In the British record, there have been only four cases during this century where an individual case involved ten or more victims. In the United States in the twentieth century, there have been over one hundred such incidents to date (Jenkins 1988a).

Known serial murder activity has accelerated since the early part of the century, but the increase had been gradual and the 1980s produced about the same number of cases as the 1940s or 1960s. It is also uncertain how current circumstances compare with longer-term trends in British history. It may be that serial murder is more frequent today than ever; but it is also possible that contemporary conditions are typical, while the relative tranquillity of the early twentieth century requires explanation. The mid-Victorian period produced a spate of major serial killers, most frequently poisoners: Celebrated instances would include William

Table 3.1.
Serial Murderers in England and Wales, 1880–1990

Name	Dates active	Victims
Amelia Dyer	1880–1896	10+
Neill Cream	1881–1892	5
Jack the Ripper	1888	5
Frederick Deeming	1891–1892	6
Robert Money	1905–1912	6
Robert Clements*	ca. 1930–1947	4?
Frederick Field*	1931–1936	2+
Frederick Gordon Cummins	1942	4
John Christie	1943–1953	8
John Haigh	1944–1949	6
Nudes Murderer	1959–1964	7
Ian Brady and Myra Hindley	1963–1965	5
Raymond Morris*	1965–1967	4?
Graham Frederick Young*	1962–1971	3?
Patrick Mackay	1973–1975	12
Donald Neilson	1971–1974	4
Peter Dinsdale/"Bruce Lee"	1973–1980	26
Peter Sutcliffe	1975–1980	13
Kieron Kelly*	1975–1983	5?
Dennis Nilsen	1978–1983	15
Michael Jamieson	1980	4
Child murderer?*	1978–1986?	5?
London pedophile ring?*	1980–1986?	9?
Michele Lupo	1986	4
Kenneth Erskine	1986	8

*May have involved less than four victims.

Palmer and Mary Ann Cotton (respectively executed in 1856 and 1873). That these were detected in an age of such rudimentary forensic science and primitive policing suggests that they may have represented the tip of a rather large iceberg.

   In historical terms, serial homicide is a rare offense in Great Britain, a picture that changes little if we include multiple killers associated with only three murders. In any given period, serial murder may account for at most 1 or 2 percent of homicides in England and Wales, compared to the 55 percent or so of killings that occur within the context of the immediate family. However, the social and emotional impact of multiple homicide can be immense, and this has been especially true in the last two decades.

Increased awareness about serial murder owed much to American ideas. The term *serial murder* was borrowed from the United States in the mid-1980s, when a distinction was drawn between serial and mass killers; and elaborate taxonomies of both types began to be constructed and circulated. New perceptions affected the attitudes of British media and law enforcement, so that unsolved deaths or disappearances were now more likely to be viewed as part of a connected sequence of crimes, behind which was a sex killer or a "ripper" like Peter Sutcliffe. Michele Lupo, or John Duffy (see below). Increased awareness of possible links may itself have promoted detection and conviction, which in turn further raised public fear about the scale of the danger.[2]

Also important in the new definition was the apparent predominance of women and girls among the victims of serial killers. The stereotype was customarily that of a ripper, a sexually motivated male murderer, though this interpretation is open to criticism. Killing for sexual pleasure is only one of the motives found among multiple murderers: Others may kill in part out of greed or in pursuit of a professional criminal career, while doctors or nurses who kill their patients may act out of motives of power and dominance that can be quite separate from sexual impulses. And female serial killers are by no means a rare type (Hickey 1991; compare Birch 1991).

Despite these caveats, cases of rape and multiple homicide became weapons in the rhetoric of sexual politics. New understanding of multiple homicide must therefore be located in the wider debates over rape and sexual violence, areas in which public attitudes were revolutionized in the decade following 1975.

THE POLITICS OF RAPE

Since the early 1970s, there has been increased concern in Britain about sexual violence against women (Soothill and Walby 1991). This upsurge of interest can be seen in part as a response to the work of American writers like Susan Brownmiller on rape as a form of mass sexual intimidation. However, British women had similar grievances about the unsympathetic attitudes of police and courts to rape victims, whose veracity was often doubted. Public attitudes suggested that women invented false charges, were "asking for it" by irresponsible or provocative behavior, and suffered little real harm in consequence of an attack (Benn et al. 1986).

Changing this situation inevitably became a prominent part of the early feminist agenda. By the late 1970s, there was a network of Rape Crisis Centers (RCCs), and a Women Against Rape (WAR) movement modeled on American precedent (C. Roberts 1989). In 1976, a Sexual Offences (Amendent) Act attempted to reduce the public humiliation that often befell a victim in court. It restricted the ability of counsel to interrogate victims about their sexual history, and imposed reporting restrictions on the media.

These changes only strengthened calls for reform that was more far-reaching, and the campaign gained strength in the 1980s (Temkin 1987; Tomaselli and Porter 1986; Toner 1982). Several events made early 1982 "a turning point in British sexual politics" (Campbell 1988a: 70). Much discussed was a television documentary on the Thames Valley Police, which showed skeptical detectives harassing a woman reporting a rape. This provoked angry reaction in Parliament and the media, and the Home Office recommended that victims should have the right to be examined by women (Borders 1982).

Also at issue were some court cases publicized about this time. In one, a woman had been repeatedly cut as well as raped, leaving wounds that required 168 stitches. The public prosecutor refused to proceed with the case, ostensibly in order to save the woman further trauma, and because she "was not in a fit state to give evidence." This apparently suggested that future rapists could avoid jail simply by mutilating their victims. Another woman who had been raped was criticized by the trial judge for her "great deal of contributory negligence" in hitchhiking late at night, and he passed a light noncustodial sentence on the attacker (Borders 1982). Taken in conjunction with the documentary, these cases suggested major failures in public reactions to rape; and throughout the decade, there would be other stories of apparent insensitivity by police or judges.

Some atrocity stories involved the lenient sentencing of sexual offenders. In 1986, the Ealing Vicarage case involved the multiple rape of a woman, while two men were badly beaten. The sentences for the two offenders were five and three years, respectively, well below the eight-year norm recommended by senior judges. Other cases were almost bizarre in nature. In one, the victims of a serial rapist named Christopher Meah received sums of £7,000 and £10,000, respectively, from the Criminal Injuries Compensation Board. The sums were generous by British standards, but they were overshadowed by the monies awarded to Meah himself. The rapist attributed his crime to a brain injury resulting from a road accident; and in 1985, received compensation of £45,000 (*Guardian Weekly*, November 22, 1985).

Estimates about the prevalence of rape varied greatly. Figures for reported rape in England and Wales rose steadily from the early 1970s, because of changes in both public attitudes and police practices (Soothill 1191; Temkin 1987). Police recorded 1,040 offenses in 1975, 1,225 in 1980, and there was a much-quoted leap to 1,842 cases in 1985. By 1988, the reported total had reached 2,855.

Survey data suggested that even this represented only a tiny part of a much larger picture (Hall 1985; Toner 1982). In 1989, an *Options* survey suggested that 80 percent of British women had been the victim of some form of assault or abuse at some point in their lives (*Times*, January 10, 1989). In 1990, a survey of over one thousand women throughout Britain implied that one woman in four in the eighteen to fifty-four age group had been raped; while one in seven married women had been raped by their husbands while cohabiting (*Guardian*, November 8, 1990; compare Renvoize 1982). The survey was undertaken for the television news program *World in Action*, which thus ensured that the item was widely publicized. Survey evidence also suggested widespread fears about becoming the victim of a rapist. By 1985, 30 percent of women described themselves as very worried about this danger.

SERIAL RAPE

These fears were enhanced by the increased reporting of cases where one man was arrested for a number of rapes, often running into dozens of incidents. Because the reporting of rape is so subject to public attitudes and police procedures, it would be rash to argue whether this was a new phenomenon; but serial rape appeared to be a genuinely new phenomenon in the annals of recorded British crime, in contrast to serial murder. When the first nationally notorious case in modern Britain occurred in Cambridge in 1974–1975, newspapers used phrases like "unparalleled in recent British criminal records," but serial rape became much more common (or better recognized) in the 1980s.

From 1983 through 1989, the newspapers often reported the career of Tony MacLean, the Notting Hill Rapist (Toynbee 1983; *Guardian*, April 14–15, 1989). In 1984, there were the celebrated cases of a multiple Disco Rapist in Southend (*Times*, September 11, 1984) and of a sinister masked attacker in Bedfordshire, christened "the Fox" by the media (*Times*, September 13–14 1984). In 1986, there was heavy coverage of the case of

M4 Rapist, John Stead. In 1987 and 1988, police in northwest England were pursuing a man in connection with some twenty sexual assaults as well as burglaries and firearms offenses, committed over a period of several years (*Guardian,* January 8, 1988). The long duration of such "careers" of rape implied yet again that the police were not treating the issue with sufficient seriousness.

News stories emphasized the extreme randomness of sexual violence. In June 1988, there was a much-discussed case when a pregnant woman named Marie Wilks suffered a car breakdown on a motorway. She walked to find an emergency phone, and in the brief interval that she was alone and on foot, she was abducted, raped, and murdered. As the crime could not have been premeditated, this seemed to confirm feminist theories about the omnipresence of a rape threat in a patriarchal society. Media coverage was particularly intense: The *Times* alone presented sixteen stories on the Wilks case in the last ten days of June.

OFFICIAL RESPONSES TO RAPE

By the early 1980s, RCCs were often successful in promoting cooperation with medical agencies and police, and established experimental project to assist victims. One influential experiment was founded in 1985 in Dublin, in the Republic of Ireland, and there were similar British groups, as in Leeds and Tyneside. Stratchclyde police set up its Female and Child Unit in 1984 (Sutherland 1986), and in 1986, Manchester acquired the country's first Sexual Assault Referral Center (Campbell 1988a:31–35). These units were important in attracting a large number of victims whose cases would otherwise have gone unreported. This supported the existence of a vast "dark figure" of sexual assault (C. Roberts 1989; Tomaselli and Porter 1986; Rape Crisis Center 1984; Toner 1982).

New views of the seriousness and frequency of rape led to calls for legal procedures to be reformed in order to make the courtroom appear a less hostile environment for victims (Temkin 1987; Adler 1987; Smart 1989). A typical critique of the existing situation appeared in the *New Statesman and Society:*

Masculinity stands revealed in [judges'] procedures and judgments. Judges quite blatantly oppose the supposed rationality of men to the unreliable witness of women, and in doing so draw not only on centuries of "common sense," but also on the work of male psychiatrists who have suggested how easy it is for women to confuse their rape fantasies with reality. (Lees 1989b; compare Lees 1989a)

There were repeated media stories on this issue, and not merely in the left or feminist press; There was a broad consensus that the prefeminist ancien régime had indeed been unfair and unacceptable.

Specific proposals were numerous. Some suggested that proof beyond a reasonable doubt should be replaced by the civil law criterion of proof on a balance of probabilities. Other less radical changes attempted to reduce the chance that a victim might be intimidated in the courtroom. Under the Criminal Justice Act of 1988, child victims were permitted to give evidence from outside the court by live video link, children being defined for this purpose as those under fourteen years of age. The following year, pressure grew for a similar protected status to be given to adult women, who had equal difficulty in confronting their alleged attackers. In 1989, some women were allowed to give evidence from behind screens.

Another breakthrough of sorts occurred in 1986, when a woman succeeded in winning a civil action for rape, after the Director of Public Prosecutions had refused to pursue the case. In 1991, a centuries-old tradition was overturned when a man was convicted of raping the wife with whom he was currently cohabiting (compare Clark 1987).

THE YORKSHIRE RIPPER

The antirape campaigns of the 1970s coincided with the Yorkshire Ripper case, in which Peter Sutcliffe killed thirteen women in northern English towns like Leeds and Bradford (Beattie 1981; Cross 1981; Burn 1984). This placed the concept of the serial killer firmly in the public mind, preparing the way for a "serial murder problem" in the next decade. It also ensured that the problem would be viewed as a subset of sexual violence. The case reinforced the connections between rape and sexual murder, so that it no longer seemed farfetched to speak of rape "survivors." There was a new emphasis on the *violence* in sexual violence, and not even the most insensitive observer would suggest that women were "asking for" mutilation and torture.

The offense of serial murder was not new in Britain, but the number of Sutcliffe's victims was very large by local standards. More significant was the issue of public awareness. In earlier British cases, the full scale of an offender's crimes came to light at the end of his or her career, perhaps with his or her arrest or death. The existence of a serial killer therefore remained unknown until he or she was safely dead or in custody. This lack of contemporary knowledge accounts for the relative obscurity of Patrick Mackay (1973 to 1975), who was at least as dangerous an offender as Sutcliffe and who claimed almost as many victims. By contrast, the existence of a Yorkshire Ripper was known for a lengthy period, which encouraged media speculation and sensationalism, with consequent public fear. In this sense, the case was perhaps unparalleled since the days of Jack the Ripper in the 1880s, but "Jack's" career lasted four months, compared to five years for Sutcliffe (Jenkins 1988b).

Sutcliffe claimed his first victim, a Leeds prostitute, in 1975, and by the end of 1977 he had killed a total of six women in the industrial areas of northern England. The murders were usually accompanied by grotesque sexual mutilations. From at least 1976, it was generally recognized that a sexually motivated serial killer was at large in northern England. The early police investigation was a model of its kind: The police made an extensive collection of apparently insignificant pieces of information, hoping that they would lead to the offender. At one point, tracing a banknote led police to inquire at Sutcliffe's place of work, and he would be interrogated on a number of occasions in the inquiry. On the other hand, the investigation went astray, partly through the sheer volume of evidence collected. In retrospect, it now appears that enough separate indications of Sutcliffe's guilt existed in police documents, only awaiting recognition and collation.

Also fatal was police acceptance of spurious audiotapes purported to come from Jack the Ripper, which if genuine would establish that the killer could be traced by his dialect to a distinctive geographical origin. Between 1978 and 1980, the police made these tapes extensively available, but this only served to distract the attention of those who already suspected Sutcliffe's involvement. By 1980, the police were increasingly frustrated and humiliated by their failure to catch the Ripper, whose final arrest occurred largely by accident, when he was stopped for an unrelated matter.

SERIAL MURDER AS SEXUAL MURDER

The Ripper case contributed significantly to changing perceptions of social menaces. In earlier decades, the violence of serial killers like John Christie or John Straffen was seen as a warning of the evil of particularly disturbed individuals, and perhaps as a symbolic call for extending psychiatric intervention to detect such offenders before they could cause real harm (Rolph 1980). Now the focus shifted to the underlying sexual conflicts that appeared to form the essential context of serial murder. It has been justly said that "the case of Sutcliffe familiarized feminist analyses of sexual violence to an unprecedented degree" (Cameron and Frazer 1987:33; compare Eardley 1985).

The wave of jokes and legends surrounding Sutcliffe indicated that rippers were only acting out in overt form the concealed fantasies of many "normal" males. In the late 1970s, the Yorkshire Ripper's name was chanted by football crowds, in part to taunt the alleged ineptitude of the police. The Ripper trial, meanwhile, was seen by feminists as an ideological charade intended to reinforce patriarchal values. As an article in the *Feminist Review* argued in 1981,

> Sutcliffe's trial demonstrated men's collaboration with other men in the oppression of women. . . . The trial refused to recognize the way in which Sutcliffe's acts were an expression—albeit an extreme one—of the construction of an aggressive masculine sexuality and of women as its subjects. This cover-up exonerates men in general even when one man is found guilty. (Holloway 1984:14)

He claimed to have been driven by voices, "but the voice that Sutcliffe obeyed was the voice not of God or delusion, but of the hoardings on the streets, of newspaper stands, of porn displays and of films. It is the voice which addresses every man in our society and to that extent, as the feminist slogan claims, all men are potential rapists" (p. 22).

Feminists argued that police and press accounts of the killings reinforced ideologies harmful to women: "The constant publicity about [the Ripper] terrified women and made him into an anti-hero. Police warned women in northern towns not to go out at night alone, while newspapers branded Peter Sutcliffe's various victims as 'innocent' or 'guilty,' further setting limits to women's behavior" (Clark 1986). The media apparently accepted Sutcliffe's evaluation of prostitutes and loose women as fair game for murder, unlike "good girls." This can be seen from reactions to the death of a sixteen-year-old schoolgirl, killed by Sutcliffe in a rare departure from his normal pattern of killing prostitutes. Was it suggested that the other women had somehow deserved their fates? Prosecutor (and prominent politician) Sir Michael Havers remarked of the victims that "some were prostitutes, but perhaps the saddest part of this case is that some were not" (Holloway 1984:21). Sutcliffe provided a powerful case study for American feminists, who focused on these issues of male attitudes (Caputi 1987:94–95, 145–146; compare Walkowitz 1982).

CONSTRUCTING SEXUAL VIOLENCE

Rape and serial murder were seen as part of a common problem of sexual violence, which also incorporated other perceived abuses. In the late 1970s, the domain of the sexual violence problem expanded enormously. In 1978, for example, Mary MacIntosh wrote, "Like rape, like contemporary forms of pornography, like beauty competitions, like much of our public culture, prostitution contributes to the casting of women as object and men as subject, and thus to the prevailing ideology" (quoted in Matthews and Young 1986:200). Rape and sexual murder often played a symbolic role in debates over legislation and social policy (Smart 1989; Rape Crisis Center 1984). Susan S. M. Edwards wrote of the need for legal reform to challenge "the all-pervasive rape ideology" (Edwards 1991:210).

One of the most sweeping examples of problem convergence was provided by lesbian activist Sheila Jeffreys, writing in the *Leveller* in 1979:

> All men are potential rapists. . . . Every man benefits from the actions of every rapist. . . .
> The spectrum of violence by men towards women, all aspects of which serve the twin purpose of male gratification and political control of women, includes: wife-beating, sexual abuse of children, frotteurism (rubbing the penis against part of a woman's body—common at Wimbledon tennis matches and in the tube), voyeurism (often reconnoitring for a rape victim), obscene remarks, pornography, touching up, Boston Strangler and Bradford Ripper, wife-murder, obscene telephone calls, father-daughter incest and rape. (Jeffreys 1979)

In the late 1970s, such concerns led to the emergence of a network of separatist women's organizations opposed to male violence, some of which campaigned for the castration of rapists (Stanko 1985; Hanmer et al. 1989). These groups asked why women were told to observe an effective curfew by staying off the streets during a serial murder crisis. Why not take truly effective preventive measures by imposing a curfew on men? In 1980, the National Women's Liberation Conference was held in Leeds, in the heart of Ripper territory. Its subject was "Sexual Violence Against Women." The 1981 venue was London, where the theme was "Women Against Violence Against Women" (Rhodes and McNeill 1985).

Defining the problem in terms of gender placed a new emphasis on sexually explicit material, which was believed to stimulate aggressive male behavior. This was important in that pornography offered tangible targets for feminist anger, which reached a peak between about 1979 and 1982. The mood of the time is suggested by the *New Statesman:*

> times like the present when sexual violence is felt to be increasing and when the media seem determined to make rape and wife-battering appear acceptable male practices. Feminists will not evade this battle, or fail to respond to the female rage which is making itself felt in attacks on sex cinemas, in "reclaim the night" marches, and in demonstrations in areas terrorized by male Rippers acting out the ultimate male fantasies of a violent male sexual culture. (January 23, 1981)

The Reclaim the Night movement demonstrated aggressively against the sale of pornography, while towns like Leeds and Barnsley were the scene of several acts of arson and sabotage against sex shops (see, for example, *Times*, February 10, 1981; August 27, 1982; Kanter et al., 1984:49). It was peculiarly appropriate that the incidents occurred in northern industrial towns with a strong tradition for political radicalism, where traditional socialist views were being challenged by a dynamic feminist element.

But rape and sexual crime continued to motivate antiporonography campaigns throughout the decade. In 1984, for example, serial rapist Malcolm Fairley was convicted for a series of rapes, burglaries, and various sexual offenses. As customarily happened in the aftermath of such incidents, there were immediate calls for tighter restrictions to be placed on sexually explicit material. Right-wing Tory M.P. Jill Knight was supported in this cause by left-wing and feminist politicians of all parties (Tysoe 1985; C. Roberts 1989:134). Rape would be a central issue in the video nasties debate of the early 1980s, and in subsequent attempts to regulate the cinema and broadcasting (see Chapter 2).

THE FEMINIST ANALYSIS OF SERIAL MURDER

The most ambitious British analysis of sex murder as a manifestation of male patriarchal power is provided by Cameron and Frazer in *The Lust to Kill* (1987), which was frequently cited in following years. This "feminist investigation of serial murder . . . began from a simple observation: there has never been a female Peter Sutcliffe" (p. 1). The image of Sutcliffe runs through the book, and provides a vehicle for remarkably sweeping observations about the mass of "normal" men.

Many men "shared the Ripper's pleasure in female fear. . . . Though few men could do what Sutcliffe did, many men share some of Sutcliffe's desires" (p. 33). The portrayal of the killer as a sort of hero was indicated by a spate of books in 1987–1978, to mark the centenary of the Jack the Ripper case.

Feminist ideas were accepted by large sections of the criminological profession within Britain. This caused some ideological contradictions, and a shift away from earlier positions that were broadly libertarian in nature. Early books like *The New Criminology* (Taylor et al. 1973) and *Critical Criminology* (Taylor et al. 1975) were seen as Marxist or anarchist tracts profoundly hostile to the criminal justice system and to most aspects of the political status quo. In the 1980s, however, feminist demands for protection against sexual violence were a key factor in pushing radicals toward "left realist" views, sympathetic to strong action against violent criminals. In some instances, this might mean proactive policing and severe sentencing [see Matthews and Young (1986), and especially the essays of Phipps (1988) and Box-Grainger (1986)].

Ian Taylor (1981:191–192) accepted that the Yorkshire Ripper incident had to be seen as an essential foundation of any future attempt to reformulate policy toward sexual violence. He also agreed that serial murder should be viewed in a spectrum that included rape and domestic violence, all of which receive at least tacit support from violent and pornographic media: "What is crucial about pornography is what it legitimates ideologically" (p. 200).

Even the law and order rhetoric of the sort traditionally associated with conservatives was now employed by leftists. It was the radical Labour M.P. Gordon Brown who listed growing sexual violence as a consequence of Thatcherite economic policies, employing highly questionable statistics in the process: "Over the last ten years the incidence of violent crime has doubled. Rape has more than doubled. In some surveys, nine out of ten women have said they are afraid to go out alone. Fear is widespread, both in the home . . . outdoors and on public transportation" (Brown 1989:159).

Even when scholars disputed specific aspects of the feminist agenda, they usually accepted the broad outlines of the analysis (Box 1983). Moreover, there was little work done from rival positions. Journals like the *British Journal of Psychiatry* published important work on extreme violence and homicide offenders, but the more sociologically oriented outlets offered little. In the prestigious *British Journal of Criminology* and *British Journal of Sociology* virtually the only mention of serial murder or rape was in the form of favorable reviews of *The Lust to Kill*.

ANNE LOCK AND SUZY LAMPLUGH

In the years following Sutcliffe's trial, there were a number of instances of multiple murder in Great Britain, some of which closely recalled the Ripper's threat to women and teenage girls. The sense of menace was focused by several highly publicized disappearances, which led to enormous media speculation, though none involved a serial killer in conventional definition (none of the culprits was involved with a sufficiently large number of attacks to quality for this dubious honor). Concern reached its height in 1986, with the disappearances of Suzy Lamplugh and Anne Lock. Both became major national incidents, which would culminate in the arrests of (unrelated) murderers John Cannan and Railway Killer, John Francis Duffy (Keel 1988; Stephen 1988; Newton 1990)

The figure of the Railway Murderer entered the national news in May 1986, with the disappearance in London of Anne Lock, a secretary working for a television network. Her body was discovered close to the suburban railway station were she had last been seen alive. The proximity of the rail line was intriguing, in that it linked the crime with two other murders in the London area during the previous six months. Alison Day had been raped and murdered in December 1985, and fifteen-year-old Maartje Tamboezer perished in April.

Police now hypothesized that not only were these murders connected, but that they might in turn be related to a series of twenty or more rapes committed in the previous two years, usually near railway stations. These crimes were already the focus of a major police task force organized as Operation Hart. In November, police arrested John Francis Duffy, a British Rail carpenter, charging him with seven rapes and the three murders in the alleged series of attacks. He was convicted on several counts, but was acquitted on the Anne Lock murder due to insufficient evidence.

The Duffy case served once more to attract attention to the image of the serial killer as sexual monster, a theme that was repeatedly stressed during the coverage of his trial through early 1988. The inclusion of the teenage girl among his victims also reinforced emerging stereotypes of the anonymous wandering sex fiend who preyed on children, an idea that will be addressed in the next chapter. But above all, the theme that emerged from Duffy's story was that of specifically male violence against women. In the words of the *Guardian*, "If ever a case illustrated that rape is about terrorizing and humiliating women, rather than sexual gratification, it was the series of brutal assaults carried out by John Duffy" (Keel 1988).

Equally frightening was the incident of real estate agent Suzy Lamplugh, whose disappearance provided one of the longest-running and most sensational stories in the British media; and the case remains unresolved to this day. She vanished shortly after making a business appointment with a man she had nicknamed Mr. Kipper. The media speculated freely about whether she had fled or been abducted, and there would be controversy about the prurient tone of many of the investigations into Lamplugh's personal life (Stephen 1988). These suggested yet again that a woman who was probably the victim of a brutal sexual attack might have drawn her fate upon herself by her immoral conduct.

Evidence that she had been the victim of violence grew with the 1987 arrest of John Cannan in connection with a recent abduction and murder in Bristol. Though never formally connected with Lamplugh, he was widely cited in the media as the chief or only suspect in this affair, as well as in a series of attacks on women in several parts of the country since 1979 (Lane 1991:211–226). The case remained officially open and Suzy Lamplugh's mother Diana capitalized on the continuing public concern to build a pressure group to campaign for the victims of violent crime.

THE EVENTS OF 1986

These sensational reports appeared to represent a small fraction of a new wave of crime by serial offenders, in which sexual violence provided a common theme. There was also the trial of the M4 Rapist, John Stead, convicted of several rapes in addition to the murder of one woman; while a series of murders of old people in the Stockwell area of London led to the arrest of the Stockwell Strangler, Kenneth Erskine (Westwood 1991; Newton 1990). Another case involved Michele Lupo, a sadistic homosexual killer who claimed at least four male victims; while Colin Pitchfork was arrested in connection with two murders of young girls in Leicestershire. This followed an investigation in which the forensic use of DNA technology received a widely publicized test (Wambaugh 1989). There were also several continuing serial rape investigations in various parts of the country.

The issue of children as murder victims was highlighted by a number of inquiries that were publicized during 1986, which will be discussed in Chapter 4. In April, the police announced the creation of a national task force, Operation Stranger, to explore possible links between some fifteen unsolved murders and disappearances. Later in the year, two schoolgirls were found murdered in Brighton; and the notorious Moors Murders story of the early 1960s was revived with a renewed search for the bodies of additional child victims.

Table 3.2. The Events of 1986

January	Disappearance of Alison Day
March	Disappearance of Sarah Harper leads to announcement of Operation Stranger inquiry in April
April	Arrest of Michele Lupo
April–July	Main media overage of Stockwell Strangler (Kenneth Erskine arrested in August)
May	Disappearance of Anne Lock; body found in July. Police in North London organize Operation Alleyman to arrest a serial rapist, later identified as Shaun Francis.
July	Murder of Dawn Ashworth in Leicestershire linked to earlier (1983) murder of girl in the same area. Suzy Lamplugh disappears
September	Five members of Hampshire family murdered in robbery
October	Bodies of two schoolgirls found near Brighton
November	Police reopen search for bodies in Moors Murders John Duffy arrested Trial of John Stead for murder and several rapes
December	Murders of two women in Wiltshire believed to be linked to another killing in Portsmouth Police announce search for man and woman in Operation Stranger

These events can be summarized in the form of the chronology shown in Table 3.2. As can be seen, each month brought a new front-page story about multiple sexual murder, while arrests, trials, and other developments kept these cases in the news well into 1988. There was a new sensitivity to "linkage," and while possible connections might have been ignored in the past, there were now occasions where they were exaggerated. The Operation Stranger series is one example, but there were several other incidents in these years where police and media dubiously hypothesized a single "maniac" offender in groups of unsolved murders (Campbell 1991b). One possible series was suggested in London and Essex during 1987, perhaps connected to a series of rapes in the Colchester area. In December 1986, there were two murders of women in Wiltshire, and another unsolved death in Hampshire (Newton

1990). Police were swift to suggest that this was yet another serial murder, but the charging of two unconnected men made it apparent that this view was false. In 1991, a number of unsolved murders and disappearances of women led to extensive speculation about a second ripper active in Yorkshire, as well as about a perceived wave of violence directed specifically against women (Alderson et al. 1991)

The new approach was enthusiastically taken up by the media and by popular crime writers. Investigators began to speculate freely about links across jurisdictions, in Europe as well as within the United Kingdom. One author has linked Peter Sutcliffe to a number of crimes in continental Europe, while Lupo is plausibly believed to have carried out attacks in other countries. In 1986, the Stockwell attacks led to media speculation about a possible relationship to the contemporary "granny murders" in Paris, which also involved the murder of solitary old people (Deer 1986).

It was during mid-1986 that the media began seeing the serial killer less as an issue of a few disturbed individuals, and more of a social phenomenon, which required urgent action. It was strongly implied that this was a wholly new phenomenon, and earlier cases were ignored or forgotten. The *Sunday Times* was typical of press coverage in its remark that "with thousands of police in the hunt for the Stockwell Strangler and the Railway Killer in London, the spectre of the serial murderer, now common in America, has been established in Britain" (Deer 1986). There was "growing alarm . . . that Britain could be seeing the growth of what their American counterparts are calling recreational murder, where there is no apparent motive" (*Sunday Times*, July 27, 1986; compare Holmes and DeBurger 1988; Levin and Fox 1985).

HOMOSEXUAL SERIAL KILLERS

Media coverage was influenced by a number of distinct political agendas. Sensational crimes were naturally of interest to the media, but there were also moral or political lessons, by no means confined to the feminist perspective. This is illustrated by two of the most celebrated cases of these years, the crimes associated with Dennis Nilsen and Michele Lupo. Both were promiscuous London homosexuals, who chose their victims among the casual sex partners they found in London's active gay scene (Lisners 1983; Masters 1985).

Both, in addition, offered political ammunition for the tabloids. Nilsen was active in leftist and radical union politics, and naturally supported the radical GLC, which was a recurrent bugbear for the tabloid press.

Nilsen himself parodied the coverage of his case in papers like the *Sun* by composing a satirical composite news story, that was uncannily close to the real reporting. It read:

RED MONSTER LURES YOUNG MEN TO THEIR DEATHS IN
HOMOSEXUAL HOUSE OF HORROR . . .

Nilsen . . . once believed to have close links with the Militant Tendency and the Socialist Workers Party (and personal supporter of Red Ken) . . . has been to East Berlin . . . a misfit and extremist trade union agitator. (Masters 1985:20)

Lupo's crimes (the "gay sex killings") were said to have been inspired by his suffering from AIDS, which once more seemed to stress the unnatural and unhealthy nature of the homosexual life-style, and metropolitan permissiveness in general. Lupo was also tailor-made for populists and moralists, as he was a well-connected figure with many friends and clients in society and show business (the *Daily Express* headline reported "Stars in Murder Quiz"). This suggested an image of a degenerate predator hiding behind a high society screen, a stereotype that will again be encountered in the context of real and alleged pedophile rings.

THE DEBATE OVER NATIONAL POLICING

Both feminist and conservative attitudes affected attitudes to serial homicide and rape, while concern can also be seen as a response to changes in police procedures and attitudes. The Sutcliffe case had been traumatic for the police, but the new emphasis on linkage should not only be seen as overreaction to one unfortunate incident. The idea fit well into certain bureaucratic agendas that were currently the source of great controversy and, above all, to the debate over national policing.

British police are under the supervision of the Home Office, and there is a centralized inspectorate, but the different forces retain their local identity. However, there has been a strong trend toward unification. During the twentieth century, the number of police forces has been steadily reduced due to mergers and amalgamations: There were 117 forces by 1962, and by 1974 there were only 52 units throughout Great Britain, mainly based at county level. By far the largest force was the Metropolitan Police in London, with about 20 percent of total police strength, and some of its units acted on a national basis. There were also some national institutions designed to combat interjurisdictional menaces such as drug trafficking and illegal immigration. In 1992, these agencies were superseded by the new National Crime Intelligence Service (NCIS), which was seen as a possible step toward a British counterpart to the American FBI, responsible for operations as well as intelligence (Campbell 1991a).

There was great resistance to any further movement toward national policing, and the founding of NCIS was attacked from many directions. Critics included not just the predictable leftists and civil libertarians, but also the Police Federation, the union of the police rank and file. National organization was unpopular in terms of the loss of local autonomy and fears of hegemony by the Metropolitan Police. There were serious worries about dangers to civil liberties: Could a national force be democratically controlled (Hain et al. 1980; Hillyard and Percy-Smith 1988)?

These fears were enhanced by the large centralized databanks in vogue, and the expansion of explicitly political police units to combat subversion and terrorism. Ulster was already a disturbing example of the creation of a virtual police state within part of the United Kingdom. When the police acquired a sophisticated national computer system in the 1970s, it had to be named the Police National Computer rather than the National Police Computer, for the latter could not exist if there was not a "national police" to use it, and even the term was politically unacceptable. Another title that many found alarming was the Integrated National Computerized Intelligence Service, which would provide a basis for the work of the new NCIS (Campbell 1991a).

The "technology of political control" had been a source of alarm to the political left at least since the mid-1970s (Hain et al. 1980; Ackroyd et al. 1980; Aubrey 1981; BSSRS 1985; Campbell and Connor 1986). Fears of national and political policing reached a climax during the miners' strike of 1984–1985, when authoritarian national policing defeated a major industrial threat (Coulter et al., 1984; Derbyshire 1988). The police had temporarily been administered by an ad hoc national command center in the form of the National Reporting Center (NRC), and even those who wished the strike to fail were often troubled by the tactics employed. The NRC was virtually free of democratic or parliamentary control, and was responsible to the Association of Chief Police Officers (ACPO), a group that critics readily characterized as a "police junta."

Further development of police national capabilities was therefore controversial, especially in the area of gathering and collating intelligence. On the other hand, the Yorkshire Ripper and other instances of serial violence indicated the need of extensive interagency cooperation and national intelligence gathering, perhaps mobilized through specialized task forces. The new investigations would require the collation of data through a massive computer network, modeled in part on the "Violent Criminal Apprehension Program" (VICAP) system of the U.S. Justice Department (Jenkins 1988a, b; Doney 1990).

American influences were important, though they are little recognized in the literature on policing. One example was the idea of catching serial offenders through "profiling," which implied the collation of large amounts of data; and in 1984, the Metropolitan Police consulted FBI behavioral scientists in connection with two ongoing serial rape inquiries (*Times,* July 3, 1984). In July 1986, it was announced that "Scotland Yard and the American FBI have launched an unparallelled joint campaign to give Britain the benefit of the FBI's experience of serial murders, where the same killers strike again and again" (*Sunday Times,* July 27, 1986). U.S. innovations were popularized in Britain through several channels, especially the FBI Legat, based in the U.S. Embassy. Senior British officers attended courses and conferences at American police academies, the most prestigious of which is the FBI academy at Quantico, Virginia.

HOLMES

The Thatcher government had pledged to increase public expenditure on the police in the form of personnel and resources, at a time when most other arms of government were being reduced severely: Between 1978–1979 and 1986–1987, the Home Office budget actually rose by 50 percent, from £3.8 to £5.7 billion (Derbyshire 1988:176). The administration was therefore likely to look sympathetically on police pressure for a large computer network; and by 1986, this became operational as the Home Office Large Major Enquiry System, or HOLMES (Peace and Barrington 1985).

HOLMES had many uses, and proved invaluable during the complex reconstruction of the remains of Pan Am 103, the airliner blown up by a terrorist bomb over Lockerbie in 1988. On the other hand, its first and best publicized use was in the Operation Stranger affair of 1986, the first case in British history where the activities of a wandering serial killer were postulated without overwhelming evidence of connections between known murders. By March 1987, HOLMES held forty thousand names in the investigation. At the same time, computers were used to find links between apparently unconnected rapes, with some success. Few could object to so laudable a goal as the apprehension of child killers and serial rapists.

This is suggested by the 1989 novel *Devices and Desires* by P. D. James, who was a prominent Home Office administrator in addition to being a thriller writer. In a fictional serial murder investigation, a detective remarks.

> The press and public know about HOLMES, of course. I get that at every press conference. "Are you using the Home Office special computer, the one named after Sherlock Holmes?" . . . They think that you've only got to feed in your data and out pops an identikit of sonny complete with prints, collar size and taste in pop music. (pp. 70–71)

The new focus on linkage helped defuse potential opposition to a major development in police technology.

Serial murder and rape inquiries also helped popularize other trends in interjurisdictional and even national law enforcement, which were rarely criticized because of the public consensus against this sort of crime. Modeled on the Yorkshire Ripper task force, groups like Operation Stranger proved to be an increasingly common device in promoting national police cooperation. These confirmed the need to allocate resources in the direction of computers and other high-technology responses to crime.

One of the child murder investigations also publicized the latest forensic technology in the form of DNA testing, which served not only to convict Colin Pitchfork, but to clear another man falsely accused of the crimes. The tool also proved valuable in some rape inquires: For instance, this was decisive evidence in the trial of the alleged Notting Hill Rapist. The triumph came at a singularly opportune time for British forensic science, which had recently been heavily criticized. Some leading scientists had been forced to resign, and many convictions of the past decade had been overturned due to flaws in forensic testimony. Between 1982 and 1984, a wide-ranging scandal had resulted from a reexamination of the work of Home Office pathologist Dr. Alan Clift, and it became apparent that forensic errors had led to the conviction of several innocent people in major terrorist incidents. A *Guardian* study in 1988 headlined "The Sorry State of a Scientific Art" (January 29, 1988; compare *Guardian*, November 14, 1987). From 1986, the spectacular claims for DNA testing offered the troubled profession a precious new veneer of reliability and public respect.

It is not proposed that the police deliberately created or exaggerated a serial murder menace to promote the cause of new technologies, and police statements about these incidents were usually admirably restrained. We do not find British police officials making sweeping estimates about the scale of a general serial murder threat, and where erroneous claims or linkages were made, they were based on understandable misinterpretations of evidence. On the other hand, the growth of national policing and intelligence gathering that occurred over the decade would scarcely have received so little criticism had it not been for the social danger they were believed to be combatting. Police interests combined with widespread social fears to enhance public perceptions of a serial murder crisis.

NOTE

1. At the time of writing, a nurse named Beverley Allitt is awaiting trial for a series of crimes committed against patients in her care, including the alleged murders of four children.

2. Part of this chapter has previously appeared in the *Journal of Contemporary Criminal Justice* (Jenkins 1991b).

Preying on Children

Pedophilia and Child Murder

— 4 —

New attitudes to rape and multiple homicide would contribute to a transformation in traditional perceptions of the sexual exploitation of children. From the late 1970s on, the image of the rather pathetic child molester would be fundamentally altered into a new and far more threatening stereotype: the sophisticated and well-organized pedophile. In the new view, the offender belonged to a predatory ring, and wrought untold physical or psychological harm on his victims. As the 1980s progressed there was a growing suspicion that the children would not emerge from their ordeal alive. Pedophilia was thus brought within the larger ambit of sexual violence in general, and serial murder in particular.

The new perceptions of pedophilia can be seen as a sequence of developmental stages. Changing attitudes and beliefs can be briefly outlined as follows:

Stage I: 1976–1982

- Child pornography is a growing menace, which is linked to the sexual exploitation of children. Both activities are often the work of organized groups of pedophiles.
- Pedophiles (whether individual or organized) are often drawn from social and political elites.

Stage II: 1983–1986

- Pedophiles, individual and organized, molest very large numbers of children, possibly in the thousands.
- Pedophiles sometimes abduct their victims and assault them forcibly.

71

- Pedophile rings are associated with the abduction and murder of children across a wide geographical area.
- Pedophilia is thus linked to the problems of sexual violence and serial murder.

State III: 1987–1992

- Pedophile murder rings are a common phenomenon.
- Murders are sometimes recorded to create a clandestine industry of snuff films and videos.
- Pedophile rings are using subterfuge and disguise to locate and seize victims, often by assuming the role of official figures like social workers.

INVENTING THE PEDOPHILE

Childhood is a socially constructed phenomenon, the definition and limits of which vary greatly in different epochs and societies (Rogers et al. 1989:23–29; Feierman 1990). Perhaps no aspect of childhood is so liable to the impact of changing social and economic patterns as the age of sexual maturity. This in turn decides what law and public opinion consider deviant in terms of appropriate sexual activity with younger people (Best 1990; Tucker 1987; Seabrook 1987a; Ellis 1986a). In England, the heterosexual age of consent was twelve for most of the nineteenth century, during which time there is abundant evidence of avid interest in young girls. In 1871, a royal commission remarked: "The traffic in children for infamous purposes is notoriously considerable in London and other large towns" (Pearsall 1971:359).

The age was raised to fourteen a few years later, and raised again to sixteen in 1885. This followed a scandal about a flourishing overseas trade in young English virgins, who were sold to houses of prostitution (Weeks 1981). Celebrated pornographic works like *My Secret Life* and *The Pearl* often record encounters with girls as young as nine or ten, yet there is little suggestion that these were specifically catering to a distinct child pornography market. Nor were the men portrayed seen as a special category recognizable by a distinctive term such as "pedophile". The younger girl, especially if a virgin, was regarded as a particularly valuable trophy for a roué, whose tastes would also run to girls and women of almost any age (Pearsall 1971).

Male homosexuality was, of course, illegal whatever the ages of the participants, but here too a widespread taste for boys and young teenagers is indicated both by recurring Victorian scandals and the surviving pornographic literature (Reade 1970). The child molester was for most of the twentieth century a familiar figure in the British press. In the 1920s, the novels of Evelyn Waugh assumed that the case of "another naughty scout-master" would be the normal fare of sensationalistic papers like the *News of the World* (Parker 1969).

Pedophile was an extremely rare word in Britain before the 1970s, in contrast to *pederast*, which had a classical lineage. As recently as 1973, *pedophile* was not included in the *Shorter Oxford English Dictionary*; as a topic in the *Times* index, it dates only from 1977. The term originated with Krafft-Ebing: It was used in scholarly works of the 1970s, usually American, in the sense of a lone male sexually interested in children [see, for example, Kempe and Kempe (1978) and Kraemer (1976), for a British perspective]. The emergence of the current image (and term) of the pedophile can be dated with some precision to debates that occurred in 1977 and 1978.

In 1977, the media began to publish many stories about an alleged upsurge in child pornography, largely imported from the Continent, though occasionally manufactured in Great Britain. The major activist was Mary Whitehouse, who in June began demanding legal controls to halt the spread of "kiddie porn." Mrs. Whitehouse and her group, NVALA, had been protesting permissive broadcasting standards since the mid-1960s, and had enjoyed limited success (Tracey and Morrison 1978). The new campaign proved to be a public triumph, as it circumvented traditional libertarian objections to censorship. The focus on children made it difficult to argue that producing and selling such material was simply a private matter that only affected freely consenting adults.

NVALA formed the subgroup Action to Ban Sexual Exploitation of Children (ABUSE) which began a lobbying movement in alliance with other groups like the Festival of Light. Throughout late 1977 and early 1978, Whitehouse was agitating for laws against parents who permitted their children to be used in pornography, and urging the extirpation of the whole genre. There were close ties with the contemporary American movement against child pornography, which had been active in testifying at a number of hearings of the U.S. House Judiciary Committee that year (Burgess and Clark 1984:8–10). The leader of the American activists was psychiatrist and lawyer Dr. Judianne Densen-Gerber, who alleged the existence of a vast international child pornography industry linked to the abduction of children for use in snuff films (Best 1990:72–73). She was flown to Britain to address meetings and press conferences.

The campaign attracted political support from both traditional enemies of permissiveness and from the new radical right of the Conservative party, including Margaret Thatcher. Parliamentary action to prohibit the production, importation, or sale of child pornography followed swiftly, in the form of the Protection of Children Act. The measure was essentially unopposed, except for some procedural points, and it became law in April 1978.

THE PEDOPHILE INFORMATION EXCHANGE (PIE)

Speedy action over pornography in the 1970s was assisted by the contemporary furor over the Pedophile Information Exchange (PIE), an organization that campaigned to abolish the age of sexual consent. Founded in 1974, the group had originally presented itself as advocating the right of men to have sex with children. In the late 1970s, PIE's rhetoric changed to the more successful approach of children's rights, arguing that children should have the right to decide their sexual behavior and orientation (O'Carroll 1980a). The group drew an important distinction between the molester and the pedophile, based on whether the child in question consented to sexual activity.

From a libertarian perspective, this was at least superficially credible. PIE leader Tom O'Carroll enjoyed some success in his attempt to portray his cause as part of the radical assault on traditional patriarchy; and for some time the group received a surprising platform in left/feminist journals like the *Leveller* (O'Carroll 1980a, b). The old-established anarchist/pacifist journal *Peace News* also offered a platform, and copublished the memoir of one of its former editors who had been tried for a sexual offense with a ten-year-old boy (Moody 1980).

PIE's advocacy work was legal, though controversial, but it was widely assumed that the group had clandestine motives: to manufacture, import, and distribute child pornography, and perhaps to create a database of likely victims. In early 1978, it was alleged that the names of British children had been found on lists circulating among pedophiles as far afield as the United States. Media exposés about PIE reached a height in the fall of 1977, at the same time as the Whitehouse campaign was reaching full steam. There is evidence that the media were expressing authentic public hostility, and PIE meetings were often prevented by protests from secretarial or maintenance staff at the meeting sites.

Tom O'Carroll was suspended and ultimately dismissed from his job with the British Open University, a conflict that led to extensive media coverage during the next year or two, while further stories concerned his growing legal difficulties over child pornography charges. The movement remained in the news: In 1984, there were attempts to extradite PIE's leader from The Netherlands, and several other members were jailed for the importation of child pornography (see, for example, *Times*, September 10, 1983, and November 14, 1984).

For the antiobscenity campaigners, PIE was evidence that pornography was no simple matter of private enjoyment: it had consequences in the real world, and specifically in the molestation of children. The right-wing magazine *Private Eye* satirically imagined whether the libertarians who defended PIE would be equally likely to support a "King Herod Society," whose members claimed merely to be discussing their interest in the multiple murder of children. This would be an ironic foretaste of some real concerns of the next decade.

PIE appears to have been a tiny cell of activists, but the social importance of an information exchange was enormous. The mere existence of the group changed not only the image but the title of the molester: It not only familiarized the general public with the word *pedophile*, but ensured that it would usually have connotations of organized activity.

PEDOPHILES AND HOMOSEXUALS

Pedophilia was an effective vehicle for attacking both homosexuality and leftist politics, with which it was frequently linked by conservative critics. Of course, *pedophile* is a term used for adults whose sexual orientation attracts them to children of either sex, and there is no necessary link with homosexuality. On the other hand, this connection was often made in popular stereotypes, and this was reinforced by the behavior of some groups in the gay rights movement.

In the 1970s, the pedophile movement was one of several fringe groups whose cause was to some extent espoused in the name of gay liberation. Jeffrey Weeks, for example, wrote sympathetically of oppressed sexual minorities like "sado-masochists, paedophiles, transvestites, prostitutes," while the Gay Youth Movement asserted the rights of "transsexuals, transvestites and paedophiles" (quoted in Jeffreys 1990:164, 188). Even the mainstream homosexual rights movement, Campaign for Homosexual Equality (CHE), was divided over attitudes to PIE, and this ambiguity caused at least some of the child molester stigma to adhere to ordinary homosexuals. In November 1977—at the height of the child porn panic—CHE's conference passed a resolution condemning press harassment of PIE and urging open discussion on issues of children's sexuality. As late as 1983, CHE asserted PIE's right to "free discussion" (*Observer*, 11 September 1983). This sympathy earned the increasing ire of feminists, especially in the years after 1980 when child abuse became so central to feminist theory. CHE's attitude was described by Emily Driver as "a shame" (Driver and Droisen 1989: 59); Sheila Jeffreys saw it as a major symptom of "the failure of Gay Liberation" (Jeffreys 1990:188–210).

Homosexual sympathy for PIE arose partly from the legal means used against the pedophiles. The 1967 act that decriminalized adult homosexual behavior had not granted full legalization, and there remained a number of earlier provisions that could be used by police or prosecutors. In the early 1970s, the newspaper *IT* had been convicted of "conspiracy to corrupt public morals" through publishing gay contact advertisements, and the judges had made it clear that homosexual advocacy or propaganda might still be covered by this offense. There was therefore real concern when PIE leaders were convicted of the same crime in 1981 (Galloway, 1983; Weeks 1977).

Meanwhile, there was a specific legal paradox that benefited the right-wing attempt to connect homosexuality and pedophilia. The liberalization of homosexuality laws in 1967 had been progressive by contemporary standards, but it had left the age of homosexual consent at twenty-one, rather than the heterosexual sixteen; and shortly afterwards, the age of majority for all other purposes had become eighteen. The problems encountered by homosexuals aged eighteen to twenty-one were apparent, and the anomaly gave the police latitude to continue to investigate and prosecute adult homosexuals.

Pressure to reduce the homosexual age of consent was depicted by moral conservatives as advocacy for pedophilia. O'Carroll thus appeared to represent only an extreme wing of the broader gay rights campaign. In the mid-1980s, police clampdowns against pedophile rings often made little distinction between such activities and the operations of adult gay clubs or societies. In 1990, Tim Tate's journalistic account of child pornography used the alleged pedophile menace as a vehicle for an attack on nudist groups and publications, as well as the Gay Liberation Front (see the discussion in Wilson 1990; Cant and Hemmings 1988).

The association with adult homosexuality posed real problems for some investigators of pedophile activity, as they feared contributing to the further stigmatization of gay rights. At the same time, social workers and pediatricians were strongly committed to the protection of children from abuse. This conflict was especially sharp in London, where a major sex ring investigation in 1987 occurred in Brent, one of the more radical areas of the metropolis. This explains the careful distinction made by one of the investigators: "We're not talking about homosexuality. We're talking about adults abusing children, that it's an abuse of power and the same as any other situation where there's sexual abuse going on" (Redding 1989).

ELITE CRIMINALITY

But the PIE furor did not simply involve a more or less covert assault on homosexual rights. There were other political agendas at work, based on the apparent evidence that child sex rings might be extremely powerful and well-connected. Through the 1970s, the ready availability of pornography of all kinds in Britain was in large measure a consequence of pervasive police corruption. This was authenticated by the numerous trials of high-ranking officers in the mid-1970s, so the Whitehouse campaigns concided with some of the most embarrassing revelations about police tolerance of obscenity. (The main trials of the police Obscene Publications Squad had culminated in July 1977.) Child pornography was available because of bureaucratic malfeasance, a theme that fit well with the contemporary ultraright perspective that successive governments had presided over a general decline of traditional moral standards.

When abuses were discovered, there was suspicion among the Left and the Right that the crimes of the upper classes would be concealed by a cover-up by an ubiquitous "old-boy network." Traditionally, pedophilia in Britain had been associated with a religious context, specifically the established Church of England, and the old-established stereotype of the vicar assaulting his choirboy had been a powerful image in anticlericalism (McCalman 1984:86–91). Between 1975 and 1990, the *Times* on average reported at least one case each year involving abuse by vicars, choirmasters, or other clergy. In 1988, a Hampshire case suggested the existence of a sex ring of clergy and churchmen (*Private Eye* 700).

Now, however, there was a different and still more sinister stereotype, which linked homosexuality with treason. In 1980, it emerged that the highly placed Soviet spy Sir Anthony Blunt had been exposed by British intelligence in the early 1960s, but had continued to enjoy his honors and social position (Blunt was also a flamboyant homosexual). Throughout the decade, there were similar charges that the Soviets had suborned Sir Roger Hollis, the head of the British Security Service, MI5. The charge remains unsubstantiated, but it enjoyed much acceptance, and it received worldwide publicity in the mid-1980s during the government's attempt to ban Peter Wright's book *Spycatcher* (from a large literature, see, for example, Pincher 1981, 1984, 1988; Glees 1987; Wright 1987).

It was commonly assumed that homosexuality played a major role in forming these elite networks, which often owed their origins to long-standing acquaintance at all-male public schools or Oxbridge colleges. This idea had been strengthened in the 1950s and 1960s by the tale of the Burgess-Maclean-Philby-Blunt spy ring. In the late 1980s, it was post-humously revealed that MI6 chief Maurice Oldfield had been homosex-ual, though there was no suggestion of treason in this case. We also find the 1982 case of Geoffrey Prime, from very different social origins, who was arrested for several sex attacks against young girls. Prime served in the Government Communication Headquarters (GCHQ), the equivalent of the U.S. National Security Agency, where it transpired that he had for years been a Soviet agent, responsible for one of the most damaging penetrations of Western security ever recorded (Bamford 1983:479–532)

For present purposes, these intelligence scandals are of great rele-vance because they helped condition public attitudes to the image of upper-class perverts whose activities were concealed by their col-leagues. This was a powerful weapon in populist rhetoric against the entrenched ruling elite. Politicians were repeatedly involved in scandals involving homosexuality, pedophilia, or frequenting "rent boy" male prostitutes.

Between 1977 and 1979, the Liberal party was the focus of charges that its leader, Jeremy Thorpe, had hired an assassin to kill a male model with whom he had been sexually involved (Chester et al. 1979). In 1984, homosexual scandals involved two M.P.s, one Labour, one Conserva-tive (*Daily Telegraph*, January 31, and May 14, 1984). In 1986–1987, Conservative M.P. Harvey Proctor was forced to resign in the aftermath of a scandal involving underage rent boys and sadomasochistic spank-ing sessions. Rumors (entirely false) suggested that the scandals reached as high as the cabinet, where two successive home secretaries were said to be involved in criminal activities, one as a master satanist, one as a pedophile. High-society scandals were fare for the popular media throughout the decade: Even the reputable *Guardian* on occasion offered headlines such as "Celebrity Guests at Rent Boy Orgies Snorted Cocaine through Banknotes" (January 16, 1988). One London detective epito-mized popular prejudices when he remarked that "people always want their paedophiles to be judges or politicians" (Dalrymple 1991). The pedophile ring has often been used in fictional works as a powerful symbol of contemporary British decadence, for example in Isabel Cole-gate's recent novel *The Summer of the Royal Visit* (Colegate 1991).

THE WORK OF GEOFFREY DICKENS

One of the most enthusiastic campaigners against pedophilia and child pornography was Geoffrey Dickens, Conservative M.P. for Huddersfield West, who emerges as a classic moral entrepreneur through his vigorous accusations of deviance among the wealthy and powerful. In March 1981, Tom O'Carroll was convicted of conspiracy to corrupt public morals by publishing newsletters and contact materials. At the trial, there was a veiled reference to a certain figure, cited under the pseudonym Peter Henderson, whom Dickens named under the shield of parliamentary privilege. This action exposed the distinguished former British diplomat Sir Peter Hayman as a contributing member of PIE, who had handled pornographic materials (*Times*, March 14–28, 1981).

The incident raised a number of questions. As with Blunt, Prime, or Oldfield, Hayman must have been subject to frequent vetting procedures, and it is difficult to believe that his predilections could have been kept wholly secret (though Hayman's political loyalty was never questioned). Dickens revealed that the police had questioned Hayman as long ago as 1978; while in the present case, considerable pressure had been placed on the M.P. not to reveal the name, again suggesting the possibility of an establishment cover-up. Also, it was unclear why Hayman had not been prosecuted; and finally, the source of Dickens's information gave rise to speculation.

Dickens himself would often be involved in such exposés, which he regarded as an effective means of drawing attention to the dangers of pedophilia and child pornography. He employed the same tactics repeatedly: using parliamentary privilege to name a specific individual and demand prosecution. Typically, he would threaten to reveal the name, which would cause protests, and the ensuing debate might continue for several days before the individual was actually cited; so the scandal might keep the issue in the news for some time. This exposé or investigative approach suggested both that cover-ups existed, and that Dickens had access to secret sources, which he was courageously revealing in the public interest.

In 1983, he asked Home Secretary Leon Brittan to investigate pedophilia in the royal Court, at Buckingham Palace, and in the diplomatic and civil services. He claimed to have extensive private information on this: "I am going to give him a glimpse inside my private files, where people have written to me with information." In one case, involving a civil servant, "there appears on face value to have been a cover-up" (*Times*, November 24, 1983). In 1986, he used privilege to name a doctor and a vicar, both of whom were said to be involved in sexual offenses against the young (*Times*, March 15–21, 1986).

Other charges were more general, as when he demanded an investigation into the existence of possible child brothels in London (*Times*, February 14, 1986). In 1984, Dickens introduced a parliamentary bill to suppress pedophile organizations, remarking that "adults in every walk of life from the highest in the land to misfits in society were involving themselves in paedophilia" (*Times*, June 28, 1984). It was partly through such claims that pedophilia became a component of conspiracy speculation.

Dickens himself had strong right-wing convictions, but the concern about pedophilia cannot be seen simply as a weapon of the political Right. The issue owed much to divisions within the ruling Conservative party. Under Margaret Thatcher, a right-wing and populist strand of opinion had risen to power, and this group had little sympathy for the traditional upper-class leaders of conservatism. The Thatcherite elite benefited from the recurrent association of their predecessors with degeneracy and cover-ups; so there were many besides Dickens active in promoting concern about sex rings and scandals, and the extravagant claims that often emerged.

In 1984, the moderate Conservative Home Secretary Leon Briitan, was smeared by fictitious rumors that associated him with a pedophile ring. The source of these tales was eventually exposed by he magazine *Private Eye*, which traced them to extreme rightist circles within MI5, the security service. (They were also said to dislike Brittan's Jewish origins: *Private Eye* 588, 1984.) The same sources had also disseminated equally false allegations about the homosexuality of the Thatcherites' archrival, former prime minister Edward Heath, and the supposed conspiracy to conceal the treason of Sir Roger Hollis.

If this interpretation is correct, then the intelligence services emerge as important clandestine claims-makers, generating rumor for the explicit purpose of spreading political disinformation. This was a tactic that had already been employed by British intelligence agencies in Northern Ireland, specifically in the Kincora affair, where the main charges again involved organized pedophilia (Foot 1989; Compare "PM Adviser in Smear Campaign," *Guardian*, December 14, 1989).

THE BRIGHTON CASE

Concern about pedophilia reached a new plateau with the Brighton incident of 1983, in which three men brutally attacked and abused a young boy and then escaped. The crime gave rise to outrage in the media, in part because of its novelty. This was no simple molestation by a single disturbed individual, but a forcible physical attack by a group of men, perhaps organized as an ongoing conspiracy. This did much to ensure the typification of pedophilia as an organized criminal threat.

After the initial reports on August 16, the story remained on the front pages of most papers over the next week, with details of every new lead—anonymous telephone tips, a possible link with a German car, the search for the boy's shirt. There was also an increase in other pedophilia-related stories from various parts of the country in the month following the attack, and incidents that would otherwise have attracted merely local attention now earned national reporting. And for years afterwards, the media were anxious to link the Brighton case to subsequent instances of child abuse and murder, and of course to PIE and its affiliates. The week after the attack, Geoffrey Dickens launched a campaign to declare PIE a prohibited organization.

The story also brought to light other possible dimensions of the pedophilia danger. One troubling context was Brighton's role as a gay center, and the press gave prominence to early police remarks about attempting to contact regulars at a nearby gay pub. This element soon faded from view, however, and the press began publicizing fund-raising by the local gay community to help find the attackers. For years afterwards, though, there continued to be references to this "savage homosexual attack" ("Homosexual Clue to Boys' Deaths," *Times*, April 17, 1986).

Another element in the attack on pedophilia was xenophobia. The geographical context alone suggested that the offenders might have slipped out of a British port to the Continent, implying that European nations might be infecting Britain with their child molesters no less than their pornography. The child abuse stories that received the most attention often included one or more of these foreign elements, and several involved molesters who held or claimed diplomatic immunity, and who were therefore exempt from British criminal jurisdiction. In January 1987, there was controversy over a case involving an American with diplomatic immunity, who could not be extradited to stand trial for indecent assault on a young girl. Other perpetrators were from European or Middle Eastern countries (see, for instance, *Times*, March 5, 1987).

CHILD SEX RINGS

Beginning in the late 1970s, there was an increased awareness of the existence of child sex rings, which came to be perceived as a problem for

police and social service agencies. Some police forces developed specialized units to investigate such crimes: They followed leads and possible
links that might have been ignored in earlier years, thus increasing the
visibility of such alleged conspiracies.

Leeds offers one example. From the early 1980s, a specialized police
team (two male officers, two female) had begun working on abuse cases
in the south of the city, in close and unusually friendly association with
officials from health and social service departments. Twenty-one men
would ultimately be arrested, in crimes involving two hundred children
aged eight to sixteen, though the actual number of groupings or rings
involved is far from clear (Campbell 1988a:103–111). The South Leeds
cases succeeded because police had been proactive, and had worked
strenuously to explore links between known victims and other children,
in order to examine chains of recruitment. Moreover, Leeds at this time
was a prominent British center for the study and treatment of child
sexual abuse, in which pediatricians and social workers were likely to be
sympathetic and supportive (Wild 1986; see Chapter 6).

Another example occurred in London, where a police and social
services team organized Operation Hedgerow in 1987 (Redding 1989).
This exposed a "major network of child sexual abuse," in which at least
fourteen men were involved in offenses against perhaps 140 boys,
mainly aged between ten and fifteen. Unlike earlier cases, police
responded to relatively minor complaints against an alleged pedophilia,
keeping him under intensive surveillance. The police then followed
boys and men with whom he was in contact until the nature and size of
the ring became apparent. The success of this operation led to suggestions that it could be the model for a citywide scheme, perhaps a
centralized police pedophilia squad incorporating social workers.

The following trial led to six convictions (Ellis 1989). Once again, those
guilty appeared to represent a broad section of social classes, from a
barrister (Colin Peters, seen as a mastermind) and a company director to
cabdrivers and caretakers. The *Times* noted that "in the year-long police
investigation, a vicar and a senior official at the Palace of Westminster
were questioned." Though the group was London based, arrests were
made over several counties of southern England. "The group's tentacles
reached out into the Home Counties" (Ellis 1989). The *Daily Mirror* was
one of many papers to urge public vigilance to meet the menace of
organized pedophilia: It urged its readers to "report anything suspicious
to the police."

Examples of such rings recurred throughout the late 1980s, and
bureaucratic changes contributed to the accelerating pace of detection
and prosecution. The Metropolitan Police took an explicit decision to
"make child pornography a number one target" in 1986 and made this a

priority of the Obscene Publications Squad, TO13. The squad undertook five child pornography investigations in 1985, thirty-seven during 1987 (Foster 1988). However, there were protests from those who wanted a separate unit with the full-time responsibility of combating child pornography, and thus pedophilia.

To satisfy this demand, the domain of the child pornography problem was expanded to cover broader areas of danger to children, even extending to murder. To quote one detective, "Wherever you find child pornography, you are likely to find paedophiles quite capable of attacking or abusing children. It is frustrating to know that without the right background, we could be investigating a problem only when it reaches murder inquiry level" (Foster 1988). This danger came from "small close-knit cells, obtaining pornography and child victims through word of mouth contacts." In 1989, the Metropolitan Police formed a specialized Child Pornography Squad, responsible for maintaining a register of suspected molesters and pornographers. There was thus an institutional base to the "war" on pedophilia, which encouraged more proactive investigation. By early 1990, the new unit was on average requesting a new search warrant every week.

This interventionist attitude by the police was encouraged by recent legal changes. In the 1970s, antipornography measures had usually met with mixed success: The then commissioner of the Metropolitan Police had written that "much pornography is almost impossible to define, that definition changes continually, that contested prosecutions are no more certain of outcome than a game of chance, and that the reaction of the courts was a virtual licence for its continuance" (Mark 1979:267–268). This apparent lack of a public consensus has been cited as one reason for the thoroughgoing corruption of the "Porn Squad" in that era; but attitudes were very different where children were concerned (Tomlinson 1982:149–151). In 1987, a panic about importation led to measures that would criminalize the simple possession of child pornography, a proposal implemented in the 1988 Criminal Justice Bill. Britain is the only European country with so sweeping a prohibition, which makes it relatively simple to prove an offense in court.

TYPIFYING THE PEDOPHILE

Elaborate and expensive investigations suggested the degree to which pedophilia had come to be seen as almost a form of subversion (indicated by the use of words like *cell* in this context). The *Times* remarked that the Hedgerow operation "has only scraped the surface of the paedophilia menace in Britain" (Ellis 1989). The police officer in charge of the inquiry said, "The trouble with paedophiles is that they work underneath the community. It's a very effective subculture. They work themselves into key jobs which bring them into contact with children. . . . The scale of this activity across London is colossal, and I'm sure it's replicated in other major cities." Within such groups, "the secrecy would make a masonic lodge look like supporters of the Freedom of Information Act" (Bibby 1991).

It was further suggested that abused boys graduated to become homosexual prostitutes, a phenomenon much discussed in the media during the decade (Redding 1989). Boys were thus initiated, prior to becoming rent boys or abusers themselves; and the consequences might be devastating. In 1986, David Pithers of the National Children's Home (NCH) claimed that eighteen boy prostitutes were deliberately spreading AIDS in London, in revenge for having been abused as children (*Times*, November 25, 1986).

The degree of organization or coordination within a particular ring was a critical issue, but one that was usually taken for granted by media and police. It is rarely clear whether the groups were as large and close-knit as it often claimed, or whether we are dealing with one or two chief activists and a number of friends and loose associates. One account claims that the Leeds investigations "unearthed seventeen sex rings involving 21 men. . . . It was one of the biggest rings ever discovered in Britain," which seems contradictory to the point of absurdity (Campbell 1988a: 103).

For the press, like the police, rings were numerous and well-defined. There was a tendency to exaggerate both scale and structure, in order to depict a more threatening enemy whose removal could be depicted as a substantial achievement. Successive stories of rings reported the detention of sizable numbers of suspects, though often only a few of these would actually be charged. The Hedgerow ring of 1987 initially involved twenty-three arrests; forty were arrested in a European ring distributing child porn videos (*Times*, January 28, 1988; *Sunday Times*, September 18, 1988).

Everything contributed to a picture of a criminal conspiracy, possibly interconnected in a national framework, and linked by sophisticated technology. CB radios were often mentioned in the Hedgerow affair. From 1987 on, there were reports that pedophile rings were communicating by means of electronic mail and computer bulletin boards, the legality of which was ill-defined (*Times*, July 29, 1987; *Sunday Times*, August 2, 1987). The media also tended to concentrate on prosecutions involving men of high social status, which strengthened the apparent link between pedophilia and elite decadence.

Another theme was the geographical extent of the rings. The discovery of pornographic videos seemed to confirm the existence of international cells or syndicates, with The Netherlands often cited as a headquarters for the child porn industry. One of the most active spokesmen on this topic was Ray Wyre, who headed the Gracewell clinic, the first in Britain entirely devoted to treating sex offenders (Wyre 1989). Wyre lectured extensively to police, social workers, and NSPCC gatherings, and his message was one of major conspiracy. He emphasized the vast international links of the pornographers, extending throughout Europe and the United States (Foster 1988). Sex offenders were thus dangerous and elaborately organized; and one solution was a "national register of convicted paedophiles."

OPERATION SPANNER

One by-product of the new concern about organized conspiracies was that the police began to devote more attention to what would earlier have been regarded as merely consensual vice rings, treating them on a par with the child exploitation groups. The reporting of such cases is often difficult to interpret. In September 1989, for example, a story noted that "sixteen men including a United Nations lawyer, a lay preacher and a missile designer have been arrested after a two-year investigation by Scotland Yard's Obscene Publications Squad" (*Times*, September 16, 1989). A lengthy and bewildering range of charges included a reference to the Protection of Children Act, and early reports implied strongly that this was in a sense a child pornography or pedophile ring.

The scale of the investigation, Operation Spanner, supported such a view of the seriousness of the charges, and the police had engaged in unusually proactive techniques, for example, responding to advertisements in gay magazines. The ring, if genuine, seemed like a true national conspiracy, with men from Wales, Hereford and Worcester, Shropshire, Bolton, Cleveland, Suffolk and London.

However, details that emerged during the trial make it clear that this was not a child sex ring, and most of the actions involved were morality offenses rather than crimes. When the prosecution concluded in late 1990, the group appeared to be a homosexual sadomasochistic ring, where members were guilty of acts such as "aiding and abetting actual bodily harm on himself" (*Independent*, November 21, 1990). In other words, the violence was inflicted with the consent and at the request of the "slaves" concerned. Most of the participants were middle-aged, and children were only mentioned in the context of a small number of indecent photographs. The accused presented a plausible defense that their acts were consensual and victimless, only to have this dismissed by the judge. The media were thus able to present this as the conviction of a sex ring on a par with the Hedgerow group.

THE CHILD MURDERS

During the 1980s, concern about sexual abuse turned increasingly to fears about child murder. These allegations represented both a new element in perceptions of the problem of child abuse and a dramatic escalation in the rhetoric. At first sight, this fear was curious. Homicide in general is far less frequent in Britain than in the United States, and in the 1970s and 1980s the annual number of under-sixteens who perished as a result of homicide was usually between seventy and one hundred in the whole of England and Wales (*Criminal Statistics* 1985). The age group between five and fifteen was in fact the least likely to fall victim to homicide, and the figures had not been growing significantly over time.

On the other hand, there had been several celebrated child murder cases in the 1950s and 1960s, involving legendary villains like John Straffen, Raymond Morris, and especially the moors murders, of whom more below (Molloy 1988). These affairs left a residual identification of the pedophile with a multiple killer, a notion that survived in popular fiction and television police dramas. In the 1980s, this idea was enhanced by a new concern with the threat of serial homicide, a theme addressed in Chapter 3. Police began to feel a need to discover links between unsolved crimes, in the hope of finding a possible multiple offender. In the summer and fall of 1985, the police response to several murders and abductions proceeded on the assumption that one or more multiple killers might be involved. This is suggested by a front-page news story from that September:

> Police last night widened their search for Tina Ashbrook, aged seven, the missing London schoolgirl, amid growing fears that her abductor may be a double killer. The body of her friend Stacy Kavanaugh, aged four, was found early yesterday in a park in Rotherhithe. . . . Police are not ruling out a link between these incidents and the disappearance of Barry Lewis, aged six. . . . Information is also being exchanged with detectives in Suffolk seeking the murderer of Leoni Keating, aged three, who was abducted from a caravan at Great Yarmouth last Friday. The Suffolk

police have also contacted Essex police to investigate a possible connection between the murder of Leoni Keating and the abduction three years ago of Pauline Coe, an Essex schoolgirl. (Dowden 1985)

Most of these alleged linkages soon proved spurious, but the average reader would be left with the impression of widespread activity by multiple child killers or abductors.

The best-known aspect of the new policy was the "stranger" investigation publicized in 1986. This grew out of two apparently genuine series of child murders. In one, three small girls (Caroline Hogg, Susan Maxwell, and Sarah Harper) were abducted between 1982 and 1986 in southern Scotland or northern England, and their bodies were then found in the English Midlands, in the counties of Nottinghamshire, Staffordshire, and Leicestershire. When the third such incident occurred in April 1986, suspicion of an active serial killer became very strong, and a national investigation began. This was merged with another inquiry in the London area, Operation Stranger, launched after the discovery in late 1985 of the gravesites of two boys, Jason Swift and Barry Lewis, who had been buried in the Essex countryside near Waltham Abbey. The new task force had about fifty officers from sixteen forces (Davenport and Tendler 1986).

In the media, Operation Stranger became the generic and somewhat misleading name for the whole child murders inquiry. The quest for linkage led to the collection of information on all recent unsolved murders and disappearances of children; and connections seemed strong enough to suggest the activity of one killer or group of killers in all the incidents. Police statements made in April suggested that about fifteen incidents might be linked, and the original list included the names given in Table 4.1. Some reports put the number of victims at over twenty and linked several other incidents, including the 1983 Brighton attack, but most lists focused on these attacks.

"Stranger" was a major story through much of 1986. In the *Times*, there were seven stories in the week following the disappearance of Sarah Harper in April, with another wave of stories following the finding of her body, reported on April 20. Like Harper's original disappearance, the announcement of the "stranger" inquiry was generally front-page news. It received much attention over the next two weeks, and there were another dozen reports by the end of the year. The murders would be a frequent theme in the media for years to come. Sometimes, there would be a new theory as to how the children had met their deaths; on other occasions, suspects would be detained and questioned, and the media would yet again report the major allegations of linked child murders. In the deaths of Hogg, Maxwell, and Harper, for example, suspects were questioned in 1987 and 1990

Table 4.1. The Child Murders Inquiry

Victim	Age	Location	Date	Status
1. Genette Tate	13	Devon	1978	Missing
2. Sean McGaun	15		1979	Murdered
3. Martin Allen	15	London	1979	Missing
4. Marion Crofts	14	Hampshire	1981	Murdered
5. Vishal Mehrota	8	London	1981	Murdered
6. Susan Maxwell	11	Coldstream	1982	Murdered
7. Caroline Hogg	5	Near Edinburgh	1983	Murdered
8. Imran Vohra	9	Lancashire	1983	Murdered
9. Colette Aram	16	Notts	1983	Murdered
10. Lynda Mann	15	Leicestershire	1983	Murdered
11. Chris Laverack	9	Hull	1984	Murdered
12. Mark Tildesley	7	Berkshire	1984	Missing
13. Barry Lewis	6	London	1985	Murdered
14. Jason Swift	14	London	1985	Murdered
15. Sarah Harper	10	Yorkshire	1986	Murdered

This ongoing coverage maintained public interest in the notion of a serial child killer; and yet it is far from certain that was ever a single "stranger." In retrospect, it is likely that these were the victims of at least three unconnected killers or groups of offenders, and even at the time it was not obvious that police had really uncovered a single lengthy series of killings. Links between the various crimes were sparse, and the victims came from a wide range of ages, social classes, and geographical settings. In addition, victims were of both sexes, which is unusual though not unheard of in cases of multiple child murder. On the other hand, there were similarities. The bodies of Maxwell, Hogg, and Harper were all dumped in Midland counties, which made it plausible that the same killer might have claimed the other victims murdered in that region, Colette Aram and Lynda Mann (Newton 1990; Marriner 1989; Wambaugh 1989).

Other connections were more tenuous, though suggestive. Vohra and

Mehrota were both Londoners of Asian extraction. Jason Swift's body was found buried in Essex, a few miles from the gravesite of Barry Lewis; and both showed evidence of the use of the same type of muscle relaxant drug prior to sexual assault. Some of the crimes seemed to have occurred near streams used by anglers; and there were persistent reports of red cars seen in the vicinity of an abduction. Other connections between the victims involved the proximity of circuses or funfairs to the sites of abductions (in seven cases). If valid, this would establish a link between the northern murders of little girls, and the London murders of Swift and Lewis, and possibly confirm the activity of one individual or group.

Several recent British cases helped to form perceptions of the child murder series, but by far the most influential was the moors murders of 1963–1965. Ian Brady and Myra Hindley had killed at least four children in circumstances involving sexual abuse and torture and buried the bodies on Saddleworth Moor, near Manchester (Ritchie 1988; Harrison 1987). The investigation and trial, which made frequent headlines in 1965 and 1966, caused a national sensation, and numerous books and articles took the crimes as a paradigm of absolute evil, on a moral par with the worst atrocities of the Nazis. Popular rumor linked the case with witchcraft, black magic, and ritual crucifixion (Williams 1968:348).

The story was much in the news in 1986 because of continuing rumors that the offenders might admit to more killings than the three for which they had originally been convicted. Brady confessed to two more child victims in late 1985, and a much publicized search would later produce the body of one of these, missing since 1963. The grave sites happened to be in the constituency of Geoffrey Dickens, who now presented the police with evidence that a third person might have been involved in this prototypical "pedophile ring" (*Times*, August 26, 1987; Topping and Ritchie 1989; Harrison 1987).

Interviews with the imprisoned Brady further suggested that he might have committed several other murders that had never been linked to him before. These alleged acts had occurred over many years and in scattered parts of Britain: If they were true, Brady might have been guilty of as many as ten or twelve murders (Harrison 1987), though Ritchie (1988) casts doubt on the confession. For Operation Stranger, the moors murders made it plausible that the known crimes might be part of a series spread over many years, requiring the police to pay attention to links that might have seemed tenuous. The case further raised the possibility of involvement by more than one individual, with a woman being used to entrap victims; and police statements about "Stranger" in 1986 explicitly described a pair of suspects, a man and a woman.

Fears about a child murder menace were reinforced yet again by a third and unconnected event during 1986, the discovery in October of the bodies of nine-year-old schoolgirls Nicola Fellows and Karen Hadaway, in Sussex. This illustrated what appeared to be the inadequacies of the justice system in confronting child assault and murder. Russell Bishop of Brighton was arrested in December 1986, but was acquitted in a controversial trial. He remained under deep suspicion in the local community, and arson attacks were made on his home. In 1990, he received a life sentence for another offense, this time for the molestation and attempted murder of a seven-year-old girl.

TYPIFYING THE CHILD MURDERS

In the mass media, the child murders were seen as part of a new problem, different in scale and nature from crimes hitherto. The size of the problem might be immense, an "epidemic of child abductions and sex killings" (Marriner 1990:412). The *Times* listed the major incidents, but noted that "the tragic toll of children missing and murdered continues to grow. These are just fourteen of the hundreds of unsolved cases that police officers are still working on" (Davenport and Tendler 1986). For the *Sunday Times*, child murders sometimes occurred when a pedophile panicked during a sexual assault; but "even more worrying . . . is the second, much larger and now growing group who appear to torture, murder and often mutilate children according to plan. Although their plans have a strong sexual aspect, they are nearly always about discharging bottled-up aggression, rather than a pedophile's distorted expressions of affection" (Deer and Rayment 1986).

The new problem was linked inextricably to the issues of pedophilia and child sexual abuse, a model example of what Hall et al. describe as "convergence." The *Sunday Times* described a problem of "serial abuse and murder," in a story entitled "Slaughter of the Lambs" [a reference to the fictional sex killer of *The Silence of the Lambs* (Dalrymple 1991; see also Masters 1991)]. This linkage was repeatedly emphasized in the coverage of child murders, like the notorious 1985 case of Leoni Keating. Fortuitously, this was reported the same week that NSPCC statistics depicted a large increase in child abuse cases, and the phenomena were inevitably connected. The *Times* report began,

One day after the body of Leoni Cornell (*sic*), aged 3, was found in a Suffolk ditch, the NSPCC yesterday released figures showing another distinct increase in the number of physically and sexually abused children in England and Wales.

The National Children's Home also launched a campaign called Children in Danger. . . . And Mr. Geoffrey Dickens, a Conservative MP, promised to reintroduce his Bill during the next session of Parliament to protect children from adults seeking sexual relationships, which failed for lack of parliamentary time last year. He said it had been "a dreadful summer of child abuse and murders." (Fletcher 1985)

Claiming that "Britain has more child murders and rapes than any other country in Europe," the *News of the World* was one of many papers to try to explain a national streak of callous brutality toward the very young (Soothill and Walby 1991:113–115).

When Operation Stranger became news some months later, a major *Times* article simultaneously addressed "the psychology of the killers" and "the making of a molester," as if the two types were virtually identical. Parents, if noted, must ask themselves whether "it might be your child who is sexually assaulted and battered before being dumped in a river" (Rodwell 1986). To prevent the murder threat, parents should study current efforts at protecting children from abusers by "streetproofing" books like the American *It's OK to Say NO*. Homosexuality was another scarcely veiled theme. The *Times*, for instance, noted that the killer of Lewis and Swift was "a homosexual who could strike again" (*Times*, April 17 1986). Significantly, the little girls were not similarly characterized as victims of a heterosexual killer.

MISSING CHILDREN

In attempting to understand the danger of an anonymous child killer, British media often resorted to experts from American journalism and law enforcement, who naturally tended to project the experience of their own country onto the different setting of Britain. This was apparent in attempts to import the American concept of a far-reaching problem of missing children. This implied that a substantial number of young people went missing each year, either through their own volition or through abduction and murder. Operation Stranger led to several imitations of American responses to this perception. A British Parents of Murdered Children group was established; and in November 1986, Central Television broadcast a program, "Missing Kids" (Marriner 1990).

Linked to this was the moralistic theme that children were disposable in a dehumanized contemporary society (compare Best 1990:22–44). The *Sunday Times* claimed that

thousands upon thousands of children, some in the 10–13 age
group, vanished from their homes each year, often heading for
London, and there was no central register or tracking unit to
control the search for them. . . . At the moment nobody knows
how many young boys and girls—known to pimps and paedophiles alike as "mysteries"—have been swallowed up in large cities
such as London in the last decade. Nobody knows how
many . . . have come to the attention of men who regard them as
free-range products on the hoof to be either bought for pleasure or
taken by force, used and disposed of in shallow graves. . . . That's
the kind of society we have now. (Dalrymple 1991).

From about 1990, we find the first tentative and poorly substantiated
attempts to quantify the problem. The *Daily Express* presented "the
tragic truth behind Britain's 98,000 missing youngsters" (July 20, 1991).

This had obvious policy implications. For the police, the missing-
child phenomenon was a powerful argument for closer coordination
between forces, and between police and social service agencies (Boseley
1991; Dalrymple 1991). It was also used to advocate a new national
computer system, which would centralize and coordinate data about
missing persons, a function previously undertaken by individual forces
(compare the debate over police centralization described in Chapter 3).
This was finally accomplished in 1992.

In feminist writing, the notion of disposable children ("free-range
products on the hoof") was especially applied to girls who had fallen
victim to pervasive sexual violence. The book *The Lust to Kill* (Cameron
and Frazer 1987) refers to one of the Operation Stranger victims in terms
that suggest that multiple child murder is an almost commonplace
occurrence in Britain: "Genette Tate is one of the many young girls in the
United Kingdom who are missing, believed murdered, but whose fate
remains a mystery" (p.185). One could easily read this passage without
appreciating that "many" in his context does not run into double
figures. The authors are simply appropriating the language common to
American claims-makers in this area.

RESOLUTIONS?

By 1990, there would be a great deal more information about the fate
of the various children on the "stranger" list. In some instances,
resolution of a case appeared to settle debate; but other evidence seemed
to present a still more damning picture of threats to the safety and lives
of British children.

The most straightforward incident involved Lynda Mann, who was the victim of a sexually motivated killer named Colin Pitchfork (see Chapter 3). Other names remained longer on the list. In July 1990, police from ten forces met in Scotland to discuss new evidence on the deaths of Hogg, Maxwell, Harper, Tate, and Crofts. Shortly afterwards, there were extensive press reports about the trial of Robert Black, a London van driver, who had abducted and assaulted a six-year-old girl near a Scottish village. He was described in a *Times* article as a sex offender and pedophile: "The court heard that he travelled to the Netherlands and Denmark to satisfy his interest in child pornography" (Gill 1990). The *Times* story made no explicit mention of other cases, but concluded elliptically: "Detectives involved in the Black case are to meet officers investigating the unsolved murders of three girls between 1982 and 1986. A man is expected to be questioned" in the killings.

PEDOPHILE MURDER GANGS?

The murders of the boys on the "stranger" list took even longer to resolve. Operation Stranger had focused initially on the death of Lewis and Swift, which appeared to be strongly connected. The police had also found evidence of a child sex ring operating from Hackney, one of the poorest areas of inner London, where they found victims from among the young poor and homeless. Several members of the group were charged with abuse, and police reports implied that a powerful conspiracy had been in place for several years:

> A well-organized and financed group of pedophiles operating in east London, which has international links, is believed to have recruited up to sixty boys into their ring. From their headquarters, a shoe-shop in Hackney, they produced manuals on how to entice and gain the trust of youngsters before seducing them. (Tendler 1989).

One of the ring was a fairground worker, which raised police suspicions about connections with the "stranger" murders.

By June 1987, several of the men were charged in the killing of Jason Swift, and the trial continued into 1989 (Tendler 1989). According to the courtroom account, Swift had left his sister's home in 1985, and had lived for several months as a street hustler and rent boy. In November 1985, he had arranged to meet several men in a cheap apartment in Hackney, in the East End of London, where he died in what the newspapers repeatedly termed a homosexual orgy with six men. (The association of homosexuality with pedophilia and child murder here emerges strongly.) Swift died either by suffocation or strangulation, but it was not clear if his death was intentional, or an accidental consequence of sadomasochistic sexual activity, aggravated by drug use. His body was then secretly buried in Essex. Four men were thus convicted not of murder, but of manslaughter (failing to obtain medical help) and perverting the course of justice (by concealing the body).

Coming so soon after the Hedgerow convictions, the Swift trial helped form a link in the public mind between sex rings and child murder (for group activity in serial homicide, see Jenkins 1991a; Hickey 1991). The connection was reinforced when another of the group, Leslie Bailey, was charged with the Barry Lewis murder. This had taken place in particularly grim circumstances. At the trial in 1991, it was stated that "Barry Lewis was snatched from the street in Walworth, south London, as he played with friends, taken to a council flat, drugged, stripped and buggered by seven or eight men. . . . He was left covered in blood and apparently dead" (quoted in "Snatched Boy Killed after Orgy," *Guardian*, June 15, 1991). However, he remained alive until strangled by Bailey, who then buried the body. Most media accounts used the same photograph of Bailey, whose disheveled and wild-eyed appearance epitomized popular stereotypes of the sex killer (Dalrymple 1991).

OPERATION ORCHID

But still wider ramifications were suggested, and the allegations made by at least one of the Hackney group in early 1990 led to a national sensation. Police statements implied that one gang was responsible for most or all of the murders of the boys on the "stranger" list, and possibly others as well: Bailey was said to have described up to twenty killings (Dalrymple 1991). An emergency police headquarters was established at Arbour Square, and the public gave an "overwhelming" response to a special police request for information via a telephone hotline. The new Operation Orchid was headed by Chief Superintendent Roger Stoodley, who became a widely quoted public spokesman on the dangers of pedophilia, homosexual orgies, and missing children.

By May, there were urgent attempts to find the bodies of alleged murder victims buried on the site of a parking lot next to a deserted synagogue at Clapton, a mile away from the flat where Swift and Lewis had died. Speculation ran rampant, but the only bone fragments found at the Clapton site proved to be animal remains. There were suggestions of other grave sites in various parts of London and the Home Counties (*Times*, December 19, 1990; Boseley 1991). The image of the secret cemetery now became a powerful part of the child abuse myth, a picture that no doubt owed something to memories of Brady's victims on the northern moors.

SNUFF

Concern over pedophilia had in part originated with fears over child pornography. In late July 1990, this issue returned vigorously, with a new emphasis on snuff as the explanation for the Clapton cases. There had been rumors that the incident might involve "child pornography and all sorts of other pornography"—a rather cryptic police statement believed to refer to snuff films and videos (*Times*, May 26, 1990). It was rumored that Jason Swift's death had been preserved on video, and that this tape enjoyed underground circulation.

The snuff film has enjoyed a lengthy history in popular mythology since the first example was said to have appeared in the United States about 1976, although it remains unclear whether there is any validity to the story. On the other hand, there is nothing intrinsically impossible about the concept, and the moors murders offered an authentic near precedent. On at least one occasion, Brady and Hindley had recorded the torture, abuse, and murder of one of their ten-year-old victims by means of the technology available to them at the time, which was audiotape. The thirteen-minute tape was played at the trial in 1966, contributing substantially to public horror at the crime (Ritchie 1988: 96–98).

London police announced that they "were investigating the disappearances of twenty children in Britain since 1984" (*Times*, July 28, 1990). Of course, the story was well covered in papers like the *Sun* and *Star*, but even the qualities gave it major play, and on the front pages. The *Times* said, "Suspicions that between six and twelve youngsters were filmed as they died after being enticed to parties are being investigated. Victims as young as six years have been abused and tortured before being killed, police believe." The *Guardian* headlined. "'Nine Killed' in Child Porn Ring" and reported, "Scotland Yard detectives investigating child snuff movies and the murder of nine boys were last night hoping to question a number of men whom they suspect belonged to two paedophile rings operating in the south east" (July 28, 1990).

The *Sun* offered a vivid account: "Evil snuff videos of real child murders are sold to paedophiles at prices that depend on the victim's age and color. . . . The videos of death are advertized for sale in well-known magazines—using coded messages known only to paedophile customers" (*Sun*, July 28, 1990). The suggestion here is that pedophiles not merely viewed children as objects to be bought, sold, and destroyed, but even accorded them a different worth depending on the "quality of the item." Dozens if not hundreds of children had perished at the hands of pedophiles and pornographers.

There were several sources for these allegations, in addition to the members of the Hackney ring. One involved a teenager named Andrew, whose testimony was presented to police by the National Association for Young People in Care (NAYPIC; *Sunday Times*, July 29, 1990). Andrew had allegedly been abducted to Amsterdam, where a group of London men had forced him to participate in making a film in which a twelve-year-old-boy perished. Andrew had presented evidence to NAYPIC workers, and had recorded testimony on tape. NAYPIC claimed that similar stories had been told by other runaways. It further alleged the existence of a group named the "elite twelve," which would pay several thousand pounds for young people to feature in snuff films.

NAYPIC had a social agenda in presenting its account. The group had experienced some difficulties the previous year, when its government grant was suspended due to "a lack of accountability within the organization" (*Community Care*, February 1989). It acquired a new lease on life from the perceived need to protect the young from pedophiles, and was campaigning in 1990 for the establishment of a network of safe houses.

Incidents of this sort would often be used by well-intentioned pressure groups. In 1989, for example, the Jason Swift trial had given rise to much writing about the young homeless falling victim to pedophiles, and there was a new emphasis on the rent boy. It was a spokesman for the NCH who drew the moral, "In the old days, runaways used to turn to pickpocketing. Now, they become rent-boys or prostitutes—it pays well" (Tendler 1989).

Other activist groups had a clear moral agenda in making claims in this area. Many of the background stories about child pornography and snuff can be traced to Childwatch, a pressure group led by activist Diane Core, who had a strong religious and anticult motivation. Childwatch asserted that the main danger was forcible abduction: "Paedophiles target the children and sell them for thousands or even hundreds of thousands. It can be any child. They see him or her walking to school and decide to target it." Children might then be sold abroad, or tortured and killed within the United Kingdom, while Core would also claim that many children—including Christopher Laverack—became victims of human sacrifice cults (Eaton et al. 1991). After the Hedgerow trial in

1989, Childwatch representatives stated on television that pedophiles had many thousands of children trapped in "cells" of abuse (Campbell 1989). Childwatch allegations on snuff films were supported by Ray Wyre, who claimed direct knowledge of such films in the United States.

Such charges reinvigorated the campaign against child pornography in general. Geoffrey Dickens called on the prime minister to offer a "grave and personal warning" to parents on the subject of snuff. Valerie Howarth of the organization ChildLine denied any direct knowledge of snuff, but saw an urgent need to ensure that Britain would not be flooded with child pornography when European border controls were reduced or removed in 1992. The same fear was expressed by Leslie Bennett, head of the Child Pornography Squad (*Times*, March 13, 1990).

The snuff story appeared to have all the potential to create a major national panic, drawing together as it did so many concerns and interest groups. It is possible that the next stage would have involved the search for other homicidal rings elsewhere in the country, and perhaps more graveyards. The London story was front-page news in most dailies on July 28 and most Sunday papers the next day, but it faded rapidly in the following days, as it was overwhelmed by coverage of the Iraqi invasion of Kuwait on August 1. In the *Times*, for example, the story abruptly vanished with the Bailey indictment at the end of July, and allegations of British snuff videos vanished without any confirmation.

BOGUS SOCIAL WORKERS

By 1990, the popular concept of the child abuser had become increasingly fused with the image of the pornographer and even the child murderer. Investigations like Operation Orchid "have only just begun to illuminate the murky and savage world of paedophilia" (Boseley 1991). Meanwhile—at least in the popular imagination—the pedophile gangs were expanding their repertoire of subterfuges. From March 1990, a growing number of reports told of teams of self-described social workers demanding entry to houses to investigate the welfare or health of children. It was alleged that at least some of the impostors had access to genuine information about the families they approached. Once access was gained, the "officers" undertook medical inspections, purportedly looking for signs of sexual abuse, which involved stripping and assaulting the children concerned.

It was feared that other crimes might be intended, and some parents were allegedly told that their children were being taken "into care." The *Sunday Times* headlined "Police on the Trail of Child Snatch Group"

(April 1, 1990). In the words of a Yorkshire police officer: "It may be that these people want a child of their own. More sinister, the child may be taken away for some form of sexual gratification. It is even possible a child may be killed" (*Sunday Times*, April 1, 1990).

The bogus social workers outbreak rapidly acquired national dimensions, with some seventy reports from all parts of the country by May 1990. There were incidents in Wiltshire, Sussex, South Yorkshire, Manchester, Cheshire, London, and in the southwest. The *Times* had two reports on the case in March, two in April, and no less than eighteen in May. This culminated on May 1 with four items, including a front-page headline and a leading article. June offered a mere two reports.

There was speculation that a national network or conspiracy, a "suspected gang of pedophiles," was responsible for the attacks, though this would be formally denied by police in early June. The most common version of the story involved a team of a man and a woman, reminding the public both of Brady and Hindley and perhaps of the couple originally sought by Operation Stranger. However, other allegations involved a pair of women. Detectives from twelve police forces were involved in a hunt by mid-May, and police composite pictures were issued. The panic declined thereafter, though sporadic reports or sightings recurred through the latter part of the year.

The pedophile had become a source of enormous public fear; and it was in April (near the height of the bogus social workers case) that a riot in Manchester's Strangways prison turned into a savage mass assault on "Rule 43" prisoners—sexual offenders and molesters. Attacks were so violent that early reports suggested ten or more deaths, though, in fact, only one died (*Guardian Weekly*, April 15, 1990; compare Priestley 1980).

The exact meaning of the bogus social workers case remains unclear. No arrests were made, no names traced, and no conspiracy detected. It is in fact uncertain whether there was any truth to the alleged sightings, and later writing on the topic has been skeptical. It is interesting that *New Statesman and Society* presented a highly critical account of the case. In 1991, this journal would be one of the chief upholders of the theory of widespread child abuse, and even of abuse by ritual or satanic cults; yet an article now suggested that the social workers were wholly imaginary. The sightings were "phantom bogies," Fortean myths on a par with UFOs, spontaneous human combustion, and rains of frogs. (Coward 1991). They belonged in the well-known literature of urban legends.

It can be argued that the story of the bogus social workers represented a classic urban legend, a tale that becomes popular because it serves to focus contemporary fears and concerns. Best argues that such a legend should be seen as an "unconstructed social problem," and the bogus social workers phenomenon was intimately related to current British panics (Best 1990; 131–150). Specifically, the reported impostors focused the public's ambiguous attitudes to the controversial figure of the social worker, who was simultaneously criticized for busybody interference in the lives of ordinary citizens, while failing to protect the truly vulnerable. It is significant that the case followed the publicity accorded to the mass child abuse cases in the county of Cleveland, in which (according to popular stereotypes) social workers had almost randomly seized children from their homes in response to spurious charges of child abuse (see Chapter 6).

There was genuine public uncertainty about the powers of the social service agencies, which seemed to have limitless discretion to invade homes and seize children. Either this might have been exploited by cunning pedophiles, or else it led to a hysterical wave of alleged sightings of these feared predators[1].

Whatever its origins, the bogus social workers affair indicates the extent of real popular concern over pedophilia, the degree to which the most extreme conspiratorial claims had been accepted. The danger was no longer confined to London and the cities: It could strike at any time, in any village or suburb. And no amount of streetproofing could safeguard children from abduction, assault, or murder. The figure of the pedophile had become one of the most terrifying folk-devils imagined in recent British history.

NOTE

1. There had been authentic precedents where offenders had used social work as a means of gaining access to young sexual partners, and in 1975, the television documentary *Johnny Go Home* gave national celebrity to one such scandal. Roger Gleaves was a multiple sex offender who had adopted a variety of aliases, and had become a self-styled "bishop" of a fringe church. He established a number of hostels in the early 1970s, ostensibly to assist the flood of poor and homeless boys then flocking to London from all parts of the British Isles. Gleaves and his followers adopted a pseudomilitary uniform, and found homeless boys in rail stations and other public places. He was assisted in his endeavors by the Charity Commission, and various London borough authorities. A number of scandals ensued, involving sex with underage boys. Gleaves was imprisoned for acts of indecency, and a number of his associates were jailed for crimes that included the murder of a teenage boy (*Sunday Times*, July 27, 1975).

Enemies Within

Reformulating Child Abuse

— 5 —

Public concern about child sexual abuse reached new heights between about 1984 and 1988. Unlike the panic over pedophilia, however, the problem was now thought to derive not from sinister strangers, but from intimate members of the family circle. As in the United States, it was increasingly believed that the sexual abuse of children was a frequent event, and that the major culprits were parents or close relatives (Best 1990; Crewdson 1988; though see Eberle and Eberle 1986; Jenkins and Maier-Katkin 1988). Attention thus shifted from pedophilia to incest: Any child could be abused, and any male could be an abuser. The view rapidly gained credence, but it is striking how important a departure this represented from views accepted before about 1980. The discovery of sexual abuse was a sudden event that requires explanation.

As in earlier chapters, the emergence and definition of the problem can be more clearly understood if we present changing beliefs and assumptions as a broadly chronological sequence of statements:

Stage I. 1972–1979

- The battering and physical abuse of children are common phenomena, affecting families of all social strata.
- Battering and abuse can pose a lethal danger to children.
- Recorded cases of battering represent only a tiny fraction of the actual occurrences. This shows that it is possible for a vast social problem to be ignored by society if it appears inconvenient or dangerous to confront the issue.
- The protection of children must be the first priority for the criminal justice system and social service agencies encountering abuse cases.

101

Stage II. 1979–1984

- Sexual exploitation is at least as widespread a problem as physical abuse.
- There is a vast "dark figure" of domestic sexual abuse, at least as large as for physical abuse.
- The family is often the setting for sexual abuse, with the father and other male relatives the most common offenders.
- Police and social services must place a high priority on fighting incest and sexual exploitation.

Stage III. 1985–1988

- About one child in ten is the victim of sexual abuse. This implies one million child victims at any given time in contemporary Britain.
- This mass sexual exploitation normally takes the form of incest or intrafamilial abuse.
- Children's statements and courtroom testimony are crucial evidence in the detection and reduction of child abuse. This testimony must normally be elicited by skilled professionals. Children have neither the will nor capacity to lie in such matters.
- Police and court practices must be amended to take account of the insights of social and psychiatric workers skilled in dealing with the child abuse problem.

THE CHILD PROTECTION MOVEMENT

The recent interest in child abuse has led to a number of important historical studies of the issue in earlier eras, and these suggest the cyclical nature of concern and activism (Behlmer 1982; Parton 1985a; Jeffreys 1985). Eighteenth and nineteenth-century literature contains many references to child neglect in Britain, in addition to the cases of infanticide and "baby-farming": These were usually publicized following scandals like the Amelia Dyer trial of 1896 (Rose 1986). Disraeli remarked of Victorian London that "infanticide is practised as extensively and legally in England as it is on the banks of the Ganges" (quoted in Parton 1985a:21). Incest and sexual abuse were less commonly discussed, but there were periodic waves of concern, especially in the early 1920s.

In the 1880s, the protection of children became the focus of a number of movements, such as the campaign to raise and enforce the age of sexual consent; while the Children's Society was created in 1881 to rescue waifs and the homeless from the London streets. There were also attempts to prevent physical abuse and neglect, and the most important group of this type was the National Society for the Prevention of Cruelty to Children (NSPCC), which would over the next century play a dominant role in defining child-related problems (Allen and Morton 1961). Interestingly, in light of later developments, the NSPCC was founded in direct imitation of an American model, the New York Society for the Prevention of Cruelty to Children. Early societies in Liverpool and London were consolidated into a national society in 1884, which received a royal charter in 1895. Through the early twentieth century, the NSPCC's uniformed inspectors (the "cruelty men") operated extensively in working-class areas, in close association with the police and (later) social welfare agencies.

Initially, the society's work concentrated almost entirely on physical abuse and neglect, and its work had a strong criminal justice focus. This was also reflected in successive cruelty acts from the pioneering legislation of 1889 onwards. By midcentury, however, there was a perception that social improvements and the welfare state had resulted in a significant betterment in the lot of children. The 1956 NSPCC report noted that "cases of physical ill-treatment are less severe than they were" (Parton 1985a:46). In the 1950s and early 1960s, it was often implied that the NSPCC should concentrate its work in the area of neglect among poor and dysfunctional families on the margins of the welfare system, while physical abuse was declining (and sexual abuse was scarcely mentioned as an issue). The questions of broken homes and single-parent families were often discussed in this context. By the 1960s, the NSPCC became steadily more oriented to professional social work approaches rather than "child policing." The uniforms were abolished between 1965 and 1969, and more intensive training was introduced.

Meanwhile, professional social welfare agencies were developing under the auspices of local authorities. In 1945, a boy's death that resulted from physical abuse led to the Monckton investigation, which recommended the creation of centralized children's departments to coordinate social services (achieved under 1948 legislation). In the 1950s and 1960s there was a steady growth of a social work approach to the issues of children and youth. This trend culminated in the Scandinavian-influenced Children and Young Persons Act (CYPA) of 1969, which revolutionized procedures toward both child abuse and delinquency. It established a system of statutory orders mandating the care, protection, or supervision of a young person, and attempted to abandon the distinction between the troubled or neglected child and the delinquent (Harris 1991; Blagg et al. 1989).

However, the whole concept of child abuse was undergoing a transformation during the 1960s. In the United States, there had since the beginning of the decade been medical interest in the topic of baby battering, or nonaccidental child injury. This "discovery" has been the subject of scholarly attention, and it has been suggested its new definition as a problem reflected the interests of groups within the medical profession, including pediatric radiologists and forensic pathologists. The same groups can be found active in British writing on the subject, and the *British Medical Journal* discovered the so-called battered-baby syndrome in 1963 (Kempe et al. 1962; Pfohl 1977; Kempe and Kempe 1978).

From the mid-1960s, the NSPCC acted as the conduit by which American perceptions of a problem (and soon a crisis) were introduced to Britain. [The stages of this process are ably described by Parton (1985a), on which this account is largely based.] NSPCC director Arthur Morton visited the United States in 1964 and spent time with Dr. C. Henry Kempe, who would long be a major influence on British child protection policy. Morton and his associates believed that battering might be a substantial problem, and the society established in 1968 a Battered Child Research Unit at Denver House (*Denver* referring to the American project that it imitated; Baher et al. 1976; Franklin, 1977).

Researchers and other officials began making frequent visits to the United States to study changing perceptions of child maltreatment. The various researchers published extensively on the topic, and there was interchange of ideas and personnel between the NSPCC and the child welfare section of the Department of Health and Social Security (DHSS), the department of central government with overall charge of the welfare system. Joan Court of the NSPCC Research Unit actually moved to head the relevant section of the DHSS. From 1970, DHSS circulars began to adopt NSPCC ideas on the prevalence and symptoms of battering.

MARIA COLWELL AND AFTER

The British child protection system had emerged in a rather unsystematic way, with occasional scandals and sporadic waves of public enthusiasm providing the incentive for change (Dingwall et al. 1983; Rogers et al. 1989: 158–164) By far the most sweeping changes followed the death in 1973 of seven-year-old Maria Colwell of Brighton. She had earlier been removed from her home for fostering, but was subsequently returned only to be starved and repeatedly beaten before eventually being murdered by her stepfather. The inquiry continued into 1974, and led to intense media criticism of social workers and to extensive administrative reorganization.

The Colwell case was crucial in the discovery of physical abuse in Britain, and helped popularize the work done by the NSPCC in the previous decade. The speed with which the idea was accepted may have owed something to current notions of Britain becoming a violent society. This concept originated with the celebrated crimes of the 1960s—the moors murders, the Shepherd's Bush police murders, the organized crime rings of the Krays and Richardsons—now reinforced by the threat of political violence and IRA terrorism (Hall et al. 1978; Parton 1985a: 81–82). In 1973 and 1974, Britain experienced one of its sharpest political crises of modern times, with a Conservative government brought to its knees by a political miners' strike. The rhetoric of the two 1974 elections repeatedly addressed the issue of a nation out of control, threatened by "men of violence." The Colwell case seemed to confirm that not even the youngest and most innocent were immune to the threat of pervasive violence, while battered children themselves grew up to accept violence as normal behavior.

The consequences of the Colwell case have been described as a moral panic over the theme of physical abuse, a topic frequently addressed in books, documentaries, and fictional works during the next three years (Frude 1980; Carver 1978; Inglis 1978; Franklin 1977; Borland 1976; Renvoize 1974). In 1976, a Parliamentary Select Committee on Violence in the Family produced a report with a separate volume on violence perpetrated against children. *Child abuse* entered public debate as a concept and as a term. In 1970, the central problem was *battered babies; nonaccidental injury* came to the fore by 1974; by 1978, *child abuse* established itself as the dominant phrase (Parton 1985a:111). The usage was consolidated and popularized by the British publication during 1978 of *Child Abuse*, by R.S. and C. Henry Kempe.

The affair naturally had an impact on the organization of child protection efforts. The "post-Colwell" system was based on the Area Child Protection Committees of local authorities, and the interagency case conferences that met to decide appropriate intervention for particular incidents. The committees had substantial discretionary powers, under the general supervision of the DHSS. The committees prepared and distributed manuals of conduct and procedure; and they also supervised the Child Protection Registers maintained in each area, a list of children determined to be at risk by medical and social work agencies. The register was intended to ensure that "warning signs" detected by one agency would be made available to other interested parties, who would then be able to determine if a pattern of abuse or neglect existed (M. Campbell 1991). This would avoid the problems in cases like that of Maria Colwell, where a failure of interagency coordination contributed to abuse or even death.

CHILD DEATH INQUIRIES

Obviously, the system was not perfect. The Colwell inquiry was the first of some 35 such investigations in the next thirteen years, each of which led to varying amounts of what was often termed "social-worker bashing" in the press (*Child Abuse*, 1982). There was by the mid-1980s a litany of cases where children had died because social and medical workers had failed to heed signs of abuse, usually physical in nature. Year after year, the names of Tyra Henry, Heidi Koseda, Jasmine Beckford, and Kimberly Carlile came to symbolize official bungling in the face of domestic brutality (Laurance 1985, 1986a).

These inquiries proved traumatic for the profession, and they are useful for illustrating the complex public attitudes toward social workers (compare Harrison 1983). An overwhelmingly conservative press took the opportunity to list the customary stereotypes about social workers (Franklin and Parton 1991). They were intrusive busybodies who held extreme and faddish notions about the alleged horrors of the traditional patriarchal family. On the other hand, they were frequently denounced for failing to intervene sufficiently in specific cases. At the same time, they sought to intervene too much, and too little (Reed 1986; Hill 1990). Fears about their powers to enter homes and remove children may be reflected in the legends and stories that grew up during the bogus social workers panic of 1990 (discussed in Chapter 4).

The most extensively reported case was that of four-year-old Jasmine Beckford, killed by her stepfather in 1984 in the London Borough of Brent. Shortly after birth, Jasmine and her sister had been removed from their natural parents under a care order because of evidence of physical abuse. Jasmine was fostered in a loving family, but was returned to her parents, in part because social workers were anxious to have her brought up in an appropriate racial environment (the Beckfords were Afro-Caribbean). The following inquiry produced a substantial report of some 450 pages, and its harsh criticisms of social services were reported at length by the press during 1985. The media also followed the process of internal inquiries and calls for disciplinary action that were made through the first half of 1986 (*Child in Trust* 1985; Parton 1986; Dingwall 1986; Franklin and Parton 1991).

A quest for politically correct solutions had led social workers to neglect obvious signs of abuse or starvation, and even to determine facts as basic as Jasmine's real parentage (they believed her stepfather to be her real father). The chair of the inquiry, Louis Blom-Cooper, referred in a much quoted phrase to "a naiveté almost beyond belief" on the part of the social workers. For the media, the case confirmed the worst stereotypes about social workers as left-wing zealots of dogmatic feminist and antiracist views. These attacks focused on one social worker in the case, Gun Wahlstrom, whose foreign origins were stressed. The setting was peculiarly appropriate, as the borough of Brent was one of the heartlands of the radical left, which would later offer a parliamentary constituency to GLC chairman Ken Livingstone.

For the purposes of the sexual abuse panic, cases like those of Maria Colwell and Jasmine Beckford left a powerful legacy. On the one hand, they suggested that huge amounts of abuse could go on barely noticed by the public, and that for many the family might be a lethally dangerous environment. Social service agencies were strongly motivated to intervene early to prevent tragic consequences, while the wave of inquiries had stressed that the interests of the child must remain paramount in investigations. But the successive inquiries also indicated to social service agencies that mistakes would be politically dangerous, in that they would simply add to the media arsenal of criticism (Franklin and Parton 1991).

FEMINISM AND SEXUAL ABUSE

From the early 1980s, fears of child abuse shifted from the predatory stranger to the molester—almost invariably male—within the home (for the debate on the prevalence of abuse by women, see, for example, Barwick 1991; Kelly 1991). Of course, there had been a long awareness of incest, usually in the context of very remote or poor areas, but child sexual abuse played very little part in the debates of the 1970s. As late as 1985, in Nigel Parton's notable study *The Politics of Child Abuse*, sexual activity was referred to only in passing references. In the Kempe tradition, child abuse was virtually synonymous with physical violence, and any British study of abused children prior to the early 1980s almost certainly focused on family violence (see, for instance, Fowler and Stockford 1979).

But attitudes were changing. To some extent, this recognition reflected a growing awareness of the feminist critique, in which child sexual abuse was seen as a nearly universal characteristic of male dominance (Roberts 1988a, b; MacLeod and Saraga 1987a, b, c, 1988a, b, c; Miller 1984). This had been a sporadic theme since the mid-1970s in publications like the *Leveller* and *Spare Rib*, but it was at the height of the concern about sexual violence between 1980 and 1982 that the exploitation of children came to the fore [see, for instance, Jeffreys (1982), Bowen and Hamblin (1981), Pizzey and Dunne (1980); once again, it is striking that Parton's account makes no mention of feminism or of women as a distinct interest group].

The new feminist self-help institutions also played a role, as both RCCs and battered-women's refuges reported finding numerous cases of child sexual abuse, both within the family and outside: In 1982, the London RCC found that 24 percent of its clients were under the age of sixteen when attacked (McFadyean 1986; compare Herbert 1989). In response to growing reports of domestic abuse, RCCs and other feminist groups created a network of support programs: an Incest Crisis Line (1978), and the first of many incest survivor groups (1981; compare Armstrong 1991). In 1982, the National Women's Liberation Conference was held in Manchester, with the theme "Male Power and the Sexual Abuse of Girls" (Rhodes and McNeill 1985). This disseminated much current American theory, including work on child pornography.

To illustrate the new activism, we might single out Emily Driver, a "play therapist" dealing with abused children. She was a founder of the Incest Survivors Campaign, and in 1984 began the Child Sexual Abuse Prevention Education Project (CSAPEP), under the auspices of the GLC. For Driver, like many others, sexual abuse was in a sense the foundation of the patriarchal family and of the society based on it: "In fact, child sexual assault has been widespread for generations. Without it, the West would not have the society it does—the family organization, the male-dominated religion, the abuse of women in pornography, even the Hollywood film stars" (Family Rights Group 1988:34).

The phenomenon affected every class and region, and was not merely confined to stigmatized "outsiders." To quote Beatrix Campbell:

> Child molesters or murderers are legitimate targets for moral panic when they're poor. Resolutions are piously passed against them at Tory party conferences, where from the fastnesses of respectability antique punishments are invoked for crimes which they think they never commit themselves. The survivors know better. (Campbell 1987)

> Sexual abuse . . . now presents society with the ultimate crisis of patriarchy, when children refuse to protect their fathers by keeping their secrets. (Campbell 1988a:71)

As with rape, the domain of the child abuse problem steadily expanded. Sheila Jeffreys argues:

> The issues of incest and marital rape strike blows at the fundamental institution of male supremacy itself, the heterosexual family. . . . If indecent exposure, various forms of abusive touch and the use of pornography are included in our definition of sexual abuse, then it is unlikely we will discover many women who have survived childhood without experiencing it. (Jeffreys 1990:242)

To quote an activist with the London RCC:

> Sexual assault of children . . . is part of all the sexual assaults, verbal and physical, that all women and girls suffer in our daily contact with men. These assaults range from being shown pornographic literature or videos, to being touched by or being forced to touch a man's genitals. . . . It will stop only when the very fabric of our society changes, and when men and women are truly equal. (Family Rights Group 1988:19)

The feminist attack on child abuse raised searching questions about the means of proceeding with offenders. Why was it the woman or child victim who was removed from the household, as opposed to the culpable male? Why did investigators implicitly blame the child victim for conduct that might somehow have provoked the abuse? More fundamentally, why did social service agencies try so hard to save the family unit, when the institution of the family might well have played a significant role in causing the abuse to occur? In this, British feminists were often influenced by R.D. Laing's theories about the family as a arena of psychic conflict that gives rise to psychiatric illness, no less than physical manifestations such as battering and abuse.

The feminist voice received a favorable hearing within the crucial audience of the social and medical services dealing most directly with children. Such feminist themes were by no means the only interpretation or ideology, but they were frequently presented in the crucial journals, publications, and presentations most likely to win the attention of social workers. Particularly important in this regard are magazines like *Community Care* and *Social Work Today*, which offer news and articles on the one hand, and extensive job listings on the other. They thus remain essential reading for both social work administrators and staff.

Since the mid-1980s, *Community Care* has reported frequently on sexual abuse, and in terms that suggest a social crisis. Increased statistics represented not changes in reporting practice, but revelations of the real scale of the problem. As NSPCC team leader Judy Fawcett wrote in the magazine, the issue was inextricably linked with gender roles:

> Society traditionally requires the male to be dominant and power-ful. When this is coupled with the male tendency to sexualize all emotional needs and the lack of strong criminal sanctions against offenders, the atmosphere is ripe for an emotionally arrested individual who feels the need to be powerful in his family and to consider sexually abusing his or her child. (Fawcett 1987)

More academic in nature is the *British Journal of Social Work*, which in 1989 presented a remarkable article by Lena Dominelli. This offered a far-reaching radical feminist critique of child abuse and the society that produced it (Dominelli 1989; compare Dominelli and McLeod 1989; Dominelli 1987; Davies 1991). She argued that the social work profession had to reconstruct itself fundamentally to meet the feminist critique, to challenge "the ideology of professionalism which places the views of the detached 'experts' above the voices and experiences of those who have undergone abuse." The proposed model would attack "theories of the family which assume that it inevitably functions in the best interest of its members." Dominelli emphasized "the significance of gender and other social divisions including adultism, ageism, racism, classism and het-erosexism in sexual abuse" (Dominelli 1989:305–306). By exposing "the misery and pain forming an integral part of the fabric of the lives of women and children who are abused within the 'normal' family," feminists were challenging "the patriarchal family which provides the bedrock of the white Western world order" (p. 295).

Throughout the decade, anyone following the social work literature would encounter such an analysis in more or less vigorous form. In 1988, the British Association of Social Workers published a guide to child abuse which blamed the problem on the "emotional illiteracy" that led *all* men to see relationships in sexual terms, so that abuse was only a mild exaggeration of normal male behavior (Glaser and Frosh 1988).

AMERICAN INFLUENCE

It is also possible to see the British encounter with child abuse as a reflection of American influences. One key name here was C. Henry Kempe, who would so often shape NSPCC attitudes (Kempe was German-born, but spent most of his professional life in the United

States). In 1976, Kempe founded the International Society for the Prevention of Child Abuse and Neglect (ISPCAN), with its journal, *Child Abuse and Neglect*. These institutions provided a forum for British specialists and activists and an opportunity to exchange ideas with their American and European counterparts (see the articles in Mrazek and Kempe 1981). In 1978, the society held its conference in London.

One interesting account of Kempe's impact comes from Arnon Bentovim, who would become Britain's leading medical authority on sexual abuse. In the 1970s, he had favored the Freudian view that accounts of childhood abuse were often the outcome of fantasy:

> He was jolted out of this comfortable illusion at a London confer-
> ence in 1979, addressed by Henry Kempe. Bentovim had worked
> with families involved in child abuse—including some of the most
> notorious cases from Maria Colwell on—since the early seventies.
> Listening to Kempe, he realized he wasn't seeing cases of sexual
> abuse at all. (Laurance 1986b)

He began seeking evidence of the crime; and from 1981 to 1986, six hundred cases of sexual abuse were seen at his institution, the Great Ormond Street Hospital for Sick Children, in London. Bentovim in turn became a leading spokesman about the dangers of child abuse, and published some of the most influential British textbooks and articles (Bentovim et al. 1988; Furniss et al. 1984; Mrazek et al. 1983; see also Bentovim 1988).

When sexual abuse was increasingly "discovered" as a major theme from the early 1980s on, British activists naturally turned to the extensive American literature that was so readily available. By 1984 and 1985, papers and books on British conditions were already regarding American experts as their chief source: We repeatedly find the names of scholars like David Finkelhor, Roland Summit, and A. Nicholas Groth, as well as literati like Maya Angelou and Alice Walker (Finkelhor et al. 1988; Finkelhor 1984; Summit 1983).

When an influential conference was held at Teesside Polytechnic in 1984, important speeches were provided by American researchers Ann W. Burgess and Danya Glaser; and the proceedings were later made available in video form. In 1987, Glasgow University organized a child abuse conference on the theme "Learning from American Experience," with speakers including David Finkelhor, Lucy Berliner of Seattle, and Astrid Heger of the abuse clinic at the University of Southern California. Also present were several of the British doctors and social workers from the recent Cleveland controversy (see Chapter 6). Glasgow University served as cosponsor with the Los Angeles–based "Children's Institute

International" (CII), the therapists who had been at the center of the McMartin case and whose diagnostic techniques would occupy so controversial a role in this lengthy trial (Murray and Gough 1991).

Through such means, British writing on the subject of abuse soon became littered with references to terms like *rape trauma syndrome* and *child abuse accommodation syndrome*, and also disseminated more fundamental concepts from the American literature. Once again, this writing stressed that abuse was a common, perhaps nearly universal phenomenon; and investigation had to proceed on the assumption that allegations were likely to be true (Bray 1991). Above all, children tended not to lie about such occurrences, and the legal and therapeutic systems had to act on the basis of "believing the children," "listening to children," phrases that were often cited (NSPCC 1989). Feminist assumptions combined with American academic models to encourage belief in the ubiquitous nature of sexual exploitation.

THE NSPCC

Also vital to the establishment of new ideas about sexual abuse was a group that was neither feminist nor radical in nature, the NSPCC. The society had succeeded in projecting its agenda in the 1970s, but there had also been significant internal problems. Alan Gilmour had become director in 1979 in the middle of a crisis: "Its Inspectors, no longer in uniform, were diminishing in number and in some areas losing credibility because they were too few and too scattered to provide a coherent service; and this service was too vaguely defined" (Gilmour 1988:133–134). Gilmour's directorship produced a near revolution, focused especially on the society's centenary in 1984. This offered abundant opportunities for fund-raising and publicity. No less a body than advertising agency Saatchi and Saatchi produced the slogan "The faces change . . . the bruises don't." "Taking advantage of its centenary in 1984, the NSPCC was able to restore its finances, and restructure and expand its services." Gilmour launched an aggressive and more proactive effort at child protection, in intimate alliance with public agencies.

He was assisted in this (once more) by Dr. Kempe, who was currently on sabbatical with the society. In addition, the NSPCC's Ray Castle was a prominent member of Kempe's ISPCAN. In consequence of Gilmour's reforms,

> a new pioneering development began, of Special Units, which were teams of child abuse workers, established and usually funded

jointly with Social Services Departments. Beginning in Manchester, and spreading to a dozen other cities and counties, these teams worked to a clear remit of managing the child abuse processes, including management of the register and case conference procedures, providing treatment to a limited caseload of selected serious abuse families, and offering a training and consultancy services to others. (Gilmour 1988:133–134)

In the late 1980s, the NSPCC managed the registers for Area Child Protection Committees in eleven areas, covering 9 percent of the child population in England and Wales, and operated sixty-six child protection teams. It had also opened a Child Protection Training Centre in Leicester. By 1989, the society was drawing about 11 percent of its £26 million ($45 million) budget from central and local government, the balance being raised from fund-raising and investments (NSPCC 1989). The society's budget had increased over the decade by 1,000 percent. In terms of social problems theory, the NSPCC possessed a degree of ownership over the child abuse issue that it would retain through the end of the decade (Maher, ed. 1987).

GROWING CONCERN, 1980–1985

By the early 1980s, academic studies of sexual abuse in Britain began to appear (Mrazek and Kempe 1981; Lynch and Roberts 1982; Creighton 1984, 1985; West 1985; Baker and Duncan 1985; Berridge 1985; Dale et al. 1986; Ennew 1986b; Franklin 1986). From 1981 on, a child abuse study group meeting under the auspices of the CIBA Foundation included figures like Arnon Bentovim, Christine Cooper, Margaret Lynch, and Tilman Furniss. In 1984, this group produced a textbook that would long be regarded as the definitive British work in the area (CIBA Foundation 1984).

There were also a number of important conferences, such as the Teesside Polytechnic gathering in May 1984, which has already been discussed. In 1980, a British Association for the Study and Prevention of Child Abuse and Neglect (BASPCAN) was founded by, among others, Arnon Bentovim and NSPCC leaders Alan Gilmour, Joan Court, and Ray Castle (Franklin 1981). BASPCAN held an inaugural conference in April 1982, and presented its views through the journal *Child Abuse Review.*

Some of this activity found a base in academic institutions. In 1980, the Open University introduced a course, "Conflict in the Family," aimed at professionals in social services and education, which placed a heavy emphasis on the variously defined forms of *abuse*. In April 1987, a Child Abuse Studies Unit was founded at North London Polytechnic: this group, headed by Mary MacLeod and Esther Saraga, specialized in "alternative feminist policy and practice" (MacLeod and Saraga 1988c). In 1987, Hull University was one of several institutions to introduce training for professionals handling child abuse cases.

The upsurge of interest in child sexual abuse was reflected in a host of books, readers, textbooks, technical manuals, and polemics, which reached flood proportions at the end of the decade. (From a great many examples, see Bray 1991; Furniss 1991; Meadow 1990; Doyle 1990; LaFontaine 1990; Chesterman 1990; Fairclough 1990; Hobson 1990; Rogers et al. 1989; Driver and Droisen 1989; Blagg et al. 1989; Jehu et al 1988; Search 1988; Bentovim et al. 1988; Corby 1987; Greenland 1987; D. J. West 1987; Jay and Doganis 1987; Jones et al. 1987). There is evidence of greatly increased sensitivity to the issue of children's sexuality; and in 1992, public outrage forced several leading retailers to withdraw lines of lingerie and other clothing designed to make children appear sexy or alluring (Bedell 1992).

Concern about abuse was reflected in the changing priorities and methods of bureaucratic and charitable agencies. There were increasing fears in the child protection agencies that concentrating on physical abuse might lead to undervaluing other forms of equally traumatic maltreatment, including sexual abuse. In an important 1980 circular, the DHSS urged extending the coverage of child protection registers to "children who suffer severe mental or emotional abuse" and extended the age limit up to seventeen years (Parton 1985a:112). By 1981, known or suspected sexual exploitation was included as a separate category for inclusion on the registers. This marked an important transition, a stimulus to investigation and to the recording and collation of statistics.

The police were also affected. Since the mid-1970s, police forces had come under pressure to extend more helpful and sympathetic treatment to adult victims of rape, which implied increased police cooperation with doctors, therapists, and social workers. There had also been collaboration with medical and social services in the investigation of pedophile rings. Such inter agency investigations involved problems far removed from traditional police practice. In order to study procedures in child abuse cases, the Metropolitan Police established a pilot project in the London borough of Bexley in 1984 (Bexley 1987). The final report on this experiment was generally seen as a model for future operations (though radical feminists criticized the project for its use of male investigators; Kelly and Regan 1990; compare Byrne and Patrick 1990).

MEDIA COVERAGE

From 1984 on, child abuse ceased to be a matter of interest chiefly to specialists and pressure groups and became an issue of major public excitement. Reports of child abuse cases became far more common in journals and national newspapers, and there was a deluge of stories from 1985 onwards. Words like *panic* were freely used by critics (Dibblin 1987; Seaton 1987; Laurance 1987 a,b; Smart 1986; Caudrey 1986; Corby and Mills 1986; McFadyean 1985; Tucker 1985, 1987).

In the *Times*, it is possible to assess the coverage of a topic in terms of the length of column entries in the annual index. Some material on child molestation and domestic sexual abuse appeared under topics like pedophilia, obscenity and pornography, rape, and murder, but by far the largest number of stories appeared under the heading of sexual offenses. Between 1977 and 1982, the total length of the *Times* index columns under that heading covered a total of 78 centimeters; from 1983 through 1985, the total was 90 centimeters. The figures for successive years were:

Year	Coverage in Times index (centimeters)
1986	57
1987	198
1988	159
1989	93
1990	103

This rough guide suggests that the *Times* published considerably more stories on sexual offenses in 1987 alone than during the nine years from 1977 through 1985; and the vast majority of such stories addressed child sexual abuse. It will also be noted that the dearth of stories in the early part of the decade occurred during Rupert Murdoch's proprietorship, and so the increased reporting cannot simply be seen as a response to new journalistic standards.

It might initially be thought that this was solely a response to the Cleveland scandal of 1987, discussed in the following chapter. This affair—one of the major domestic news stories of the year—did much to enhance public awareness of a "crisis," but less than 40 percent of the

1987 stories concerned the Cleveland case and the subsequent inquiry, and the remainder were unrelated. Most of the stories reported individual incidents and trials that would presumably have gone unnoticed in the national press in earlier years.

This explosion of miscellaneous stories continued in subsequent years. Coverage again increased to near Cleveland levels during 1990 and 1991, largely in response to the newly perceived menace of ritual or satanic abuse. Put another way, in 1977 and 1978, the *Times* published about twenty to thirty stories each year on the related topics of child sexual abuse, child pornography, and pedophilia. By the beginning of the 1980s, that number had fallen to an annual average of about ten, but then there was a remarkable increase. In 1987 alone, there were almost 400 such stories, 150 of which dealt with Cleveland. By 1990, the number of stories appearing each month exceeded the annual total a decade previously.

An impressionistic survey of other papers confirms the impression of a general surge of reporting during 1985 and 1986, climaxing in 1987. Apart from general reporting, the newspapers published feature articles and investigative pieces. The *Times* and the *Sunday Times* published no such articles between 1978 and 1983. In 1984, however, there was a surge of articles with titles like "The Menace of Pedophilia" and "The Sad Secrets of Abused Children." The year 1986 offered "Bringing the Child Molester to Book," "Child Abuse Challenge," and "The Making of a Molester."

In 1987, twelve substantial pieces were published, which presented a diversity of views about the reality of the crisis, especially in light of Cleveland. Attacking the "panic" over false abuse charges were articles like "Could a Child Mistake a Parent for a Sexual Abuser?" "Cashing in on Gullible Teachers," "An Unhealthy Obsession," and "Guilty! Until Proven Innocent." Other pieces were more supportive of the claims-makers, and the *Sunday Times* in 1988 proposed "Why We Must Now Start Listening to the Children." Outside the newspapers, magazines like *Woman's Own* and *Woman* offered major outlets for such stories.

The visual media were equally active in promoting the theme. During 1985, Channel Four broadcast a trilogy of films about the sexual exploitation of children, which was also the subject of a documentary in the series "File on Four." In December 1985, the investigative television program "TV Eye" broadcast an interview with a man who claimed to have molested some two thousand children in his "career" as a pedophile. Another "TV Eye" (*The Secret Crime*) depicted a ring of fifty teenage and subteen prostitutes in Leeds. All the major television news programs addressed these topics between 1985 and 1987, notable examples including a 1985 "Panorama" on the Beckford case, and a 1986 edition on sexual abuse; and a July 1987 "Cook Report" on child pornography. In 1988, the series *Protecting the Children* documented the work of the NSPCC. Child abuse was a recurrent theme on the national BBC radio program "Woman's Hour," one of the most widely heard shows in Britain.

Often, media accounts were strongly parti pris documents. In 1986, Channel Four presented *A Crime of Violence*, produced by film-maker Audrey Droisen, of the Feminist Coalition Against Child Sexual Abuse. In 1990, feminist writer Beatrix Campbell produced a "Dispatches" documentary (again on Channel Four) on the perils of ritual child abuse.

CHILDLINE

Media and government agencies were increasingly talking of a national drive against pedophilia and child abuse, but it was a television program shown in October 1986 that brought the movement to a new plateau. Television personality Esther Rantzen had long introduced the investigative show "That's Life," which used sensationalistic rhetoric to expose fraud and crime. A special investigation in October focused on sexual abuse and offered the figure of up to one million abused children in Britain. "Child sexual abuse was suddenly transformed into the occupational hazard of any young child (especially female child) living in a family" (Seaton 1987).

The results were sensational, especially when Rantzen sponsored a ChildLine telephone hotline, for the use of any child wishing to report abuse or to seek counseling. The idea was not new, and there had been earlier experiments such as the feminist Incest Crisis Line, or the anticult Childwatch. ChildLine was, however, the first national endeavor, and it was heavily publicized. The news media treated the opening of the hotline as a major event, and were well rewarded in terms of news coverage when the service received a reported fifty thousand calls on its opening day. This seemed decisive confirmation that the known abuse cases were but the tip of a very large iceberg, and children's calls and letters were extensively reported and quoted. This became an important news story in early November, but calls continued to come in at a rate of eight to ten thousand a day through mid-1987 (Laurance 1987a).

ChildLine was not without its critics, who soon pointed out that the charges made by children were often trivial in nature and fell far short of even the most flexible definition of abuse. News stories suggested that children were being encouraged to see quite innocent behavior as abusive and to report it accordingly. Nor could ChildLine cope with the problem it had apparently discovered, and the number of trained volunteers was quite inadequate for the task.

Social service agencies also complained about the emergence of a two-track system of child protection, "a local authority one and another run by a self-appointed body which is doing what it likes" (*Community Care*, December 18–25, 1987; *Times*, January 9, 1987). Of the first 16,000 children to seek the help of ChildLine, only 250 had been referred to social workers. Meanwhile, the social workers within the organization protested the employment of volunteers. The charity was also questioned about the allocation of its resources, and it underwent a thorough structural reorganization in early 1987. The new director was Valerie Howarth, the director of Brent social services at the time of the Beckford case.

Whatever its own problems, the ChildLine phenomenon played a central role in shaping a social problem and in decisively shifting the definition of child abuse in the direction of sexual exploitation In the aftermath of Cleveland, the panic over child abuse would be explained by *Community Care* in terms of three main causes: "the NSPCC's centennial, the launch of ChildLine, and public criticism of social work following three successive child abuse inquiries" (*Community Care*, July 7, 1988). As child abuse became a common topic for radio and television talk programs, Esther Rantzen emerged as a vital spokeswoman on the issue, sharing "ownership" of the problem with the NSPCC. ChildLine itself now joined the proliferating range of pressure groups and organizations whose whole raison d'être involved detecting and publizing child abuse. In 1990, Health Minister Virginia Bottomley remarked that organizations like ChildLine had been responsible for making "children increasingly believe they should be free from terror, torture and neglect" (interview in *Social Work Today*, September 13, 1990).

RESPONSES

By 1987, Margaret Thatcher spoke of child abuse as "the biggest blot on civilization" and suggested a "crusade" to combat it. American models were much in evidence in this campaign, which got under way in 1985. Michelle Elliott, an American educational psychologist living in Sussex developed a Child Assault Prevention Program for schools (Tucker 1985; Elliott 1985). She also founded the organization Kidscape, to train children to resist abuse and molestation, and to report it as soon as it occurred. Elliott was involved in a Home Office working party on the subject.

Psychologist Gerrilyn Smith wrote in 1985 that "Streetproofing—as it is called in America—is on its way across the water" (Family Rights Group 1988:1). By the mid-eighties, Britain offered a substantial market for the numerous "self-protection" books that had already become such a vogue in the United States, among them *I Like You to Make Jokes with Me, But I Don't Want You to Touch Me* (1981), *It's My Body* (1982), and *No Is Not Enough* (1984) (Smart 1986). British imitations soon appeared, with *It's OK to Say NO!* activity book and coloring book (both 1985), and Oralee Wachter's bestselling *No More Secrets for Me* (1986). British publishers also reprinted works like *No Is Not Enough* (1985).

In 1985, National Children's Homes helped make and distribute a video, *Strong Kids, Safe Kids,* a version of an American production. NSPCC made a series of videos aimed at different age groups, and featuring show-business celebrities such as Rolf Harris. The society also produced and distributed booklets like *Protect Your Child: A Guide about Child Abuse for Parents.* The Home Office distributed the film *Say No to a Stranger* for use in schools; and the Church of England's National Society devised a *Better Safe . . .* campaign for the use of teachers, featuring the cartoon character Fred the Fish.

These educational efforts were much publicized in the media and the specialized press addressing teachers and social workers, and the television networks broadcast similar material. The Education Department recommended that there should in every state school be at least one senior teacher trained to look for the signs of abuse (*Times,* July 7, 1988). It would have been surprising if such a systematic propaganda campaign had not stimulated public awareness and in turn increased investigation and reporting of suspicious activity.

THE USE OF STATISTICS

Child abuse activists used statistical evidence to support their views about the prevalence of the problem. Sexual abuse is naturally difficult to quantify: To all the problems involved in judging the scale of any type of crime, must be added changing definitions and public perceptions, and the central dilemma of reporting. On the other hand, the various studies that have been undertaken are perhaps less important than the way in which they were summarized by the media and various pressure groups.

There were various attempts to assess the scale of abuse by surveys that asked adults whether they had been abused as children. This type of measure often produced figures that were startlingly high, though there were always methodological issues about exactly how abuse was defined. As in most surveys, the exact phraseology of the questions was vital. In 1986, Dr. Jane Wynne of Leeds told the British Paediatric Association

> Figures from the United States show that one in three children has some sort of sexual experience such as being flashed at, one in ten has something more serious and one in a hundred suffers incest. We are missing the vast majority of sexual abuse if these figures are correct, and we think they are. (*Times*, April 17, 1986)

(This story may have received particularly heavy coverage because it coincided exactly with the announcement of Operation Stranger.)

British surveys were not so sweeping in their implications, but the statistics they produced were higher than what might have been predicted a few years earlier. The most quoted British instance was a Market and Opinion Research International (MORI) poll carried out in September 1984 and reported the following March. [MORI is broadly equivalent to the American Gallup Poll, (*Times*, March 5, 1985; Worcester 1991).] This suggested that about one person in ten had been the victim of childhood sexual abuse. Other accounts that year said one in five; but one in ten was attractive because of its simplicity (Laurance 1988b;40–49). The poll suggested a vast "dark figure" of child victimization, and specifically implied that perhaps one million British children were currently suffering or had experienced abuse.

"We estimate that there are over 4.5 million adults in Great Britain who were sexually abused as children, and that a potential 1.17 million children will be sexually abused before they are 15 years of age" (Baker and Duncan 1985 p. 458). This was a momentous finding, reported as a major news story. Also much noted was the suggestion that "there was no increased risk associated with specific social class categories or area of residence": In other words, families in all areas were likely to suffer sexual abuse. By implication, areas or groups with low reporting rates were either unaware of their problem or were more successful in covering it up.

The structure of the poll deserves closer examination. MORI questioned 2,019 individuals nationwide, who were presented with a very broad definition of sexual abuse:

> A child (anyone under sixteen years) is sexually abused when another person, who is sexually mature, involves the child in any activity which the other person expects to lead to their sexual arousal. This might involve intercourse, touching, exposure of the

sexual organs, showing pornographic material or talking about
sexual things in an erotic way. (Rogers 1989)

This has been described as "almost a textbook example of how *not* to
write a survey question" (Rogers et al. 1989:48–49). Among the many
problems, pornography is not defined, and the survey pays little
attention to the relative ages of the abuser and the victim. By this
criterion, any form of sexual activity between an eighteen-year-old boy
and a fifteen-year-old girl would be classified as child sexual abuse.

Two hundred six subjects reported abuse and 259 refused to answer.
Of the 206, only 26 (1.3 percent of the total surveyed) reported abuse
within the family, 128 (6.3 percent of those surveyed) reported abuse
through some form of contact; while a further 15 individuals (0.7
percent) described intercourse. Nine recorded incest. Of the 206 who
described abuse, 127 were recording a single incident, which would
often involve exhibitionism by a stranger; 119 of the abused group were
eleven years of age or older at the time of the occurrence.

Analyzed in more detail, the figures suggest a picture much less grave
than initial reports implied; and abuse also seemed less likely within a
family context. The MORI poll offers no support for the image of
prevalent abuse of toddlers and small children within the family, usually
by a father or stepfather; nor were one in ten children subject to rape
and buggery. In 1987, the researchers protested at the misuse of their
work, and noted that the true rate of intrafamily abuse for girls was not
one in ten, but closer to one in 220 individuals. This report, however,
earned little media attention in comparison with the original story
(*Times*, December 2, 1987).

NSPCC STATISTICS

In his introduction to a 1989 book on child abuse, Alan Gilmour made
the statement, "The latest NSPCC research . . . shows that the number of children registered for sexual abuse has increased twelvefold
during the period 1983 to 1987" (Blagg et al. 1989:ix). The sentence
reflects an undisputed fact—that the number of children so recorded
had increased by just this amount—and this could be explained in many
ways. Gilmour himself was scrupulous in repeatedly emphasizing that
growing rates of *recorded* child abuse did not necessarily reflect actual
changes in the behavior (compare Gilmour 1988).

On the other hand, his words easily lent themselves to the popular
misinterpretation that the number of sexually abused children had

grown by a factor of twelve in a mere four years. The NSPCC naturally made great play of figures in its publicity and fund-raising, and media reporting often treated its claims as if increased numbers did reflect an increase in actual abuse. Detailed analyses were customarily oversimplified to a simple headline statement, as in December 1986, when most papers quoted the NSPCC as claiming a 125 percent growth in child abuse over the year. In 1989, the *Times* report of the society's latest statistics headlined "Sex Abuse Cases up by 24 Percent" (April 13, 1989; compare the frequent reports during the decade, for instance, *Times*, September 19, 1985; March 22, 1986; December 10, 1986; January 5, 1988).

The NSPCC possessed a curious semipublic status, as the society was a private and charitable adjunct to the work of police and social services. This ambiguous role would be important because the group played a leading role in assessing the scale of abuse by recording and generating statistics. This is not to suggest that the society distorted or exaggerated information in order to promote its views or interests, but it should be made clear that this was a pressure group as opposed to a theoretically neutral bureaucratic agency. It is not therefore surprising to find the NSPCC at the forefront of campaigns to stress the seriousness and ubiquity of child abuse.

There were two main sources of data generated by the NSPCC: the number of reports to the society of "children helped" and those "at risk." Both criteria showed dramatic increases in the 1980s. Just between 1987–1978 and 1988–1989, the number of "children helped" by the society rose by 12.5 percent, to a total of over 54,000. In this category, victims of sexual abuse represented 2,327 cases in 1986–1987, 3,680 in 1988–1989.

The "at risk" registers were a critical source of information (M. Campbell 1991). The total number of children currently at risk was found by extrapolating the detailed information obtained on the NSPCC-run Child Protection Registers to the nation at large. These appeared to offer a detailed and reliable statistical analysis of the endangered child population as a whole. In March 1989, for example, there were 43,100 children recorded on registers in England and Wales, representing over 3.8 per thousand individuals under the age of eighteen. Of these, 17,200 were under five years of age; 14 percent had been listed because of known or suspected sexual abuse; 13 percent for neglect; 24 percent for physical abuse; and 40 percent for various forms of "grave concern."

These NSPCC registers presented perhaps the strongest evidence of a crisis in child abuse. From the mid-1980s, overall numbers recorded in the registers began a startling growth, often by 10 percent or more a year. "The 2,137 cases in late 1986 represented an increase of 34 percent on 1985 figures, which in turn were a 43 percent increase on 1984" (Rogers et al. 1989:41). Between 1987 and 1988, the overall numbers in NSPCC registers grew from 5,341 to 5,947, a one-year increase of 11.4 percent. Between 1988 and 1989 alone, there was an increase of 9 percent in the number of cases at risk.

Once again, sexual abuse was a key area of growth. Only in 1981 was sexual abuse listed separately on child abuse registers, and thus earlier figures are not available; but growth thereafter was swift. NSPCC registers recorded 27 cases of sexual abuse in 1981, 98 by 1985, 222 by 1985, 527 by 1986 (Gilmour 1988; Blagg et al. 1989:153–162; Rogers et al. 1989:41)

INCREASED INVESTIGATION

In large measure, the growth in "children helped" or "at risk" stemmed from bureaucratic factors. There is a well-known cyclical and self-sustaining process, whereby increasing awareness of an issue leads to more resources being devoted to its investigation, which in turn promotes higher statistics, and still more public awareness. This process was clearly at work in the child protection bureaucracies in the mid-1980s.

Most social service agencies were devoting unprecedented attention to the issue of abuse, and investigations and recorded cases were both increasing rapidly. In Nottinghamshire, for instance, a huge increase in abuse reports led to the hiring of 57 new social workers in 1987 (*Times*, July 7, 1987). In Scotland, the number of child abuse investigations rose by 260 percent between 1986 and 1987. Growth in particular localities was often startling. Bradford had 9 recorded cases of sexual abuse in 1985 and 248 in 1988; Strathclyde had 4,500 in 1986 and 6,000 in 1988 (Roberts 1989a).

Many saw the rise as a direct bureaucratic response to media charges of insufficient action during the various child death inquiries. In *New Society*, Jeremy Laurance wrote in April 1986:

Child abuse referrals have risen steeply in recent months. Doctors, health visitors and schoolteachers appear to be playing it safe. In Staffordshire, the figures are up 60 percent in the last five months. In Nottinghamshire, the 1985 total was 68 percent higher than for 1984. In Norfolk, the referrals in the last six months of 1985 were more than double the same period for 1984. Sharp increases have

also been reported in the London boroughs of Merton and Green-
wich. In Brent, the figures are up 30 percent since the Beckford
report was published. (Laurance 1986a)

There are even examples of what might be called the "quota" effect:
the phenomenon of areas being criticized for failing to record a large
number of cases. Since abuse was so prevalent, the argument goes, this
must imply either unsympathetic or inefficient local authorities. This
attitude is suggested by *New Stateman and Society*: "One disturbing
feature that *This Week*'s MORI poll revealed is that while 10 percent of
local authorities have 200 or more cases, the majority of London
boroughs have around 50 or less. . . . So why is London picking up on
so many fewer cases?" (Roberts 1989a). The bureaucratic incentive to
seek out abuse cases is clearly implied. In such an environment, it would
be astonishing if the Child Protection Registers were not recording steep
increases from year to year.

One corollary of this approach was that the position could by
definition never improve. In 1989, Alan Gilmour's reaction to a decline
in NSPCC statistics for child neglect was, "We are obviously going to
have to do something about the area of neglect because the referral rate
had been slipping down. Neglect has again become a neglected (*sic*)
area" (*Times*, April 13, 1989).

The general public also played a role in this process of spiraling abuse
reports. A majority of referrals to the NSPCC derived from the public at
large as opposed to social service agencies. In 1988–1989, there were
25,133 referrals for abuse or neglect, of which 43 percent came from the
general public, with another 12 percent from anonymous tips. Greater
public consciousness increased the likelihood of referrals, which in turn
increased awareness of a problem. Inevitably, the NSPCC was given
abundant new material to prove the scale of the problem it was
encountering and its effectiveness in meeting the challenge. In reporting
this, the society was constantly feeding the media stories of soaring
child abuse statistics.

LEGAL CHANGE

Outrage at domestic abuse led to calls for remedial action, if in fact
legislation could have any impact on so vast and intractable a problem.
From 1984 onward, schemes to remedy the law in such cases were
extensively proposed and discussed by media and politicians (Rogers et
al. 1989:129–142). This in turn helped keep the issue in the public

consciousness and maintained a sense of crisis. The debates were also of interest in showing how seriously the threat of child abuse was regarded, as many of the reforms involved sweeping attacks on traditional Anglo-American legal rights and protections. Legal assumptions were challenged by what might be described as therapeutic values, the sense that neutral professionals were working in the best interests of the child and the community and should not be hampered by dated technicalities (Kittrie 1973).

This sense of conflict is suggested by social workers' resentment at the growth of legalism in limiting their capacity to intervene for the public good. On the other hand, there were a number of areas where the erosion of legal values would still cause debate. The draconian nature of the procedures made possible under child protection laws would become fully apparent in the mass abuse crises of the late 1980s, when they would be responsible for a public backlash.

There were several critical areas of policy where legal changes were felt to be necessary. Among the most pressing were the use of children's evidence in courtroom proceedings, the means of identifying and tracking known and suspected child molesters, and the procedures involved in taking children into official care (Blagg et al. 1989:163–178).

The Law of Evidence

Schemes to protect the rights of alleged child victims in the courtroom were proposed by the NSPCC as well as by organizations representing the police and social workers (Davies and Drinkwater 1988; Naylor 1989; Blagg et al. 1989:122–137). There had been long debate over the value of child testimony in criminal matters. The 1933 Children and Young Persons Act (ss. 42–43) permitted the very young to give unsworn evidence in some cases, but demanded that it be corroborated. The leading court decision in this area, *R. v. Wallwork*, dated from 1958 and was controversial in its hostility to permitting the testimony of child witnesses as young as five. In fact, it had been described as a "molesters' charter" in this regard. In the 1980s, there were suggestions that abusers escaped conviction and punishment because of these weaknesses in the law of evidence: Harrowing stories were told of witnesses declining to testify out of fear for their personal safety (Lund and Booth 1991).

Reform proposals suggested allowing the evidence of small children, and in the most favorable and nontraumatizing environment (Spencer and Flin 1990; Smart 1989; Enright 1987). Usually, this involved testimony by closed-circuit video link, which involved a considerable departure from the traditional right of the accused to confront witnesses. The practice of isolating witnesses behind courtroom screens also developed during 1987. However, demands soon went further, especially following an important article in the *Times* by the respected legal scholar Glanville Williams in November 1986. One scheme involved permitting evidence to be presented in the form of "secondhand" taped interviews between the alleged victim and a "qualified" professional like a social worker, teacher, doctor, or psychologist; and severe limitations would be placed on the right to cross-examine a child (Murray and Gough 1991; Davies and Drinkwater 1988; Naylor 1989; compare Warnock 1986; *Report on Child Witnesses* 1991). In 1989, a committee headed by Justice Thomas Pigot issued a highly praised report, which asserted that "children ought never to be required as witnesses in Crown Court, whether in open court or protected by screens or closed circuit television, unless they wish to do so."

Also controversial was the development of new means of interviewing children, for example, by means of anatomically correct dolls, and the use of play as a medium of communication. The suggestion was that children might be able to act out symbolically events that they could not put into words, though the idea has its detractors. These practices were pioneered in Britain by Arnon Bentovim, who had attracted criticism for his structured interviews of possible victims (G. Roberts 1988). As in the United States, there were fears that therapists or social workers might consciously or otherwise lead children, or even implant suggestions that abuse had occurred (G. Roberts 1988). Therapists, after all, are seeking outcomes from interviews that may or may not coincide with the quest for objective forensic evidence demanded in a trial setting, a point made in a controversial 1986 case [*Re M (a Minor) (Child Abuse Evidence)* 1 FLR 293].

The courts therefore had to confront a significant change in therapeutic responses to child abuse (Blagg et al. 1989:122–137, 163–178). By 1986, the issue of presenting children's evidence was central to a number of cases, all involving videotapes of diagnostic interviews at Bentovim's clinic at Great Ormond Street Hospital (Roberts 1988). The judges raised several objections to the evidence, noting that the therapists appeared to operate from preconceptions that abuse had occurred; while in legal terms, the child witnesses seemed to be put under pressure to testify in a certain way, and leading questions had been used [*C v. C (Child Abuse Evidence)* 1 FLR 321; *Re E (a Minor)* 1 FLR]. However, subsequent cases showed the judges as basically sympathetic to the use of video in such surroundings, as it allowed subsequent observers to assess the original interview (Roberts 1988; Blagg et al. 1989:122–137, 163–178).

Between 1988 and 1991, new criminal justice acts granted many of the calls for reform. Children under fourteen were permitted to testify by video link, while some courts permitted testimony from behind a screen until the available technology was in place. The same laws removed the need for corroboration for the evidence of younger children. This was widely felt to represent an acceptable solution, but the closed-circuit facilities were slow to be installed, and only forty-four of the hundred Crown Court centers were scheduled to be fully adapted by mid-1993. In consequence, there continued to be widely reported cases that collapsed due to the peculiar problems of taking children's evidence (Lund and Booth 1991).

Also, the new acts fell short of the Pigot Committee recommendations by requiring that child witnesses could be cross-examined; and a number of notorious abuse cases offered instances where such children were discredited by what were alleged to be the bullying tactics of counsel. One of the most controversial was a 1991 ritual abuse case, the "black magic trial," where a family was said to have abused children in circumstances that also involved cannibalism and satanic ritual in Epping Forest (see Chapter 8). The media reported the eventual dismissal of charges as a clear instance of the inadequacies of the law to address a serious social menace and to deal sympathetically with molested children, though there can be little doubt that in this particular case, the charges were quite spurious (MacIntyre 1991; L. Jenkins 1991).

Tracking Abusers

The reformers were suggesting that traditional rights and protections had to be weakened in order to promote the interests of the child, which were repeatedly mentioned as the paramount concern. This conflict of interest also occurred over the issue of identifying suspected child molesters, so that they could not gain positions of trust working with children as teachers or social workers. It was proposed to create "suspect databases" of known and suspected pedophiles and sex offenders. Improved computerization and tracking was one of the major proposals made in 1984 following the notorious case in which a released sex offender found a babysitting job because his probation officer failed to reveal his record. The individual later killed a little girl named Marie Payne (*Guardian*, December 18, 1984; *Times*, December 19, 22, 1984). The press often recounted atrocity stories along these lines.

The goal of prevention might be accomplished in several ways, including reform of the Rehabilitation of Offenders Act of 1974. This act had been intended as a liberal measure to permit offenders to "bury" minor criminal convictions after a set period of time. Such "spent" convictions would not have to be declared in employment applications and could not be mentioned by the media, or even in court. The law had never been popular with the police, and the press detested what was in effect an obstacle to effective investigative reporting.

Various groups supported calls to change the law so that child molesters could not evade their earlier misdeeds. Background checks were commonly proposed for those wishing to work with children (such procedures are far less common in Great Britain than in the United States). Perhaps a school or local authority could check the records of job applicants with the central Criminal Records Office, again suggesting a need to abandon individual protections and privacy rights in the face of a perceived menace (*Times*, July 17–18, 1986).

More serious altogether were proposals for a list of suspected abusers, one of the few areas where the courts took a stand against "reforms." In 1989, a court ruled in *R v. Norfolk County Council* that a social services case conference could not arbitrarily place the name of a suspected abuser on a register without due process, as this practice had "dangerous potential as an instrument of injustice and oppression"(Blagg et al. 1989:168).

Care Proceedings

The removal of children from parents by compulsory order involved many potential conflicts, legal and ethical, and these issues soon became central in public discussions of the perceived crisis. The key measure was the Children and Young Persons Act, CYPA, of 1969, which offered local authorities great latitude to place children into care by compulsory process (Blagg et al. 1989:163–178). Abuse that could lead to removal was defined in section (1) as conditions where "the child's proper development is being avoidably prevented or neglected, or his health is being impaired or neglected, or he is being ill-treated." In such cases, any magistrate could issue a "place of safety order" (PSO) mandating removal, and the magistrate might well be approached in an informal setting such as his or her home. This clause was only one of several catchall phrases that could be used in cases of suspected abuse: Compulsory care was appropriate if "the child is exposed to moral danger" (Blagg et al. 1989:163–178; Parton 1985b).

The operation of the child protection system had been modified over the years by the Child Care Act of 1980, and by guidelines and working papers from the DHSS. Among the most significant were the guidelines issued in 1974 after the Colwell case, but there were still a number of gray areas where social workers had a good deal of undefined powers. Procedures surrounding forced access to a home left some room for debate, as did the issue of whether the parent of a child in care could be denied access, or under what conditions (Sinclair 1984).

There was a general long-term growth of compulsory orders after the Colwell era. From the mid-1970s, local authorities tended to place fewer numbers of children into care overall, but the ones who were removed were far more likely to be taken under a PSO, and their stay in care—residential or foster—was likely to last longer than previously. This reflected the theory that long-term stability was in the best interests of the child.

Against this general background, use of PSOs grew still more sharply during the successive waves of concern about abuse, first physical and later sexual. One peak in the number of statutory orders occurred in 1980, followed by several years of decline. The year 1987 marked a recovery and a new plateau, well above the level of the late 1970s. This reflected fear about the consequences of failing to intervene in the child's interests, but also the problems of operating smooth bureaucratic procedures under a sudden overload of cases (Parton 1985b; Hillyard and Percy-Smith 1988:210–215). Under CYPA (s.1), a child was taken into care for his or her own protection while the social service agency prepared a case for longer-term action or intervention. In the first instance, the magistrate's order lasted for up to 28 days. Initially, 28 days was regarded as a maximum that would rarely be required, but the increased pressure of business during the panic of the mideighties meant that the full term of the order was usually imposed.

The procedures were highly discretionary in nature, with a substantial potential for abuse by magistrates or (above all) local authorities. The laws had originally passed with so little difficulty because of the assumption that they were applicable to a limited section of the population, where the essentially marginal issue of child neglect or abuse might prevail. Care and protection proceedings thus operated in an environment far removed from traditional legal values, where the accused person is assumed to be innocent until proven guilty and has the opportunity to confront accusers.

Of course, this objection did not in theory occur in the CYPA procedures, in that neither the parent nor the family was on trial: The only issue was the welfare of the child, in which surely the parent was as much interested as the social workers or doctors involved. Nor was there a penal element as such. On the other hand, the distinctions between intervention and punishment were often perilously thin. Case conferences were especially controversial, as they resembled secret tribunals able to inflict draconian penalties (the disruption of a family, removal of children, and the stigma of molester) without either judicial intervention or the possibility of appeal.

The British courts had a rather ambiguous attitude to care proceedings, though they tended to support the discretionary aspects of the law. In 1988, *R. v. Harrow LBC* decided that mother did not have the right to be present at a case conference at which it was decided to place her children on the register of those at risk. From the 1970s also, the courts became more directly and frequently involved in child abuse cases, as local authorities sought to place children in the position of wards of the court. This offered some advantages to the authorities, who only had to prove that the move was in the best interests of the child, but it allowed more play to legal interests and values.

Legal reforms were systematized in a Children's Act passed in 1989 in the aftermath of the Cleveland case, though it would not be fully implemented until 1991. This sought to establish the primacy of the child's interests in any abuse investigation, though calling on social workers to operate within the family framework as far as possible. Among other things, the act revised the protection system with a new regime of Emergency Protection Orders (EPO), Child Assessment Orders, and Interim Care Orders. This took account of the frequent charges that social service agencies had been hasty in taking children from their families, and attempted to limit such procedures to genuine emergencies. The new EPO would be effective for only seven days, and there would be an appeals procedure (Bell 1990).

CONCLUSION

A number of factors can be cited to explain the rapid acceptance of child sexual abuse as a primary social problem. There was, for instance, the campaigning work of the NSPCC, the growing power of feminist analyses resulting from a perceived wave of sexual violence, and the increased sensitivity of social service agencies in the aftermath of the child death inquiries. However, the triumph of the abuse issue also owed much to the lack of serious opposition. It was possible to criticize specific aspects of the campaign, such as the inadequacies of ChildLine, or the misinterpretation of the various surveys and statistical evidence. However, none of these objections affected the core issue of the perceived problem, that incest and abuse within the family were widespread.

This alleged fact could be accepted and employed in various ways by activists of all political shades, moralists and feminists, conservatives and socialists, while it was difficult to mount a counteroffensive. Even if one disagreed with the analysis, there appeared little reason or need to attack specific policies such as prevention programs or streetproofing.

The judges themselves, so often noted for social conservatism, went far toward accepting the essential implications of the abuse problem as popularly defined.

Opposition was lacking because it initially appeared that responses to the abuse problem could do no great harm, personal or even ideological, if we exclude a few individuals who may have been wrongly convicted under the new legal procedures. This perception changed fundamentally from 1987, when it appeared that a struggle against child abuse could lead to a searching, obsessive, and perhaps indiscriminate investigation of a whole community, of the sort that easily earned the title of witch-hunt. The development of such incidents shifted the balance in the media against the earlier uncritical acceptance, and permitted the return of the long-established rhetoric against social workers and the local authorities they represented.

Cleveland

— 6 —

Cleveland is a county of some 560,000 people in the northeast of England, based on Teesside industrial communities like Middlesbrough. In the history of social problems, it deserves fame as the setting for the first mass sexual abuse case in British history. In the numerous books that have appeared on child abuse in Great Britain in the last few years, we often encounter the expression "post-Cleveland." (The impact of the case is obvious in books like Richardson and Bacon 1991; Bray 1991; LaFontaine 1990; Fairclough 1990; Rogers et al. 1989; Driver and Droisen 1989; Blagg et al. 1989; O'Hagan 1989; Search 1988; Children's Legal Center 1988; Family Rights Group 1988; Laurance 1988c; MacLeod and Saraga 1988c.) In addition to confirming the existing beliefs about the child abuse problem, the Cleveland affair of 1987 also appeared to show that:

- The abuse of children commonly takes forms far more serious than hitherto imagined, with vaginal and especially anal intercourse being commonplace.
- The experience of active local authorities and social service agencies proves the widespread nature of sexual abuse within a family setting.
- Police and politicians effectively conspire to understate or conceal the evidence of mass sexual abuse.

The Cleveland affair was a fundamental event in shaping British social policy in this area, and it deserves analysis in depth.

LEEDS

Nineteen-eighty-six was the year of ChildLine and the Operation Stranger investigation. However, a medical discovery reported that year caused a still more fundamental evaluation of the threat to children. The prestigious *Lancet* published an article by two Leeds pediatricians on the topic of buggery (anal sex) symptoms in small children. In a much quoted sentence, they suggested, "Buggery in young children, including infants and toddlers, is a serious, common and under-reported type of child abuse" (Hobbs and Wynne 1986:974). One writer would later refer to this portentously as "the Leeds discovery," that "more children were being buggered than battered" (Campbell 1988a:25). If the theory were right, sexual abuse was not only more frequent than even the most pessimistic had suggested, but it was of a nature that threatened grave physical as well as psychological damage to the victims.

The study had its origins in the scare over pedophile rings. In the early 1980s, Leeds police launched one of the first major interagency projects against sex rings, and discovered that many children had been victimized. Pediatric facilities were required, to provide both medical help and therapy, and local doctors therefore had a great deal of opportunity to observe and diagnose child abuse. Since 1982, a few child abuse activists from pediatrics and social services had been arranging ocasional meetings and discussions. This group, including doctors Chris Hobbs and Jane Wynne, believed that they had discovered a diagnostic technique of great value in the recognition of child abuse (Wild 1986; Hobbs and Wynne 1987a, b).

This reflex anal dilatation (RAD) test was supposed to indicate the experience of anal penetration, though even Hobbs and Wynne stressed that the technique required careful administration and that a compliant child could imitate a positive result. Others object that some symptoms for anal abuse are not unlike those for other complaints, including chronic constipation. In light of other influences on the British discovery of child abuse, it is noteworthy that the anal dilatation test originated in the United States. Hobbs and Wynne were "first alerted to the problem by two visiting social workers from America where recognition of the syndrome was much further advanced" (Laurance 1988a). As a Leeds consultant pediatrician commented, "Emissaries began to arrive here and I sent one of our people to America" (Campbell 1988a:22).

Armed with the dilatation technique among others, the doctors began discovering a remarkably large amount of sexual abuse. Three cases of abuse were found in 1980, 9 in 1983, 30 in 1984. Numbers then mushroomed, to 100 in 1985, and 237 by 1987. In a two-year period, 1,368 children had been referred to the group, 608 of whom were suspected victims of sexual abuse. Of the latter, 337 were determined to be confirmed or probable victims of sexual abuse, and a striking 42 percent of these gave positive responses to the anal dilatation test (Hobbs and Wynne 1989).

The number of sex cases on the Leeds register of at risk children stood at 8 in 1983, 79 in 1985, and 174 by the fall of 1986. Community services were placed under enormous strain, and in 1987, a Leeds M.P. requested £2 million in government aid to provide care, counselling, and prevention work. The figure was much reported, because if extrapolated to the country as a whole, this suggested an urgent need for £140 million in central government spending on this problem (*Times*, January 9, 1987). Leeds became the first British community to experience a child abuse crisis on a pattern that would shortly be experienced in other areas.

The findings about RAD were, to say the least, counterintuitive, though the doctors rightly emphasize that they were usually accepted by judges and social service agencies. The literature on sexual abuse is now vast, and there are many accounts from victims and perpetrators. Overwhelmingly, the abuse described as being inflicted on smaller children (say, between four and nine years old) involves masturbation, fondling, and oral sexual activity. Anal sex is not frequently described, even by those most committed to unearthing an abuse problem. Nor do incest survivors often recall such activity. To take one of many examples, the Avon Sexual Abuse Center in Bristol studied 225 cases referred during 1985–1986, and found precisely one instance of anal penetration (Bate and Liss 1986). A sample like that presented by Hobbs and Wynne might be expected to produce a handful of anal abuse diagnoses—not the 140 or more actually noted. The disparity between these findings and the bulk of the literature seems impossible to reconcile.

THE INFLUENCE OF LEEDS

The work in Leeds was made available through publications from 1986 onwards, and the new ideas were adopted in other regions, such as the county of Hereford and Worcester, where diagnoses of anal abuse were running at high levels through the summer of 1987 (*Sunday Times*, September 6, 1987). One of the most important centers was Tyneside. This area had an active RCC, and there had been considerable activism following the notorious 1982 documentary on the police reaction to rape cases. In response, Tyneside formed a Women Police Surgeons' Group to support victims of sexual assault, both adult and child. One factor in promoting this was the presence in Newcastle of Christine Cooper, a pediatric consultant with a strong interest in child abuse (in 1980, she had been president of BASPCAN). The new group found what it believed to be increased evidence of incest and penetrative abuse among children, and called a conference to discuss and publicize its findings. In 1986, the first paper by Hobbs and Wynne crystallized thinking on the subject, and a growing number of doctors began applying the new diagnostic techniques.

One of those working at Tyneside was Marietta Higgs, an Australian, who in 1986 examined two children from the county of Cleveland for suspected abuse. She claimed to find evidence of the anal dilatation syndrome, which she would increasingly regard as diagnostic proof of abuse, rather than merely a suspicious sign requiring further investigation (Roberts 1989b, c). The Cleveland link was important as this was one of the areas where new ideas about the prevalence of child abuse had had a considerable influence on the social service department.

CLEVELAND

As in the United States, social work agencies in Britain are the responsibility of local and city governments, and there is considerable variation in the policies that characterize different local authorities. In November 1985, Cleveland social services director Mike Bishop had made an explicit decision to give child abuse priority over the agency's other concerns. This emphasis might at first sight seem curious in light of the area's more glaring economic problems. Unemployment had grown steeply in the early 1980s, and Bishop made dire prophecies of trouble to come: "My deep fear is that Cleveland is becoming an industrial wasteland where people don't expect to get jobs and where second generations of families are not employed. And there are real indications that the community is almost breaking down" (*Community Care*, June 12, 1986).

However, Bishop's main concern addressed the effects on the area's children: "The number of children known to my department who are subject to child abuse has doubled in the past ten years. The children who are in care because of parental neglect has increased by 30 percent in the same period. These are alarming statistics and they must in some way be correlated to the increase in unemployment" (*Community Care*, June 12, 1986).

There was already a core of interest in the child abuse issue, in health visitors and social workers like Marjorie Dunn, who had attended the conference at Teesside Polytechnic (Campbell 1988a:36; Richardson and Bacon 1991). Bishop sought to build on this expertise (Bishop 1988). In June 1986, the council acquired a new "child abuse consultant" in Sue Richardson; and in January 1987, Dr. Marietta Higgs arrived to serve as consultant pediatrician (Richardson and Bacon 1991; Bulter-Sloss 1988; Bell 1988; Campbell 1988a; Gilmour 1988; Masson 1988). She worked closely with another pediatrician named Geoff Wyatt, who had been in the area since 1983. A number of other appointments were soon made, including Deborah Glassbrooke, a veteran of the Childwatch and ChildLine organizations, who established a sexual abuse therapy center at Middlesbrough General Hospital (Richardson 1988).

THE CASES BEGIN

Shortly after Higgs's arrival, she and Wyatt began to diagnose child abuse at what seemed a remarkably high rate, and with great reliance on the anal dilatation test. By March, Higgs had positively diagnosed abuse in a two-year-old child solely on the basis of the test, without external corroboration. Also the extensive application of the anal dilatation test to children who were referred to the pediatricians for a variety of conditions apparently unrelated to sexual abuse was controversial. The most notorious instances concerned children originally referred for conditions like asthma. Higgs stated that there was a series of symptoms that might give rise to suspicion about abuse and suggested a need for further inquiry. She mentioned "conditions like soiling, constipation, sudden change in behavior, poor growth, urinary symptoms and so on" (Roberts 1989b).

Also controversial were cases in which the doctors would diagnose symptoms of apparent abuse that occurred after children had been taken to the hospital. Higgs explained these in terms of molestation actually occurring within the hospital environment: "Even under supervised access and social service departments, children have been abused. It sounds preposterous, but we do know that it takes place." In one instance, a child was taken into care on the basis of evidence of anal abuse. Shortly afterwards, it appeared that the same symptoms recurred, leading some to conclude that he must have been abused anew by his foster parents. Such stories gave rise to press charges that the diagnoses were simply false, and that the pediatricians were making up any explanation to avoid confronting this.

By the spring, Higgs and Wyatt believed they had found evidence of a sexual abuse crisis. In five months, they diagnosed 121 children as victims of abuse, from a total of 57 families. In terms of official reaction, the social service agencies were haunted by the memories of the thirty or so child death inquiries since Maria Colwell, and of the fresh wounds opened by the investigations into the deaths of Jasmine Beckford, Tyra Henry, and Kimberly Carlile. This theme is repeatedly mentioned by participants in the affair, including Bishop himself (*Social Work Today*, April 11, 1991:15). *Community Care* defended the Cleveland investigation by asserting, "No department wanted to run the risk of a child dying in the same way" (*Community Care*, November 7, 1988). Indeed, the Carlile inquiry was getting under way just as the Cleveland cases peaked.

These precedents suggested the need for intervention, and that usually meant PSOs. The volume with which such orders were sought became another troubling aspect of the affair: Magistrates were allegedly frequently approached at odd hours to issue orders, the suggestion being that they did so without proper investigation. Eighty-three PSOs were obtained in May and June 1987, and twenty-five children still remained in "care" by the middle of the following year. The crisis came to a head in May and June, with the PSOs being "issued like confetti" (Dominelli 1989:294). By the end of June, 202 children were reported to be in care. Later estimates placed the figure somewhat lower, but confirmed that over two hundred children had been referred to social services.

Many of those removed were then medically examined for forensic evidence of abuse, a procedure that was legally uncertain. In ethical terms, the intrusive tests were at least on occasion administered against strong protests from the children concerned. Also controversial was the neglect of parents, who were usually not informed of actions in their cases. Parents were present or involved in none of the 175 case conferences held between April and August, though at each meeting the social service agencies had the power to remove children from their families. In only a few instances were parents seen by the chairman of social services, and that was to explain the decision already taken in their absence.

In terms of the construction of social problems, the social service and medical agencies had apparently established an almost perfect mechanism for the continuous generation of abuse reports. There were agencies and individuals with the full-time responsibility to investigate child abuse, and thus there was a bureaucratic need to produce tangible results. Concrete evidence against a child in one family permitted siblings to be removed and examined, while intense publicity about abuse generated still more referrals. However, the cycle had points of weakness, and the "child abuse crisis" began to fall apart within a few months of its inception.

TOWARD CRISIS

Partly, the investigation collapsed under its own weight, due to the sheer numbers of children taken into custody as abuse "victims."

Middlesbrough General Hospital was rather dilapidated, with already limited pediatric facilities. Now,

> as the numbers grew to crisis proportions over the weekend of 13–14 June, nursing staff had to reorganize the accommodation. Families were crowded into a set of cubicles on the ward, but soon they too were filled. Relocation of those children and their families created the conditions of the parents' revolt. (Campbell 1988a:155)

The next step would be the transfer of children to the care of other local authorities.

There were also bureaucratic conflicts. Cleveland stood in marked contrast to Leeds, where the doctors and social services took greater care to ensure good relations with the police, and exercised greater restraint about the relative value of the dilatation test. On the other hand, relations between Cleveland police and social services had long been strained: As early as 1985, the NSPCC had attempted to design coordinated systems for dealing with sexual abuse on the model being explored in Bexley, but the proposals were rejected. In 1986, Richardson had criticized the Cleveland police for its alleged failure to support social services and to attend case conferences. The conflict with the police was a central issue in Cleveland and was the largest single reason why a scandal erupted there rather than other cities (see also Chapter 9 for the complex relationship between police and social service agencies). From March 1987 on, the pediatricians were also coming into conflict with other medical authorities, who refused to accept their findings or their methods. An important enemy was Dr. Alistair Irvine, the police surgeon, who shared his skepticism with the Cleveland police authorities.

By May, Richardson was issuing memos forbidding the use of police physicians in the examination of suspected abuse victims; at the same time, the police were advised that they should exercise great care in any diagnosis that rested on the dilatation test. The supporters of the investigation naturally focused on Irvine as a villain motivated by professional jealousy; but he was also supported by a number of other police surgeons, including Manchester's Raine Roberts. She was well regarded by feminists for her sympathetic work with rape victims, and had often been in conflict with police opinion. It was therefore significant that she rejected charges of frequent anal abuse, and bitterly criticized Higgs and Wyatt. At the eventual public inquiry, she would charge that the children suffered "outrageous sexual abuse" at the hands of the examining pediatricians.

Another source of criticism was the Teesside magistrates, who by June were beginning to reject social workers' demands for statutory orders, and the High Court, which began hearing applications for wardship. The *Middlesbrough Evening Gazette* ensured that the investigation remained in public view, running a campaign under the slogan "Give Us Back Our Children." The story was soon picked up by the national press, which reacted strongly against the investigation in general, and Higgs and Richardson in particular. Parents were mobilizing into support/defense groups, with the aid of local clergyman Michael Wright; and they found a strong friend in Middlesbrough's Labour M.P., Stuart Bell.

Bell was a crucial figure, for whom the affair reflected many ongoing controversies. He was a moderate-to-right-wing Labour M.P., of the sort who had been removed or "deselected" by radical constituency parties in different parts of the country in the last two decades. Bell was vulnerable as a defender of the "passive patriarchal fastnesses" of the northeast (Campbell 1988b). The Cleveland party had been split for some years, and in 1983 a radical Labour member took control of Middlesbrough city council. M.P. Stuart Bell thus represented the old party machine; Councillor John Bell was a young militant, who strongly supported the abuse investigation. Cleveland can therefore be seen as another episode in the Labour party's simmering civil war over sexual politics.

Throughout, Stuart Bell would be an aggressive and tireless advocate of the rights of the families against the pediatricians and the social services, whom he believed to be fanatics pursuing a vendetta against the institution of the family. He asked questions in Parliament and demanded the suspension of Higgs and Wyatt, who were "colluding and conspiring" to keep police out of investigations. He was supported by another Cleveland M.P. Conservative Richard Holt. The request for removal was denied, but the Health Minister did order an official inquiry. Meanwhile, the parents began a series of legal actions against the county council and regional health authority, which culminated in 1991 in an award of substantial damages to twenty-seven of the families whose children had been removed.

BUTLER-SLOSS

The inquiry into the Cleveland affair was chaired by Judge Elizabeth Butler-Sloss, whom the *Guardian* referred to with a certain hyperbole as "a Solomon with the compassion of Mother Teresa." The choice of a woman was remarkable in Britain, where women judges remain more of a rarity than in the United States: They account for perhaps 5 percent of the total judiciary. Hearings in Middlesbrough Town Hall lasted seventy-four days, and turned into a bewildering legal morass. Legal teams represented the parents, the police, police surgeons, Northern Regional Health Authority, the two doctors, the county council professionals represented by the union NALGO, and the South Tees and North Tees Health Authorities (Chant 1988). A seven-hundred page report was published in July 1988 (Butler-Sloss 1988). The media had been able to comment little while the inquiry was in progress, but the appearance of the Butler-Sloss report in a sense revived the whole controversy, and permitted lengthy reinvestigation of the cases. The resulting publicity undoubtedly encouraged new schemes for the detection and prevention of sexual exploitation (Pithers 1988).

The report concluded that, in essence, everyone was to blame. Social services director Mike Bishop was faulted for failing to take full command of the investigation and for inadequate coordination with health agencies and police. Sue Richardson was crucial throughout, especially since her position as consultant gave her immense discretionary power but no clear place in the bureaucratic chain of command. She had placed too much emphasis on child removal through the use of PSOs, and overall "did not have the managerial skills or foresight to control or contain the escalation of the problems that eventually overwhelmed the department," though Bishop relied heavily on her advice. Higgs and Wyatt showed "certainty and overconfidence with which they pursued the detection of child abuse," while reliance on the dilatation test was "premature." Social workers in general viewed their tasks too narrowly; the police "retreated to an entrenched position," and Stuart Bell had acted in an intransigent and inflammatory manner.

The Butler-Sloss report also offered something to everyone in terms of its final recommendations, which were heavily publicized and regarded as the basis for reform. Among the most important recommendations, the judge stated that child sexual abuse was indeed a major problem, which should be confronted by emphasizing the interests of the child. Major reforms were proposed in extending parental access to case conferences and similar procedures, and recommending that parents have access to children taken into care except where there were pressing reasons to act otherwise. There were also recommendations to improve management within social service agencies and to increase interagency coordination. The government responded by allocating up to £10 million for increased training for social workers in sexual abuse incidents. The DHSS also issued a revised version of the investigative guidelines originally published under the somewhat ironic title, *Working Together* (*Child Abuse* 1988).

One of the most important lessons cited by many observers was the need to create a nonpunitive climate, in which a family suffering from sexual abuse could turn to authorities for help without facing immediate removal of the children or possible criminal charges. It was often stated that this had been the trend in physical abuse since the harsher days of the mid-1970s, and that this was the essential direction for the future of dealing with sexual abuse.

THE CRITICS

Reactions to Cleveland and the subsequent report fell broadly into two categories, which tended to attach themselves to the personalities of Higgs, Wyatt, and Richardson on the one hand, and to Bell and Irvine on the other. The news media overwhelmingly tended to denounce the doctors and social services, and asserted the rights of the parents. The suggestion was that abuse in Cleveland was either nonexistent or limited in scale, and the great majority of the children taken into care were "abused" only by the dictatorial actions of the social services who plucked them from loving families.

Most papers exaggerated the scale of the Cleveland investigation, and the randomness of its methods. Higgs and Wyatt were portrayed as applying tests for abuse to virtually every child with whom they came into contact, and trawling the children's wards in order to find subjects to test. In addition, the papers suggested that the dilatation test had been the sole criterion for evaluation, and that any suspicious signs resulted in the immediate breakup of a family (for earlier charges of error and misdiagnosis in Leeds, see, for example, *Private Eye* 667).

A common theme in the reporting concerned the plight of the children, particularly the image of degrading forced medical examinations that were described as akin to torture. The *Daily Express* was typical in its headlines: "Hospital Chaos as Abuse Suspects Pour In," "Midnight Test Ordeal of Sex Inquiry Tots," "Agony of Families in Sex Abuse Row," "Sad Letters from Alleged Sex Victims Were Smuggled to Parents." The *Daily Mail* and *Mail on Sunday* were also consistent in their hostility to the investigators, and continually stressed the agony of children and parents in the face of a bureaucratic monster. The *Independent* headlined "The Families Broken by a Diagnosis" (compare Sharron 1987b).

The parents were depicted as innocent people confronting a powerful system, effectively lacking the battery of rights and protections that would be available if they had been accused in a courtroom of a motoring offense or even littering. This theme had emerged in the baby-battering era, with reports of parents who were castigated as abusers because their children had diseases that made them more likely to suffer bruises or fractures. In 1985, some victims of the child protection system organized into Parents Against Injustice (PAIN), modeled on the American organization, "Victims of Child Abuse Laws" (VOCAL). By May 1986, the group claimed to have files on two hundred cases of gross injustice, mainly involving battering charges; and that was before the start of the fully fledged panic over sex abuse (*Times*, December 15, 1987).

In the aftermath of Cleveland, PAIN achieved striking success in presenting its views to the mass media, and one member even had a piece published in *Community Care*. This depicted the plight of a family wrongly accused of sexual abuse and denied redress or appeal: "Several weeks later, in a tiny court room, in a few minutes, a judge allows your daughter to be adopted. You will not see her again" (Marshall 1988). The group obtained sympathetic reporting in *New Society*, with its accusations of "parent abuse" (Sharron 1987a; Hodgkin 1986); and PAIN evidence to the Butler-Sloss inquiry was favorably reported. The success of PAIN ensured that future crises would be met by early formation of parents' defense groups, as occurred in the ritual abuse cases some years afterwards.

Basic to the media critique of Cleveland was the plausibility of the charges of ubiquitous abuse, at anything like the level of the "one in ten" claim. These figures had been extrapolated to Cleveland by local councillor John Bell, but they were dismissed by M.P. Stuart Bell: "On this basis, fourteen thousand girls and seven thousand boys [in Cleveland] would have suffered this abuse, and there is no substantial evidence to support it" (*Community Care*, July 9, 1987). The *Daily Mail* asked similarly:

> How could a few well-educated professional people subscribe to a belief—namely that sex abuse was rampant and that one in ten children at least were victims of it—and treat it as a fact that governed their lives, and ended in ruining the lives of so many others, when that belief was at best an assumption and at worst a figure whose substance was based on an opinion poll? (July 13, 1987)

The critics explained the Cleveland crisis in ideological terms. The advocates of the "mass child abuse" theories were portrayed as extreme feminists and antifamily radicals. The media depicted a stereotyped conspiracy of dogmatic radicals anxious to overthrow society regardless of the human cost. Higgs and Richardson served as personifications of the "loony left," and were depicted as aggressive man-hating harridans. Male allies like Wyatt and Bishop were "wimps and weaklings in the thrall of the unseemly strength of insubordinate women" (Campbell 1988a:50). As the *Sunday Telegraph* wrote, "In the Cleveland saga, the authority of medicine has got hopelessly bogged down in the assumptions of the far reaches of left wing politics and enormous harm has resulted" (November 1987).

The critics asserted that the social workers were acting out of professional self-interest. At the height of the crisis, in June 1987, an overwhelmed department was given permission to hire sixteen more social workers at a cost of £185,000, and some saw this as part of the underlying strategy of attracting resources. Bishop had stated that he wanted to create a whole new bureaucratic establishment entirely devoted to combating sexual abuse, with "highly specialized, multi-disciplinary child abuse units in each of the county's four districts" (*Community Care*, July 2, 1987). Stuart Bell described the whole affair as a "put-up job" to build a bureaucratic empire, and claimed the social services knowingly cited false abuse statistics. He asserted, "There is evidence of councillors who were manipulated by persons known and unknown within Cleveland social services, who fed them briefs on child sex abuse in a deliberate attempt to gain more money for the service" (*Community Care*, July 9, 1987). Naturally, the charges were denied by both agencies and councillors.

SUPPORTERS

But Higgs and the social workers had many allies, who insisted that the investigators had not made the serious errors with which they were charged. In the immediate aftermath of the Butler-Sloss report, Labour M.P. Hilary Armstrong created a controversy in the House of Commons by reasserting that many children had been abused: "At the heart of this lies the fact that the majority of those children even in Cleveland were abused and that our main concern has got to be to ensure that fewer and fewer children are abused."

Armstrong had been a professional social worker, as had Conservative M.P. Virginia Bottomley, who also defended the zeal of the investigators in attempting to defend children. There had indeed been mass abuse in Cleveland, a view supported by a number of consultant pediatricians in a 1989 report (Campbell 1989). This suggested that as many as 90 percent of those referred to social services might have been victims of abuse. Even the measured response in *Community Care* used the approach of "no smoke without fire": "While it is unlikely that every child has been abused, it is equally unlikely that none has" (July 2, 1987).

It is possible to see these reactions partly as manifestations of professional solidarity, and indeed the theme of "professionalism" was widely employed by the defenders of the investigation. They suggested that the controversial decisions had been made by trained professionals who had actually witnessed conditions firsthand, and had based decisions on their expertise. So the defense of the professional element in social work was an important agenda in the debate.

On the other hand, the Cleveland investigators had more friends than might have been thought at the height of the scandal. Some papers like the *Mirror* noted the Cleveland cases that did appear to involve abuse and were proved to have in court; and Higgs was duly praised for unearthing the crime. By 1989, there was a local Cleveland Campaign Against Child Sexual Abuse (later CAUSE), which supported the reinstatement of Marietta Higgs in her old job with the local health authority (Campbell 1989; Richardson and Bacon 1991). Several accounts note that the abuse issue was a source of gender conflict in Middlesbrough for years after the height of the crisis (Jervis 1991).

CLEVELAND AS WITCH HUNT

However, most of the debate was far removed from the details of the actual cases, and much revolved around rival interpretations of how problems and panics are constructed. Stuart Bell's (1988) partisan account of the case is entitled *When Salem Came to the Boro*, and the *Mail on Sunday* reused the Salem analogy against Higgs and Richardson; but advocates of an abuse crisis often employed this language in their own behalf. This is perhaps ironic. For the historian, there are resemblances between the child abuse investigation and the witch-hunts of early modern times (Geis and Bunn 1991:31–46).

In both, we find the spreading net of allegations, often anonymous. In both, there was a dedicated core of ideologically motivated investigators, anxious to find objective signs of evil on the person of the suspect, a "witch-mark" so clear as to silence skeptics and critics. In Cleveland, however, it was the defenders of the investigation who tended to speak of witch-hunts. One reason for this is that the whole theory of moral panics and artificially constructed problems traditionally belongs to left and liberal circles in Britain, the intellectual environment most sympathetic to the reality of the child abuse issue.

In addition, social workers were already accustomed to the image. As early as 1974, the general secretary of the British Association of Social Workers remarked of media reactions to the Maria Colwell case: "It has at times seemingly become a witch-hunt seeking out those who could be blamed. . . . [I]f society is seeking a scapegoat, the vulnerable position of the social worker has been all too apparent" (quoted in Parton 1985a:85). *New Society* analyzed the Cleveland affair as a witch-hunt, but the poor witches who were under attack were not the accused parents, but the maligned therapists and social workers (McNeill 1987). The social workers were demonized in a classic moral panic stirred by "media hype" (Dominelli 1989:293–294). Driver similarly wrote of "the panic reaction of the controversial Cleveland Inquiry" (Driver and Droisen 1989:59). In *Feminist Review*, Mica Nava wrote of the portrayal of Higgs, "In this way, the spectre of feminism becomes folk-devil" (Nava 1988).

If in fact the Cleveland critics were witch-hunters, then social theory suggested that they must be projecting concerns over deeper underlying issues. For the defenders of Cleveland, the critics were overreacting to the key revelation of the case: Child abuse was more common than even the most radical feminists had ever dared imagine, and society had to come to terms with this fact. As Mike Bishop wrote, "The Cleveland crisis will force society to admit the problem of sex abuse and very often sex abuse within the family. . . . People are blaming us for unearthing a problem that they don't want to acknowledge is there" (*Community Care*, July 9, 1987 p. 3; compare Bishop 1988; Richardson and Bacon 1991).

For feminist writers reacting to Cleveland, the investigators were hated because they were revealing a fundamental flaw with the Western family. Abuse was not the result of a dysfunctional family, but in a sense the logical consequence of that family institution. These writers even attacked the mainstream of opinion within the NSPCC and social agencies dealing with abuse, because of their acceptance of existing structures: "The assumption that families exist to satisfy men's emotional and sexual needs is never explicitly stated, but scrutinize the arguments about abuse and this is what you find" (MacLeod and Saraga 1988a p. 23).

Among the strongest supporters of this point of view were writers in publications like the *Feminist Review* and the *New Statesman and Society*, both of which devoted whole issues to Cleveland. This suggests the crucial position that child abuse was coming to play in the feminist worldview. The much-quoted *Feminist Review* special number contained seventeen pieces on child abuse by theorists such as Mary MacIntosh, Mary Macleod, and Esther Saraga (MacLeod and Saraga 1988b; compared MacLeod and Saraga 1987a,b, 1988a,c; Kelly 1988). The issue included Mica Nava's study of press reaction to Cleveland, which was cited by those who argued that Higgs had suffered at the hands of a witch-hunt. Several accounts depicted grass-roots responses to the perceived abuse crisis, in the form of local projects in Glasgow, Norwich, Brixton, and Islington.

New Statesman and Society provided a platform for MacLeod and Saraga, and also for Beatrix Campbell, who would present a detailed reaction to the case in her 1988 Virago book *Unofficial Secrets*. She worked from a "red-feminist" perspective, and had written for many years for the communist *Morning Star* (see also Coote and Campbell 1987). From 1970, she had been one of the founders of the nascent women's liberation movement in Britain, and helped produce the journal *Red Rag*. In the mid-1980s, she became one of the most important advocates for the feminist view of child abuse. Cleveland for her represented the exposure of the final taboo, the massive abuse of children within the patriarchal family: It was a profoundly and genuinely subversive event.

In response to Stuart Bell's charges of social service "empire building" in the case, she responded with charges that Bell himself was so active on the parents' behalf in an effort to shore up his threatened position in the local Labour party. While the critics attacked Marietta Higgs, Campbell focused on the ideological assumptions of Bell and his supporters, which she saw as reflecting a conservative onslaught in the wider society: "Bell's campaign has exactly synchronized with Thatcherism's resurrection of the solitary, heroic parent and the besieged family—they are the innocent victims of cheating children and conniving experts" (Campbell 1988b:9). Campbell's portrayal of the critics places first emphasis on the "cheating children," while the experts merely "connive" in their lies. This serves rhetorically to set the opponents of the investigation against the children themselves, as if they had been the sources of the charges. In reality, it was never implied that children themselves had made false allegations, while all the emphasis was on the failings of the doctors and social workers.

However, this issue is critical to Campbell's stance on the whole affair, which appeared to epitomize many of the battles of the Left. It reflected interest group politics, with the pediatricians bearing the flag of the powerless and victimized, and the police surgeons and other medical specialists defending traditional authority, the parents, and police. It also reproduced the struggles of women during the 1970s to have their word accepted over issues like rape. Children were human beings, and deserved equal credibility: This was the issue of "believing the children," which would play so central a part in the ritual abuse scandals in succeeding years. Cleveland was a gender battle, and the abuse problem "demands the feminization of the police and the judiciary" (Campbell 1988a:71). While the critics had charged an antifamily conspiracy personified by Higgs and Richardson, the defenders of the inquiry reacted with their own evil stereotypes, based on Stuart Bell and the Cleveland police authorities.

"Pro-Cleveland" activists were often aggressive in their claims and rhetoric, though perhaps few went as far as Emily Driver. In 1989, she wrote that at a time of intense concern over child abuse, molesters and incestuous fathers are likely to conceal themselves: "Some have moved to the forefront of the professional anti-abuse lobby." Does this really imply, as it seems to, that people who criticize the Cleveland investigation are themselves likely to be cryptomolesters? This appears a startlingly crude way to discredit opposition, especially coming as it does a few pages before Stuart Bell is berated for his "intemperate and inflammatory remarks" (Driver and Droisen 1989:194, 199).

AFTER CLEVELAND

There was much debate about the impact of the Cleveland case on future abuse inquiries, and Alan Gilmour suggested a likely backlash. Fearing the fate of Higgs or Bishop, future investigators might be more restrained about making controversial diagnoses, or in intervening in the interest of children. On the other hand, there is little suggestion of this effect. Many writers professed to find that Cleveland reinforced their views about the prevalence and seriousness of sexual abuse, and redoubled their efforts accordingly (Campbell 1991b; Hollows 1991). Sue Richardson stressed the lesson that child sexual abuse knew no frontiers of class or region: "This was one of the fundamental truths of the Butler-Sloss report, and that recognition is one of the achievements of Cleveland" (*Social Work Today*, June 6, 1991).

From the height of the scandal in mid-1987, we begin to encounter a series of other mass abuse cases, of "little Clevelands," as at Congleton in Cheshire. In November, seventeen children were taken into care here in an alleged sex and pornography ring said to be run by parents and friends. That abuse had occurred was confirmed in court, but once again, several of the suspects were freed and their children released from care; and only three adults were eventually imprisoned (*Times*, November 25–26, 1987; July 14, 1988). In Kent, a group of seventeen adults was said to be involved in an extended family ring prosecuted in 1990 (though once again, only four were eventually convicted). Another case of mass organized abuse led to prison sentences for a number of Stoke-on-Trent men.

For many social workers and child protection officials, there was thus almost a conscious element of defiance in the post-Cleveland era. In 1989, an alleged mass child abuse investigation in Nottinghamshire was directed by Judith Dawson, who wrote, "Cleveland emphasized parents' rights, but this emphasized how we must keep the protection of children as the pivot in our work" (*Community Care*, February 9, 1989). Mike Bishop himself moved to become head of Manchester social services, where he presided over another controversial mass abuse investigation, in 1990. Indeed, the scale and seriousness of charges in abuse cases grew rather than diminished; and it is from 1988 that Britain began for the first time to encounter the phenomenon of alleged ritual and satanic abuse.

The Devil Rides In

Constructing Ritual Abuse

— 7 —

The Cleveland scandal had involved mass abuse in the sense of hundreds of generally unrelated cases in the same community. From 1987 on, there was also a growing perception of mass abuse as the work of organized rings, and the phenomenon of *organized* child abuse was much discussed. Originally, this term referred to sex rings like the pedophiles arrested in Operation Hedgerow, and perhaps the faceless conspirators who directed the bogus social workers; but during 1989 and 1990, *organized abuse* came to be shorthand for another and still more speculative phenomenon. It was increasingly charged that these groups or rings operated for ritual or satanic motives.

Though the new ideas appeared to represent a remarkable departure from British precedent, they drew heavily on themes that had been widely accepted over the previous decade, among them:

- Children often fall victim to sexual assault and murder.
- There are organized sex rings that prey on children, who might be abducted and subsequently killed.
- Children are commonly subjected to extreme sexual abuse within a family setting.
- Children's testimony about abuse and exploitation must be believed, even if it initially appears improbable.
- The experience of both battering and child sexual abuse shows that a vast social problem can be ignored or dismissed for many years.

DISCOVERING RITUAL ABUSE

In March 1990, the NSPCC issued a statement claiming, "Children throughout Britain are being exploited by abuse which is highly organized and planned. . . . The NSPCC has voiced its increasing concern as evidence is mounting of child pornography, ritualistic abuse and sex rings involving children." Ritualistic abuse was defined as "physical, sexual and emotional abuse of children in bizarre ceremonies. An increasing number of NSPCC teams are working with children who have been ritualistically abused." This ill-defined ritual was specified as "Satanic rites" in newspaper reports, even in quality papers like the *Times* and *Daily Telegraph*, while the tabloids presented headlines like "Rape Hell in Satan's Coven."

The reports noted that of sixty-six NSPCC child protection teams, seven had found evidence of ritual abuse, which allegedly involved children being forced to kill animals and drink blood; and fourteen more teams had received reports of activity by "secretive and well-organized" cults. This implied that roughly one third of child protection teams either had encountered the problem or would soon do so. The spokeswoman refused to specify which teams were involved because this would "endanger the lives of the children and the social workers involved."

At first sight, these allegations were weak even by the standards of past child abuse panics. They lacked specific names and dates, and were thus untestable. Meanwhile, the claims-makers could maintain that they had perfect grounds for withholding the information, and the police's Child Pornography Squad would not confirm the charges. On the other hand, the charges clearly found many believers, and between 1989 and 1991 there were at least six highly publicized investigations of ritual abuse rings in Britain. Courts appeared to accept at least a prima facie validity for such charges, insofar as initial attempts to have care and protection orders overridden generally failed. At the same time, investigative television programs charged that mass abuse in a satanic context was occurring in northern and midland towns like Nottingham and Rochdale. Ritual abuse was thus added to the canon of charges laid against pedophiles and child molesters (Tate 1991).

Britain began to experience the same sort of charges that had surfaced in the United States in the aftermath of the McMartin school case of 1983, and that recurred in a number of other celebrated cases over the next two years, as in Jordan, Minnesota, and Bakersfield, California. In essence, it was charged that organized groups of satanists held ceremonies in which children played a major role. Children were raped and sodomized by large numbers of participants, both male and female, and some infants were mutilated or sacrificed (Jenkins and Maier-Katkin 1992; Victor 1992; Hicks 1991). Sacrificial rituals might involve the drinking of a victim's blood or the eating of his or her flesh. Other rites involved the consumption of urine or feces. The emphasis on defiling children was said to reflect the view that the most innocent victim was the most satisfying sacrifice to the Lord of Evil. One variant of the story held that women belonging to the cults acted as "breeders" or (the British term) "brood mares," who bred children specifically to be murdered (Jenkins and Maier-Katkin 1991).

Even at the height of the American panic, there had been many skeptics, and the allegations had enjoyed a distinctly checkered career (Nathan 1987, 1988; Rabinowitz 1990; Hicks 1991; Richardson et al. 1991). The McMartin case was suggestive here, in that charges were originally made about a vast conspiracy involving seven teachers at the school, as well as unnamed others. Soon, allegations were dropped against all except one male teacher and his elderly grandmother. Following a series of lengthy and inordinately expensive trails, all charges were either dismissed or ended in mistrials. As in other cases, the ritual allegations fell by the wayside at a relatively early stage, leaving only charges of normal nonritual abuse to be heard by the jury. It is worth recording that allegations of organized ritual abuse have never been accepted by any court of law in any Western country during modern times. [However, Emily Driver appeared not only to accept the reality of all the McMartin charges as late as 1989, but inflates the number of participants to sixteen (Driver and Droisen 1989:68).]

On the other hand, the allegations led many to assert that society faced a real menace from satanists and occultists (see especially Raschke 1990). In 1988, *The American Focus on Satanic Crime* (a work especially targeted at law enforcement professionals) suggested that satanists are connected with:

> the murders of unbaptized infants, child sexual abuse in daycare, rape, ritual abuse of children, drug trafficking, arson, pornography, kidnapping, vandalism, church desecration, corpse theft, sexual trafficking of children and the heinous mutilation, dismemberment and sacrifices of humans and animals. [They are] responsible for the deaths of more than 60,000 Americans each year, including missing and runaway youth. (Peterson 1988: foreword)

In 1988, nearly twenty million Americans watched a network television program in which Geraldo Rivera publicized the most sensational charges.

Religious fundamentalists were among the most enthusiastic in disseminating the various rumors, but satanic theories also established a foothold in the psychiatric profession, where it was alleged that ritual abuse was a prime cause of multiple personality disorder (Richardson et al. 1991; Jenkins and Maier-Katkin 1992). From the mid-1980s on, many of the most extreme charges about ritual crime would be presented through national and regional conferences on "multiple personality and dissociative states" (compare Mayer 1991).

SATANISM IN BRITAIN

Charges of this sort had no real precedent in the British context before the late 1980s. This is ironic, because there is an authentic occult movement in Britain that is probably far more substantial than that found in the United States. Britain is in a sense the home of most of the occultism that would be seen as so menacing by American theorists of the 1980s. It was the land of occultists like Aleister Crowley, of societies like the Golden Dawn, and of the modern witchcraft movement revived (or invented) by entrepreneur Gerald Gardner (Tate 1991; A. Kelly 1991; Symonds 1973; Symonds and Grant 1972; Grant 1972). Even the Church of the Process, so often attacked by American critics of satanic cults, was founded by British expatriates (Bainbridge 1978). Post-1960s interest in the New Age and occult led to a boom of practicing groups and a network of occult publishers, and stores selling books and supplies (see, for example, Matthews and Matthews 1985–6). By 1984, *New Society* could speak of a "Great British Witch Boom," with pagan adherents possibly in the tens of thousands (Tysoe 1984).

There are also satanists. Genuine British ritual magicians do undoubtedly exist, and a few accept the term *satanist*. There was in the 1980s an Anglian Satanic Church, which published the magazine *Dark Lily* as an "above-ground" recruiting tool for those not yet fully initiated. However, most groups were local, self-taught, and decentralized, and it is these who were presumably responsible for most of the notorious activities of recent years. These included well-authenticated satanic desecrations of churches and cemeteries, which became quite common during the 1960s and 1970s.

"DENNIS WHEATLEY TYPES"

Modern satanism was the consequence of a revival engineered by English enthusiasts like Crowley and Gardner (though neither would himself deserve or accept the *satanic* label; A. Kelly 1991). Perhaps the most important figure was the popular British author Dennis Wheatley (1897–1977), author of novels like *The Satanist, They Used Dark Forces*, and *To the Devil—A Daughter*. Though fictional, these books played an indispensable part in shaping the new occult groups from the 1960s onwards. Wheatley himself was not a believer in the occult, which he used merely as a source of material. On the other hand, it was his novel. *The Devil Rides Out* [1934] 1966) that played a seminal role in shaping the new occultism, introducing Crowley himself as a villain in the character Mocata. The 1968 Hammer film of *The Devil Rides Out* (known in the United States as *The Devil's Bride*) was as influential as the book, and the magic disseminated by popular occultism in 1960s Britain drew more heavily on Wheatley than the more intellectual Crowley (Jenkins and Maier-Katkin 1992).

The mythology invented for Wheatley's fiction had an enormous influence on current perceptions and practices of occultism. It was Wheatley who synthesized the hitherto unrelated world of ceremonial magic (authentic) with the accounts of the medieval witch trials (largely fictitious). Thus the evil magicians in the novels do not work alone, as in tradition: They have followers who gather in covens at the great seasonal meetings, or sabbats. This idea is fundamental to the modern practitioners and critics of the occult alike, but it was invented within living memory.

Wheatley's inventions were enriched with borrowings from the literature of the witch trials throughout history, but especially from the sixteenth and seventeenth centuries. These are chiefly taken from Continental Europe as opposed to England, where organized witchcraft, devil worship, and the sabbat were virtually unknown even as rumors. English witches were punished for cursing an individual or a community, for *maleficia* rather than heresy. Wheatley, in contrast, depicts a clique of aristocratic witches who meet at an English country house, and then organize a sabbat in the best seventeenth-century French or German tradition.

In effect, this scene marked the first appearance in England of both the sabbat and the Black Mass (a French and Italian innovation of the eighteenth and nineteenth centuries). This is worth emphasizing. What most people mean when they refer to a satanic ritual of the sort implied in the McMartin case is a variant of the Black Mass, an institution wholly unknown in Britain or the United States before the mid–twentieth century (compare Ginzburg 1991). Wheatley's sabbat scene—a set piece that occupies the middle section of the novel—would be of vital importance for self-proclaimed witches and devil worshippers throughout Britain and America, and even more so for their religious critics. These thirty or so pages contain virtually all the charges that would be so popular in the literature of antisatanism in the 1980s. This makes it all the more important to stress that Wheatley's description is wholly a literary artefact.

In the novel, the satanists gather in the literal physical presence of the Goat of Mendes, the Devil himself, and begin an orgy that involves every form of perversion and inverted behavior imaginable. The "host" at this mass is the meat of a child. When Satan and the initiates begin to feast, one of the heroes asks,

"So the Devil feeds too . . ."
"Yes," agreed the Duke, "or at least the heads of his priesthood, and a gruesome meal it is if I know anything about it. A little cannibalism, my friend. It may be a still-born baby or perhaps some unfortunate child they have stolen and murdered, but I would stake anything it is human flesh they are eating." (Wheatley [1934] 1966:93)

This scene from a sensational novel probably marks the first appearance during the present century of the idea of a satanic danger to children.

SATANISM AS THREAT?

Occult movements exist as a quite genuine tradition in England, but public concern or panic has traditionally been lacking. In a more secular society, satanism and church desecration were traditionally viewed as a distressing form of vandalism without serious religious overtones. It is noteworthy that there was so little public excitement about the 1960s case of Edward Paisnel, a serial rapist with strong satanic beliefs (Rutherford 1973). The case was publicized as that of a notorious sexual offender, but with little emphasis on the occult aspects. Even in the mid-1980s, there were occasional reports of pedophiles who used occult trappings in order to attract or intimidate victims, but these were not seen as part of a satanic conspiracy (*Times*, November 9, 1982; November 12, 1983). We can only speculate how such events would have been portrayed in the very different environment of 1990 (compare Newton 1987).

This relative lack of concern can be observed from the press of the early 1970s, when occult-related stories were extremely frequent, but were largely outside the arena of public policy or concern. Sensationalist papers like *News of the World* and *The People* regularly reported on the occult. In *News of the World*, 1973 alone produced headlines like "Grim Sacrifice in Garden of a Derelict House" (January 7), "Women as Bait in New Devil Coven" (August 19), "Unmasked—The Evil High Priest of Witchcraft" (September 23), or "His Witchcraft Lost Its Magic" (September 30).

Meanwhile, there were several individual occultists whose doings provided the sensational press with regular copy through these years— "master satanist" Charles Pace, "witch king" Alex Sanders, and Robert Farrant, the necromancer and vampire hunter (Johns 1971a,b; Farrar 1971). Occasionally, there would be acts of vandalism sufficiently serious to feature in court reports. In 1971, a necromancy ritual at Walsall was reported in quality papers like the *Guardian* (Girl in Black Magic Ritual," February 26). In 1974, there was extensive coverage of Farrant's trial for desecrating Highgate cemetery in an occult ceremony. He was found guilty and imprisoned, but the tone of the reporting is suggested by the *Guardian* headline, "Capers among the Catacombs" (June 16, 1974).

With a few exceptions like these, the doings of the occult groups rarely came before the courts, and were virtually never discussed in the serious press, or in Parliament: They were routinely dismissed as the work of "Dennis Wheatley types." Even the tabloid press virtually never made accusations of serious criminal activity. The most sinister charges made against the occultists involved the rumored sacrifice of animals, while accounts of witch groups like that headed by Alex Sanders served chiefly as an excuse to publish photographs of nude participants at the ceremonies. The fundamental image was one of harmless sybarites. Serious allegations about harmful cults tended to report on American groups like the Manson family, and especially Christian fundamentalist and Charismatic sects like the Children of God.

When the occult featured in a more serious context, it was usually treated with mild anthropological interest. In 1988, for example, there was a special "Walpurgis Night" edition of the television talk show "After Dark," which featured representatives of several pagan, occult, and satanist groups. The general tone of the questioning was inquiring and nonjudgmental, and the only hostility was expressed by the "token" Christian spokeswoman, ex-witch Audrey Harper.

Before the mid-1980s, it would have appeared ludicrous to discuss British satanists as a serious phenomenon, still less a social problem. The tone of media attitudes is captured by a 1980 sketch on the popular television comedy show "Not the Nine O'Clock News." The interviewer approaches satanists who describe their activities, which include sacrificing virgins and goats:

"Every full moon we do go up to the Heath at midnight, then we
do strip naked and ravish each other passionately until the dawn."
"And this helps you summon up the forces of evil?"
"Who cares?"

It would be impossible to imagine a comic treatment that drew its humor from rape or child abuse, or anything that was regarded as an authentic threat, especially to children.

AMERICAN INFLUENCE

During the 1980s, satanism in Britain was transformed from a joke to a menace. Two major forces can be discerned in the identification and dissemination of the new problem. A group of American theorists and experts were instrumental in bringing the notion to Britain, but the growing perception of a serious problem was made possible by the network of evangelical and fundamentalist religious groups within Britain itself. Once the ideas were "domesticated," they were increasingly adopted by social work and child protection groups anxious to assert the serious and pervasive nature of child abuse.

At each stage, the new problem was shaped by American influences. The proliferation of such authorities in the United States is worth stressing: One 1988 guide to "resources" in combating satanism lists over one hundred individuals and agencies, including police officers, psychiatrists, religious activists, and leaders of "children's rights" groups (Peterson 1988). Their specialities are variously listed as child abuse/occult awareness, heavy metal/cemetery desecration, ritual crime intervention, and so on. About twenty are listed simply as mental health therapists for whom ritual crime and abuse accounts for the major part of their professional activity.

The first British newspaper citation on the topic appeared in January 1988 in the local *Colchester Evening Gazette,* and was based on an interview with Sandi Gallant (Waterhouse 1990a, b, c). Gallant is a San Francisco police officer who had since the late 1970s developed an interest in occult crime, on which she is regarded as an expert. She is one of the most quoted sources in Larry Kahaner's *Cults That Kill* (1988), a controversial book that argued for the existence of human sacrifice and ritual murder in the United States. Another "occult cop" is Robert Simandl of Chicago, whose appearance at a British conference in September 1989 was widely cited as a major factor in disseminating some of the more extreme charges about ritual crime and the murder of infants. Both Gallant and Simandl are listed in the 1988 guide to resources, respectively, under "Satanic/ritual crime expert" and "Satanic and gang crime investigation." (It should be noted that Gallant has since emerged as a critic of many of the charges of satanic and cult survivors).

American therapists were also influential in suggesting the reality of ritual abuse (Lloyd 1991; see, for example, Finkelhor et al., 1988). One of the most important was Pamela Hudson of Mendocino, California, author of a paper "Ritual Child Abuse—A Survey of Symptoms and Allegations," which was explicitly cited as a source by one of the social workers in the Rochdale affair. The writings of other authorities like Catherine Gould (of Encino, California) were also influential, as was a paper by Maribeth Kaye and Lawrence Kline, "Clinical Indicators of Satanic Cult Victimization," originally delivered at a 1987 Chicago conference on multiple personality. It was from such works that British "students" now began to compile a list of "indicators" of ritual abuse, which would become one of the most troubling (and ridiculed) aspects of the whole affair.

The most important and comprehensive list of symptoms was based on a 1987 article by Gould in the journal *California Psychologist*. In summary, a case was likely to be ritual in nature if some or all of the following features were present in the children interviewed:

> Preoccupation with urine and feces. . . .
>
> Discussion of urine and feces on the face or in the mouth. . . .
>
> Preoccupation with passing gas . . . wild laughter when the child or someone else passes gas. . . .
>
> Aggressive play that has a marked sadistic quality. The child hurts others intentionally and seems to derive pleasure from doing so. Child destroys toys.
>
> Mutilation themes predominate. . . . Aggressive words include cut, saw, slice, chop . . . acting out mutilation themes.
>
> Preoccupation with death. . . . Questions are distinguishable from normal curiosity about death by their bizarre quality.
>
> Fear of ghosts and monsters. Child's play frequently involves ghosts and monsters.
>
> Harming animals or discussing harming animals. . . .
>
> Fear of jail, or being caged. . . .
>
> Child is "clingy," demonstrates fear of being left with babysitters, particularly overnight. . . .
>
> Mentioning other people at school besides teachers. . . .
>
> Writing letters or numbers backwards in the "Devil's alphabet." . . .
>
> Fear of bad people taking the child away, breaking into the house, killing the child or the parents, burning the house down. . . .
>
> Preoccupation with the devil, magic, potions, supernatural power, crucifixions. . . .
>
> References to television characters as real people. . . .
>
> Nightmares or dreams or any of the above. (Gould 1987)

This list has been widely criticized, not least because it implies a lack of familiarity with the characteristic fears, concerns, and interests of normal small children. A critic might remark that if this list is even partly accurate, it is rare to encounter a child who has *not* been the victim of satanic abuse. The problems are obvious, but the issue of subjectivity is crucial: Everything depends on the perceptions of the individual investigator, or therapist as to what constitutes an "unusual," "bizarre," or "morbid" interest in a particular topic (compare Hicks 1991; Richardson et al., 1991; Lloyd 1991).

It is also interesting that the list as disseminated in various forms made little or no provision for individual factors that might explain the occurrence of some of these phenomena: Left-handed children are likely to reverse or invert writing in the early stages of schooling, if not to create whole pages in mirror writing; crucifixion themes would be more likely to predominate in the imagery of children from Catholic or fundamentalist households; and so on. Such an ill-defined and wide-ranging catalog of symptoms offered enormous potential for abuse by investigators.

The spread of the "satanic indicators" in Britain has been traced to the work of another expatriate American claims-maker. The *Independent* placed particular attention on the work of Pamela Klein of Chicago in popularizing the notion of ritual abuse and the means of detecting it (Waterhouse 1991a). She had come to Britain in the 1980s and established Child Sexual Abuse Consultants, a firm offering advice and counseling. This was active in providing counseling in a number of cases that Klein regarded as satanic in nature. Klein's British associates included Ray Wyre, who has been mentioned as a prominent activist in the area of child pornography. Members of the group would act as consultants to investigators in the key Nottingham incest case, which developed on the Broxtowe estate in 1987 (Waterhouse 1990a, b, c, 1991a; Strickland and Waterhouse 1990; Tate 1991).

This case appears at the time of writing to have involved actual child abuse by a group of adults within an extended family, nine of whom received lengthy prison terms in 1989 for sexual offenses committed against twenty-three children. The Nottingham case was valuable for the believers in ritual crime, in that it actually ended in convictions, and thus the existence of a "ring" had been proven in court. However, the courtroom never heard a word about the extensively rumored "animal sacrifices, blood being drunk and sexual abuse by adults in ritual robes" (Barwick 1990). At the time, the case was treated as a "normal" mass abuse incident like Operation Hedgerow. (Coincidentally, conviction and sentencing in the two cases occurred during the same weeks in February 1989.)

In reality, it was and is debated whether there might have been any ritual element whatsoever. The first mention of this aspect occurred when "one of the senior workers, Christine Johnston, rang [Ray Wyre] early in 1988 and left a message on his answerphone asking if he knew anything about witchcraft. He gave the team the 'Satanic indicators,' a list of signs identifying satanic or ritual abuse. Mr. Wyre says he was given the list by Ms. Klein" (Waterhouse 1991a). According to the *Independent on Sunday* and other newspaper investigations, the "indicators" were soon disseminated to a number of other social service departments (Waterhouse 1991a). Whatever their basis in fact, the charges that surfaced made Nottingham the model followed by other ritual cases, the British equivalent to the McMartin affair in the United States.

American perceptions were also popularized through the work of Tim Tate, a British journalist who was studying the topic of child pornography. In 1987, he began to encounter American allegations about satanic rings, including charges of infanticide and ritual cannibalism. He presented these views in a controversial book, which apparently uncritically accepted as fact the charges brought against supposed witches and diabolists in the historical witch trials (Tate 1991; compare Ginzburg 1991). Tate was also significant because he worked as a researcher for Central Television's "Cook Report," which in 1989 presented a sensational (and influential) documentary entitled *The Devil's Work*. Tate wrote extensively on the topic of ritual abuse, and acted in an advisory capacity in the Nottingham investigation (Waterhouse 1991b).

FUNDAMENTALISTS

The satanism panic originated in the United States, but such stories could not have attained the power they did unless there was already in existence a domestic audience willing and eager to hear them; and this was found among the swelling ranks of fundamentalist and Charismatic Christians within Britain itself (Thompson et al., 1989; Thompson 1989, 1990). The concept of spiritual warfare and the ministries of exorcism, spiritual healing, and deliverance had existed among British evangelicals for many years, increasingly associated with glossolalia, or speaking in tongues (White 1990; Lawrence 1990; Harper 1976). From the mid-1960s, both exorcism and glossolalia became a source of recurrent controversy within the established church (Welsby 1984:246–248). These ideas were practiced by interdenominational Christian fellowship groups operating under a variety of names. Such "base communities" rapidly spread throughout the country during the 1970s, and would provide the building blocks for the revivalist movement in the following decade.

In 1975, there had been a notorious case in Barnsley (South Yorkshire) where problems had developed in such a fellowship group, and this provides insight into the beliefs and assumptions of the movement. A Methodist minister and an Anglican cleric performed an all-night exorcism on a member of one group named Michael Taylor, who had supposedly fallen under the influence of satanists. Some hours later, Taylor responded by killing and mutilating his wife, and he was subsequently diagnosed as criminally insane. The ensuing trial was extensively reported in the quality press no less than the tabloids (Longley 1975; Deeley 1975).

For most readers, it was one of the first glimpses into what appeared at the time to be a curious religious fringe, with an unfashionable belief in the reality of demons and possession. In view of later developments, it is interesting that the media casually dismissed the charge of satanic involvement, and concentrated entirely on the dangers to mental health of practices like exorcism and glossolalia. Exorcism was characterized as "macabre," and most papers cited approvingly the remark by defense counsel that the crime resulted from "grotesque and wicked malpractices posing in the name of religion." The Anglican hierarchy attempted to place stringent restrictions on the future use of exorcism; but even this was denounced by many liberal clergy, who felt it dangerous to grant any degree of recognition to the phenomenon (Welsby 1984:246–248).

THE EMERGENCE OF THE ANTISATANIC MOVEMENT

But groups like that in Barnsley flourished and proliferated, as did ideas like demons, exorcism, and spiritual warfare, which provided an essential background for the new emphasis on the satanic danger (Lawrence 1990:130–157). An interdenominational Christian Exorcism Study Circle was founded in 1972, and in 1985, one of its leaders claimed that each year the group was counseling some two hundred defectors from satanic and occult groups (Luhrman 1989:82). The group's secretary warned "that some Satanic groups will sacrifice a human being if they possibly can: often these victims are unwanted babies or tramps taken from the streets at night. . . . Satanists can be found at the highest levels in our society, in political life and on the boards of multinational companies" (Newton 1987:153–154). Satanists were said to operate behind front organizations of a theosophical or New Age nature.

The intellectual outlook of the anticult groups can be illustrated by the work of the Reverend Russ Parker, who had worked with the Manchester Deliverance Advisory Group before being appointed to the care of two Leicestershire parishes within the established church. In his 1990 book, *Battling the Occult,* Parker asserts a belief in possession by evil spirits and discusses exorcism. He stresses that the battle against satanism was an urgent necessity for contemporary Christianity. The book recites all the arguments familiar from American antisatanism, with the same identification between the apparently harmless New Age and pernicious criminality. Satanism is here placed in a spectrum of activities that includes ouija boards, astrology, palmistry, meditation, Dungeons and Dragons, and occult films like *The Omen* and *The Exorcist.*

He even follows American precedents in expressing concern about the observance of Halloween, a custom largely introduced into Great Britain in the last decade. In 1982, there had been a controversy in Cambridgeshire when the schools began to celebrate Halloween, to the objections of fundamentalist parents who attempted to withdraw their children (Luhrmann 1989:82–83). This hostility to occult influences among the young was echoed by the Association of Christian Teachers, which denounced toleration of Halloween, which "does in fact encourage an interest and fascination in the occult and this invariably leads to more serious involvement and damage to the individuals concerned" (Parker 1990:36). The group also struggled against satanic or witch imagery in school books. There is some evidence that they were successful in this, and by 1990, publishers were expressing growing sensitivity about anything that could be interpreted as occult (Strickland and Waterhouse 1990). This represented a sudden and astonishing reversal in attitudes, as such pressures had never been felt before in 1980s.

But there was also a more immediate satanic threat, said to be orchestrated through powerful devil-worshipping groups or cells with direct access to demonic powers. Russ Parker notes that when he had been in Manchester in the early 1980s, "we went through a phase of ministry in which a number of people were trying hard to break free of the black magic groups to which they had belonged." These people were often characterized by "uncontrolled outbursts of verbal abuse, lying, cursing and blasphemy," which showed that they had been in the group of literal demonic powers (Parker 1990:80). These were manifested in the form of sexual perversions and various forms of addiction.

Another influential anticult activist was Kevin Logan, Anglican vicar of the Lancashire parish of St. Johns, Great Harwood, near Blackburn (Logan 1988). He is the author of several books published by the Eastbourne-based firms Kingsway and Monarch, which also produce the work of Audrey Harper, Peter Lawrence, and most of the spiritual warfare school (see, for example, Harper and Pugh 1990; White 1990; Lawrence 1990; Ellis 1990; and Logan's introduction to Miller 1990). Logan's works include *Close Encounters with the New Age*, and *Paganism and the Occult*, both British parallels to the numerous exposés currently appearing in American fundamentalist circles.

Like Parker, Logan similarly describes exorcising those who had become involved with satanic cults and constantly sees New Age activities like yoga, astrology, and meditation as part of a common spectrum that also includes satanism, occultism, and paganism. Naturally expecting to encounter skepticism, Logan repeatedly attempts to show the real secular harm done by the cults and their connection with serious and violent crime. For example, he draws a connection between cult activities and multiple homicide. American examples like Charles Manson and the Son of Sam are naturally included, with citations of Maury Terry's sensationalistic work *The Ultimate Evil*; but Logan also provides a British linkage when he traces the Hungerford mass murder rampage of Michael Ryan to the influence of a fantasy role-playing game (Logan 1988:21–23).

From this perspective, cults and demonic phenomena might also be linked to incest and child abuse. Logan describes the abuse of one fourteen-year-old girl by the "high priest" of a coven (Logan 1988:89–90). One widely read book by Anglican cleric Peter Lawrence records an attempt to exorcise a "Christian lady":

> When I asked the Spirit to come, horrific demons manifested, growling and snarling and throwing her to the floor. Like so many Christians we find with resident demons, she had been an incest victim. Not everyone we see who has suffered abuse as a child is demonized, but when demons manifest in mature Christians, we are not surprised to find a history of abuse, sexual or otherwise. With many such people we also find ancestral demons which have been in the family for generations due to black mass rites and passed on to the child at conception or birth. (Lawrence 1990:147)

In this context, it is scarcely surprising to find parliamentary activism on the issue by Geoffrey Dickens, who in 1988 sponsored an adjournment debate in the House of Commons on the topics of child abuse and witchcraft. He announced his intention to present a dossier of confidential information to the Home Office, and declared that he would attempt to introduce legislation prohibiting the exercise of the satanic religion—a point at which even Kevin Logan balked (Logan 1988; see also Dickens's highly laudatory dedication to Harper and Pugh 1990).

ELITE SATANISM

Religious concerns are evident in the wave of rumors that sinister rings or cults were well-ensconced among the highborn and politically influential, a charge of the sort popularized by some of the exposés of pedophile rings. Kevin Logan offered several case studies, for example, of "a London occult group whose members are made up of high ranking civil servants, top industrialists and prominent City figures. . . . each city and major town has its own small exclusive coven made up mostly of people in the professions" (Logan 1988:59).

Belief in elite satanism was suggested by the 1986 trial of Derry Knight, a flamboyant con man who claimed to be breaking away from a satanic cult led by the deputy prime minister, William Whitelaw. With other highly placed politicians, Whitelaw was said to lead the Sons of Lucifer, the supposed secret overlords of British diabolism (Lelyveld 1986; Vallely 1986). In reality, Whitelaw is one of the most inoffensive and generally popular characters in national politics, who is quite untainted by scandal of any kind, but the charges found powerful believers. Knight gained entrée into a circle of determined antisatanists who gave him several hundred thousand pounds to fund his campaign to bring others into the light.

Contributors included the enormously rich family that owns Britain's Sainsbury's supermarket chain, and other wealthy supporters of the Charismatic movement. One of the most prominent was the wife of Timothy Sainsbury, the Conservative M.P. and antipornography campaigner (Tomlinson 1982:146–156). She claimed to have experienced the gifts of prophecy and glossolalia "at a Bible meeting for parliamentary wives at the House of Commons" (Valley 1986). This affair suggests an entirely new degree of suspicion and hostility about cults among the social elite. As a mainstream Anglican bishop now warned, the Charismatic movement has "led in places to individuals and groups becoming obsessed by the thought of evil and believing that the Lord speaks to them and gives them direct injunctions how to deal with it. This is extremely dangerous and needs to be checked" (Vallely 1986).

Tales about the elite occultism sometimes focused on freemasonry, which is very popular among the British upper and middle classes, with a strong following among law enforcement, the legal profession, and the Church of England. The movement has also been patronized by the royal family for over a century. However, there are critics: Masonic oaths appear to include threats of death and ghastly mutilation, while Catholics and many evangelical Protestants regard the sect's rituals as heretical or pagan. Some of the wholly fictitious rumors in circulation in the 1980s reported that high initiates were required to defecate upon a crucifix; while "Prince Charles had been secretly initiated into a north London lodge that practised Black Magic" (Knight 1984:5–6). Kevin Logan notes that "Mason Grand Masters were also responsible for the founding and structure of one of Europe's occult societies, the [Crowleyan] *Ordo Templi Orientis* (OTO) in 1902. . . . The OTO, founded by freemasons, has much to answer for in the last eighty years" (Logan 1988:148–50).

Freemasonry provided an essential context for the Derry Knight affair, and many of the initial charges concerned alleged (and spurious) connections between masons and diabolists (Vallely 1986). This may explain the choice of prominent mason William Whitelaw as a prime target of the satanic slanders (Knight 1984:207). A new hostility to cults in general was suggested by the antimasonic sentiments expressed by a number of Protestant churches during these years (Short 1989:44–66, 88–107, Logan 1988:146–153).

There is also evidence of local rumors and panics, for instance in Sussex, where a series of unusual deaths in the Clapham Woods area stimulated tales of a black magic conspiracy. A group named the Friends of Hekate was said to be thousands strong, with two hundred in the inner circle alone, and they carried out human sacrifices at ancient ritual sites (Newton 1987). The rumors came to involve UFO sitings, and extremist political conspiracies.

SURVIVORS AND BROOD MARES

Concern about satanism was especially strong among the Evangelical Alliance, the umbrella federation that claims to represent up to one million adherents. In 1988, the alliance appointed a committee to investigate the charges, several members of which would be active in disseminating claims about the prevalence of ritual crime (Waterhouse 1990a, b, c). Members of this committee were especially important in shifting the emphasis of British interest toward the figure of the occult survivor or defector, a controversial figure from the American literature on satanism (Richardson et al., 1991).

British theorists began to make extensive use of American accounts purporting to recount the memoirs of such survivors, women who had been abused by satanic cults in childhood, but who had escaped with their lives. The pioneering text here was the 1980 *Michelle Remembers* (Smith and Pazder 1980), but there were a host of imitators, such as *Suffer the Child* (Spencer 1989) and Lauren Stratford's 1988 *Satan's*

Underground. The latter book popularized the theme of the "breeder," who produced children for sacrifice. The Evangelical Alliance committee included two survivors in the form of self-described former witches, Doreen Irvine and Audrey Harper (Irvine 1973; Harper and Pugh 1990).

Another member was Kevin Logan, whose Lancashire house had become a refuge for those escaping from the clutches of the occult, and one case in particular would attract national attention. When one Catherine Marchant, "Hannah," committed suicide in Logan's house, she left behind an occult memoir that draws largely on the American exposés. She claimed that she had been inducted into a satanic sect at the age of thirteen, and like Lauren Stratford, Hannah had been a breeder. Her story was reported as factual in some popular newspapers, and in March 1990 the *Sunday Mirror* offered the headline, "I Sacrificed My Babies to Satan: From Sex Orgy to Death at the Hands of the Devil's Disciples." The tale remains part of the growing mythology of antisatanism, recounted especially among fundamentalist religious groups, though an important journalistic investigation has discredited every aspect of her tale (Hebditch and Anning 1990).

The two remaining committee members were both active in offering facilities to cult members who wished to free themselves from bondage to the devil. Diane Core was the organizer of Childwatch on Humberside, while Maureen Davies ran the national organization Reachout, which had also been in contact with Hannah. Davies founded Reachout in 1983, and claimed to have found her first ritual abuse case in Britain in 1985. (Thompson et al. have pointed out that Reachout's anticult message also extended to Catholics, Jehovah's Witnesses, and other relatively accepted groups).

With Logan, Davies and Core promoted startling claims about the menace of the occult. Diane Core stated, "I am convinced that Satanic abuse not only exists but is a real danger to modern family life. About four thousand babies a year are born into covens to be used for sacrifices and cannibalism. This is only the tip of the iceberg" ("British Inquisition" 1991; *Daily Star,* September 20–21, 1990; *Mail on Sunday,* September 16, 1990). She expanded on this in a 1988 interview with the American *New Federalist,* in which she provided a broad theological context for ritual abuse:

We're in the middle of the most massive spiritual warfare. The whole satanic movement has decided to initiate as many young people as it can. We are at war. At this moment, in this country, Satan is winning, he's in the lead. Awareness has been raised. We're doing everything we can, causing reactions, receiving information, letters. If we can present a united front, and if the police support us more, I *think* we'd win. But often the police deny it is really going on.

The economic crisis creates fertile ground for recruiting kids to cults based upon despair and hedonism. (quoted in Thompson et al. 23–24).

Maureen Davies had other concerns:

In the temples or covens they have young girls or older women called brood mares. These girls are there to be made pregnant purely for the sacrifices. When they are five and a half months pregnant the birth is induced. At this stage, the foetus is alive and can be sacrificed. The blood of the infant is then drunk, then the body is eaten. What is not eaten is stored for the next ritual. ("British Inquisition" 1991; *Daily Star,* September 20–21, 1990).

Logan claimed to know of no less than eight cases where girls had been impregnated so that their fetuses could be used in this way (*Guardian,* September 9, 1990). Audrey Harper recalled several similar cases, such as that of "Rose," who "was taken into a coven by her parents, and made pregnant four times by a warlock so that the babies could be sacrificed to Satan" (Harper and Pugh 1990:214).

By the end of the decade, there was a network of organizations committed to the idea of a real occult danger that threatened the lives of thousands, and this network acted as a conduit for allegations from American conspiracy theorists. In such a setting, it was perhaps inevitable that a growing number of individuals were prepared to declare themselves survivors or defectors from cults, though often with as little veracity as Hannah. These supposed survivors helped promote and spread further tales and rumors. One activist in the cause was Sue Hutchinson, of the SAFE helpline; who claimed to know of fifty unrelated cases of satanic abuse in the United Kingdom, often featuring cannibalism (*Guardian,* September 10, 1990). Audrey Harper estimated that there were 200,000 witches in Great Britain (Harper and Pugh 1990:215).

We can discern the early stages of a process that permits the almost unlimited manufacture of survivors and their grisly tales, on the model that occurred in the United States in the late 1980s (Jenkins and Maier-Katkin 1991). Initially, ideological and theoretical changes within religious and therapeutic communities tend to increase the numbers of self-described occult survivors. These individuals are likely to find themselves interviewed and promoted by exponents of the satanic threat, including occult experts from religious groups and law enforcement. In turn, these accounts gain publicity in the mass media. As these stories appear ever more frequently in television and published accounts, so survivors and ritual crimes increasingly permeate the public consciousness, providing a vocabulary for disturbed individuals to recount in therapy or in religious confessions. The process thus becomes a self-sustaining cycle.

But the survivors also gave the religious activists an entirely new ground on which to seek official action in support of their cause. If satanism was an excuse for grotesque orgies by consenting adults (as it customarily appeared), police action against it was unlikely to win public sympathy. Taking "Dennis Wheatley types" seriously was to invite ridicule. On the other hand, the new formulation of satanists was founded on their supposed threat to children, from newborn babies to teenagers, who appeared to be the potential victims of violence and murder. If satanic groups were reconstructed in the public mind as uniquely vicious pedophile rings, then decisive action against them would become acceptable and necessary.

SOCIAL WORKERS

But ideas can exist on the religious or political fringe for many years without having a serious impact on policy. What is remarkable about the British panic is the speed with which the ideas were first noted, accepted, and naturalized, and then became the motive force for far-reaching actions by police and social service agencies. The whole cycle occurred in at most three or four years. Ideas of ritual crime came to permeate the thinking of various bureaucratic agencies.

Between April and September 1989, ritual abuse was a major theme at three conferences at Reading, Dundee, and Harrogate, with sponsors including the Association of Christian Psychiatrists. The most important of these gatherings was held at Reading University in September (Waterhouse 1990a, b, c). Among the speakers were the American experts Simandl and Klein, as well as Maureen Davies, Diane Core, and Marietta Higgs. Others noted as having made a considerable impression were Nottingham social workers Christine Johnston and Judith Dawson, who recorded their "ritual" interpretation of the recent abuse case. Johnston now became active in RAINS, a Ritual Abuse Information Network Society ("British Inquisition" 1991; Waterhouse 1990a, b, c; *Mail on Sundays,* September 16, 1990; *Daily Star,* September 20, 1990).

There were also lesser conferences and seminars, as at Lancaster, Bolton, Cardiff, and London. Apart from the meetings, the ritual abuse theorists made their views known through a number of publications. The religious press had carried this sort of material for some time, but during 1989 there was a series of articles in the social workers' "bibles," the magazines *Community Care* and *Social Work Today*.

The first article, "When the Truth Hurts," was written by Nottingham's Christine Johnston and Judith Dawson, and appeared in *Community Care* in March 1989 (Dawson and Johnston 1989). This reported extensively on the Nottingham case, which originally appeared to have involved a sex-ring. Some months later, however, the children's remarks suggested instead "a more serious and unusual type of abuse," a "vortex of evil"; children were "born into a culture of multi-generational abuse." "Children were fodder for the gratification of those interested not in sex itself but in its use as a tool for the promotion of ritualistic acts that could only be described as satanic." Specific allegations included children being abused "by adults in strange costumes; being forced to eat excreta, drinking blood from animals, which were sacrificed in front of them to gain power—this in suburban Nottingham." Acts especially occurred on certain nights of the year, suggesting a satanic calendar.

The authors explicitly say that their first response was incredulity, but they then realized that they were falling into the same trap that had befallen Freud, the deadly sin of not believing children. Considering that this was the first case of its kind known in England, it is striking how far the reports match each detail of the American precedents. This suggests either that international rings were involved in genuine activity, or else that the investigators were themselves influenced by what they knew of the American material, which helped form their expectations of what they were likely to find.

Despite the fundamentalist convictions of many of the satanic advocates, the two social workers offered no explicitly religious interpretation of the crimes (Dawson would assert that her group was a "secular team"). However, a powerful theme in the piece is the necessity for social workers to confront real evil, rather than simply social dysfunction. "It was difficult to hear properly at first—difficult to grasp how evil people can be. The social work profession derives from an optimism and belief in the innate potential for good and for change." But matters changed in face of the Nottingham charges, "vile revelations which were compared to the opening of the concentration camps at the end of the second world war. We have learned of the power of survival in the midst of evil." Must the optimism of the social worker yield to a religious belief in absolute evil?

More far-reaching in its implications was the article "Facing the Unbelievable," which appeared in *Community Care* in December 1989 (Bartlett 1989). This was in effect a straightforward summary of the views of all the major ritual theorists, but especially those from the fundamentalist Christian groups. This was important in that the theme of the article concerned belief, the necessity of having faith in allegations, despite rationalistic doubts. Prominently emphasized on the first page of the article were the words "When children relate tales of satanic rituals, they are often met with disbelief. . . . One of the most damaging reactions a social worker or any other professional can have is disbelief. Trust is eighty percent of the treatment." This approach did not augur well for a critical analysis of the tales and their sources. Bartlett stated that "The stuff of horror films is being made a reality for children all over Britain. . . . Children are being used in satanic rituals in towns and areas such as Hull, Surrey, Wolverhampton, Telford, Portsmouth, Manchester and Shrewsbury" (though Manchester is the only one of these cities where an investigation has been publicized to date).

There had been the cases of Nottingham, and a heavily reported case in the Dutch village of Oude Pekela (see below); but media and professionals were unpardonably skeptical. By contrast, Bartlett quoted a social worker as saying that "Even if what the children are saying is untrue, it is clear that if they believe it to be true something dreadful must have happened to them." Bartlett admits the Christian credentials of many of the claims-making organizations, but notes that Maureen Davies's Reachout Trust "has fast gained a reputation as a reliable source of information in a field where information is scare. . . . Social workers, police officers, GPs and church leaders from all over the country now turn to her for advice." Put another way, Reachout was acquiring ownership of the problem.

The article cited a familiar range of sources: Apart from Davies, other experts cited by name included Klein, Simandl, Wyre, and Audrey Harper. In the absence of rival interpretations, the reader is left with the impression of a clandestine menace requiring urgent action. *Community Care* again addressed the issue with new articles during 1990, as well as ongoing news coverage of the developing mass abuse cases (Sone 1990a, b).

Social Work Today was equally disturbed. In October 1989, the journal presented an anonymous article, "Networks Of Fear," which argued that "Organized sexual abuse of children—in sex rings and satanic cults—exists in various parts of the country." However, the emphasis throughout was on the satanic aspects, especially family-linked sex networks on the lines reported in Nottingham; and the illustration was a drawing of several children dancing around a six-pointed star in a forest. (*Community Care* would use a similar device, in the face of

criticism from Jewish groups who felt that this was in a sense reviving
the antisemitic blood libel; *Community Care,* April 11, 18, 1991.)

Social Work Today returned to the topic on several occasions during
1990. In May, the magazine offered a platform to Maureen Davies,
whose views were presented without comment or criticism (Cohen
1990). In October, David Pithers of NCH emphasized the need for social
workers to take account of children's fantasy lives before taking occult
stories literally; but the article still rejected charges that "satanic abuse"
originated in the minds of cranks and fundamentalists (Pithers 1990). In
November, the magazine published a sweeping account of the perceived
danger, "Exposing the Secret," by child protection officer Hazel Wood.
This was illustrated by drawings of animal sacrifices, inverted Bibles,
snakes, and ritual daggers (Wood 1990).

Wood's bibliography indicates the sources that were being used to
foster belief in ritual abuse, and this predictably includes the 1987 paper
"Clinical Indicators of Satanic Cult Victimization" by Kaye and Kline.
For the occult background, the reader is referred to the questionable
survivor accounts of "Michelle" and *Suffer the Child,* and to an article that
appeared in *Passport* magazine in 1987. A British reader would have no
way of knowing that this is an unusual and dubious source, one that is
not readily available outside fundamentalist circles even in the United
States. The magazine was produced in California by a fundamentalist
pastor named John Frattarola, who was also a major source of the
American Focus on Satanic Crime, discussed above (Peterson 1988).

Frattarola's views are distinctive. He has attacked "the gradual but
consistent displacement of Christianity by a hodge podge of occultic,
mystic, Eastern, pagan, New Age spirituality." Satanism was only part
of the broader secular ills of society:

> The outbreak of satanic crimes and worship; an epidemic of killer
> disease; the slaughter of over 22 million unborn children; the
> collapse of once solid financial institutions; the bankruptcy of
> American farmers; harsher and more unpredictable weather pat-
> terns; an increase of drug abuse, child abuse and pornography; the
> corruption and disintegration of morals, values, ethics and
> integrity . . . and the powerful rise of false religious right under
> our drooping eyes. (quoted in Jenkins and Maier-Katkin 1992)

Seen in the best light, these views represent extreme right-wing
thought; at worst, a critic might describe them as conspiracy-minded
demagoguery with more than a hint of racism. It is at least questionable
to cite such a source as authoritative without further discussion of its
nature.

THE PROFESSIONAL LITERATURE

For child abuse professionals, there were a number of possible sources to consult on this issue, and most appeared to give qualified support to the extreme of a problem. *Child Abuse Review* reported on the phenomena, and in 1991 was instrumental in alleging an entirely new satanic ring, in Sussex.

In 1991, a special issue of *Child Abuse and Neglect* discussed the controversy over ritualistic abuse and certainly presented hostile or skeptical views, by the FBI's Kenneth Lanning, and by Dr. Frank Putnam (Lanning 1991). However, other articles were strongly supportive: One was cowritten by Bennett G. Braun, a leading American authority on the phenomenon of multiple personality as a result of childhood ritual abuse; another concerned the 1987 Dutch case of Oude Pekela, which according to original reports involved mass ritual abuse (Young et al. 1991; Jonker and Jonker-Bakker 1991). This latter article basically accepts the truth of all the charges, though subsequent Dutch work on the topic has emphasized the numerous mistakes of the investigators, and the role of religious groups in shaping the media interpretation of the event. It is at least a common interpretation that the Oude Pekela affair was largely spurious in nature, but this critique does not emerge here. As Putnam comments, the article is "particularly inflammatory" in various ways.

The journal thus attempts to provide balance, but it is troubling that the one article that aimed to provide an objective balanced overview implicitly accepted the authenticity of the problem. In the introductory "Commentary," a highly respected British child psychiatrist notes that practioners have encountered "children who *have been subjected* to sadistic, perverse and sometimes bizarre practices. . . . The children were young *when first initiated into these activities*," and so on (Jones 1991:163, emphasis added). This formulation begs the fundamental question of whether indeed the children had been subject to this activity, or whether they were merely reporting events that may or may not have occurred (compare the critique in Mulhern 1991).

RADICAL SUPPORT

Respectful coverage in such sources tended to validate "diabolical" claims among community workers who might otherwise have been dubious about charges so grotesque. This neutralization of doubt was enhanced by a series of supportive articles in news media of impeccably liberal, radical, and secular bent, which had a common sympathy to feminism broadly construed.

Left-wing reactions to the panic were by no means predictable, and there was debate within the radical press. The *New Statesman and Society* debunked the charges and attacked the role of American religious groups. Scathingly, it noted in September 1990:

Does your child make farting noises, laugh when other people fart, have nightmares, play aggressively or sing rude versions of nursery rhymes? These are some of the symptoms displayed by children subjected to satanic abuse, according to Pamela Klein, American expert in the phenomenon. If applied to the nation's children as a definitive test of satanism our schools would have to be emptied, and they'd have to hold case conferences at Wembley Stadium. ("The Devil You Know" 1990)

Satanic abuse was a meaningless distraction from the reality of "every-day" abuse: "the typical perpetrator of the crime is no berobed Anti-christ, but Dad; its locus not the woodland coven but the back bedroom" (1990)

But the skeptics were to be in a minority over the next few controversial months, and a number of feminists supported the reality of the charges. They did so for a variety of reasons, but above all because of the sacrosanct tenet that children's evidence must be believed. In addition, failure to defend these charges would cast doubt on a generation of assertions about child sexual abuse in general. Without this, the movement would lost an effective rhetorical weapon against the unsavory and dangerous patriarchal nuclear family. Radical feminists therefore formed an unlikely common front with the Charismatics and Evangelicals with whom they disagreed on so many other aspects of social policy.

It was the liberal *Guardian* that at the height of the Rochdale controversy in 1990 published a sympathetic account of American therapist Pamela Hudson. This noted that since her pioneering work in southern California in 1984, no less than six cases had been proved in the United States, where ritual abuse rings had been preying on nursery schools. This statement appears to be simply groundless, as no such organized abuse has ever been accepted by an American court, but the claim is indicative of sympathy toward the ritual abuse theorists (Sinason 1990). The article concluded with a note that mail for Hudson could be forwarded via the *Guardian*, suggesting that her expertise should be better known in Great Britain.

In 1990, *New Statesman and Society* published a Judith Dawson piece on the Nottingham case, "Vortex of Evil," which argued that an "insidious and dangerous" contagion was sweeping the land, the opinion that ritual abuse was imaginary: "This contagion takes the comforting form of skeptical and rational inquiry, and its message is comforting too: it is designed to protect 'innocent family life' against a new urban myth of the satanic abuse of children inspired by evangelical fundamentalists" (Dawson 1990). Dawson thus presented the "rational" approach to the cases as effectively a willful blindness to the problem, and charges of fundamentalist influence and professional gullibility were part of a "new mythology," ultimately hostile to children.

Her argument was in a curious sense appropriate for the left-liberal environment, as the villains of her piece were generally the police, who struggled to play down the diabolical aspects of the case. *New Statesman and Society* readers were well accustomed to reading accounts of police abuses and official cover-ups; and the heroes of the Nottingham case were the ten members of all the all-female task force Team Four, set up to investigate mass abuse activity. Progressive women therefore seemed to be combating reactionary and patriarchal policemen.

Dawson's piece was followed by a supportive article by the indefatigable Beatrix Campbell, who emerged once more as the most consistent claims-maker on the left (Campbell 1990a, b, c, d, 1991). Like Dawson, she faced the unenviable task of attempting to make essentially medieval allegations palatable to a progressive left/feminist readership, and she did so by placing the controversy in a context of gender conflict: "Ritual abuse is about oppression. Part of the social workers' resilience in supporting the children and their foster mothers lies in a sense of solidarity and empathy that derives from the fact that they, as Judith Dawson puts it, as women they know something about oppression" (Campbell 1990a). Campbell would link police neglect and contempt to the satanic phenomenon itself. After describing the police desire to destroy the ritual component of the cases, she remarks, "The violence of the Chief Constable's ambition echoes the violence which was the everyday experience of 23 terrified children in one extended family in Nottingham" (Campbell 1990b).

Apart from the *New Statesmen and Society* article, Campbell was the producer of an October report on the Nottingham case that appeared on the Channel Four program "Dispatches." This presented evidence—presumably derived from the local social workers—purporting to prove the existence of satanic cults. It also attacked police skepticism and claimed that the number of children victimized was closer to fifty than the twenty-five already known.

Another defense of the ritual claims appeared in the rather inappropriate setting of *Marxism Today*, a popular left-wing journal. Campbell was writing for an audience that had struggled to accept claims of widespread child abuse, and that now gagged at the prospect of accepting satanic rings as culprits. However, the charges had to be taken seriously, or else we would be challenging the truth of what children were saying (Campbell 1990d).

In defense of the charges, she asserts that satanism is often not taken seriously, and thus only provides abusers with a more exciting setting and justification for the crimes: "Satanic rituals in a secular culture like ours aren't taken seriously. Anyone who respects children's accounts of ritualized abuse isn't taken seriously either." After all, the occult was commonplace in the culture, in the form of heavy metal music, horoscopes, and New Age shops. Her linkage of these phenomena with satanic abuse reflected (no doubt unconsciously) the connections so frequently made in the religious press.

But throughout her writing, Campbell knowingly or otherwise repeats the charges from the fundamentalist literature, most strikingly the alleged claims of human sacrifice made by Aleister Crowley, as great a charlatan and practical joker as an occultist (Symonds 1973). She is left defending the truth of human sacrifice and ritual abuse in the Nottingham case and elsewhere, and excoriates the police for their failure to pay attention: "All the progress of the 1980s in transforming the way children and women witnesses alleging sexual crimes have been treated by the police has been undermined by the notion that child witnesses should be treated as if they were the culprits and not the victims. . . . Once again, the problem of policing has confounded the struggle for children's rights" (Campbell 1990d). The appropriation of left and feminist rhetoric in such a cause is striking, but it was not untypical.

The breadth of media support—and the odd coalition of religious and radical groups that now emerged—created an atmosphere conducive to the rapid spread of ritual abuse accusations.

The Ritual Abuse Cases

— 8 —

The theory of ritual abuse emerged in the space of some three years. During 1990, tenuous and barely respectable theories provided the basis for urgent actions in several communities, as social workers and child protection teams believed they were responding to a significant menace to children. As the crisis progressed, nearly one hundred children were subject to care or wardship proceedings. By the fall of that year, ritual abuse had become a national scandal, and the story received nearly as much play in the media as Cleveland had in 1987. The *Times*, for example, reported a handful of stories in the first few months of the year; and then "satanic practices" became a major theme, with twenty-five items in September alone. The topic remained in the headlines into the following spring (Tate 1991; Eaton et al. 1991).

The chronology in Table 8.1 suggests the major events of the panic. It does not include other events of 1990 that contributed substantially to the increased belief in organized abuse, such as the London pedophile ring and the bogus social workers scare.

THE PANIC SPREADS

Information about ritual abuse was disseminated in various ways, including the magazine articles discussed in Chapter 7. Press reports of the various cases also placed great emphasis on social workers attending conferences or workshops where speakers like Maureen Davies or Judith Dawson advocated the notion of a ritual danger. The reports suggested that agencies would then be motivated to discover similar practices in their home areas. There were direct contacts with the various ritual claims-makers, who were much used as consultants or advisers. The article "Facing the Unbelievable" had concluded with information about how to contact the Reachout Trust, and a telephone number was given. This was the course adopted over the next few

177

Table 8.1. The Ritual Abuse Panic

1990

February	Harrogate seminar on ritual abuse
	Allegations of ritual abuse reported by children taken into care in Manchester
March	Four children taken into care in Langley estate, Rochdale
	NSPCC statement on widespread ritualistic abuse
June	Twelve children in Rochdale made wards of court and removed from families
July	Strathclyde police announce ritual abuse case
	Children taken into care in Merseyside
September	Rochdale cases attract national publicity and debate
	Allegations of ritual abuse in Epping Forest area
November	Eight children from Orkney family taken into care
December	Eight children freed in Manchester inquiry

1991

February	Nine children seized in dawn raids on Orkney
March	Ten children in Rochdale case to be returned to families
April	Orkney children released to families
	Collapse of mass abuse case in Aberdeen
June	New government guidelines attempt to regulate future investigations
November	Epping Forest case collapses

---

months by various police and social service agencies, who turned increasingly to such "experts" with committed beliefs on ritual abuse.

In early 1990, Rochdale social services sought the help of Reachout. In Liverpool, the police asked for advice from Kevin Logan, Diane Core, and Maureen Davies (Waterhouse 1990a, b, c). In Strathclyde about the same time, the two Nottingham social workers Dawson and Johnston were the experts consulted before events were perceived as ritualistic in nature. They had been asked for help in the Congleton mass abuse case, and in turn, the Congleton workers were approached for advice by the Merseyside social services. Nottingham's Team Four appeared as consultants in several of the major cases (Waterhouse 1990a, b, c, "British Inquisition" 1991). Official agencies were drawing on a very small body of experts for advice in such matters. Ownership of the issue was in the hands of the religious activists and the Nottingham social workers, perhaps ten or twenty individuals in all. They might have been impeccably objective and correct in their views, but the narrow base of opinion increased the chances of error.

THE EVANGELICAL ROLE

In the controversies of the next year, the media would suggest that the ritual abuse panic had originated in the minds of a handful of religious zealots and the social workers they had converted to their point of view. This is difficult to credit for a number of reasons, not least because it appears unacceptably conspiratorial. It also undervalues the attitudes and abilities of social workers around the country, who believed they were encountering a new and serious menace, and who were sincerely groping for explanations, from whatever source they could find.

There is much disagreement how far religious beliefs might have motivated individual administrators or social workers in seeking out ritual abuse. It is distasteful to many to inquire into religious beliefs in this way, and some British newspapers were criticized for their apparent suggestion that cliques of fundamentalists and Charismatics were inspiring witch-hunts. *Social Work Today* called it "snide" and "disgraceful" to comment on the religious background of Ray Wyre and others. In Nottingham, speculation focused on the religious affiliations of the foster parents in the case, who were said to have influenced the testimony of the child witnesses (Waterhouse 1990a, b, c). In the Orkneys, it was believed in the local community that some social workers were affiliated with a small sect, the Orkney Christian Fellowship, and this ground became stigmatized as the root of the islands' crisis (*Scotland on Sunday*, March 17, 1991).

On the other hand, newspaper inquiries did uncover some suggestive connections, which if nothing else might have facilitated the rapid dissemination of information and theory. Some journalistic sources suggested a link between the Nottingham abuse case of 1987–1988 and the religious beliefs of the deputy director of social services, Tony Croall (*Scotsman*, March 14, 1991). Croall denied the charges in a 1991 interview, but his remarks confirmed the strong religious agenda of some social workers. He strongly believed in the reality of ritual abuse: "When you listen to children you find them using words, using behavior with each other, behaving to other adults as well in a quite explicit way which isn't to do with watching videos—it's actually to do with behavior they've been involved in" (*Scotsman*, March 14, 1991). But this need surprise no one, as these horrible crimes might be a sign of the Bible's prophesied last times: "This is being shown, this is being revealed, and as a Christian I believe actually it is God's time for it to be revealed. I really believe it is becoming more exposed because light has to be shone into darkness" (*Scotsman*, March 14, 1991). (However, the remark that secured Croall's suspension was a direct comparison between abortion and child abuse; Ivory 1991a.)

Croall was far from unique in his strong Christian beliefs. According to the *Independent*, the list of satanic indicators was passed to various members of the Social Workers Christian Fellowship, the secretary of which worked in Congleton at the time of the alleged discovery of a mass abuse ring there (Waterhouse 1990a, b, c; "British Inquisition" 1991).

GENERATING A NATIONAL PROBLEM

In 1989 and 1990, religious and other groups were highly successful in promoting awareness of the ritual issue at grass roots level. In various ways, local agencies became familiarized with the new ideas, and modified their interpretation of phenomena accordingly. Ritual reports originated with particular teams and individual workers, who then put pressure on their respective national agencies, groups like ChildLine and the NSPCC. This transformed local fears and rumors into a national problem. It was noted in March 1990 that "after a staff training program was set up by ChildLine, workers began to detect 'bizarre and difficult to comprehend elements' in telephone calls from a number of children" (McMillan 1990). The conclusion was that this must represent ritualized activity. Val Howarth now became a restrained but influential advocate of the reality of the charges, and called for a national inquiry into organized abuse (Cohen 1990).

In the case of the NSPCC, the issue arose with individual child protection teams such as those in Rochdale and Manchester. Rochdale had been one of the pioneering child protection teams under the Gilmour regime, and some of the society's most active workers and researchers were based in this unit (for some of their publications, see Blagg et al. 1989; Bannister et al. 1991). The local social workers had sound credentials, which inspired respect when they made claims of ritualistic activity, while in turn, events here would have a national influence through the intermediary of the national society. It was such local reports that led the society to alert the Department of Health to the danger in November 1989, and then to the startling public announcement about ritual crime the following March.

When local concerns were projected at the national level, there began to be a feedback effect. Concerns originate in the localities and come to influence central authority, which in turn alters its policies or actions in such a way as to promote or encourage reporting of the supposed problem. As reports of ritual activity poured in during early 1990, national charities like NCH and the NSPCC responded with a series of seminars and workshops. There were also calls for regional and national coordination to fight the new peril: The Nottingham social workers suggested that the Department of Health establish a national advisory group on ritual abuse.

In early 1990, there were meetings on ritual abuse between the national Social Services Inspectorate (SSI) and other interested bodies: the Association of Directors of Social Services, as well as charities like NSPCC, the Children's Society, and ChildLine (McMillan 1990; *Daily Telegraph*, *Times*, and *Guardian*, March 13, 1990). By May, "officials from the SSI and the department of Health [were] gathering information and experience from a variety of agencies on this problem" (Cohen 1990). The role of the SSI was crucial as it coordinated policies for agencies throughout the country, and circulated leaflets and publications. As the *Independent on Sunday* noted in September, "Virtually every British police force has received the satanic indicators. And although they might regard them as absurd, the Social Services Inspectorate has sent similar 'memoranda' to every social service department in Britain" (Waterhouse 1990b).

Once the central government was involved through the SSI, the affair could enter party politics, which further enhanced the visibility of the topic. Demands for more intensive government action were made by Joan Lestor, Labour's spokeswoman for children, who urged that the inspectorate intervene directly instead of merely monitoring reports (McMillan 1990).

THE PANIC

By mid-1990, social service agencies around the country were report-ing a dramatic upsurge in ritual abuse cases comparable to the sudden "discovery" of baby battering in the mid-1970s. The often slow legal proceedings meant that these cases remained in progress for some months, while access to detailed information was limited by the strict British rules on matters sub judice, especially where children are concerned. This in itself tended to increase rumor and speculation about the scale of the problem. But from the end of 1990, a series of court decisions cast increasing doubt on the various cases, and the means by which evidence was obtained: And it became apparent that the panic had little substance.

Studies of the satanism panic in the United States had repeatedly emphasized how occult charges arose from flaws in the investigative techniques employed both by prosecutors and by the therapists who are employed to interrogate the children (Eberle and Eberle 1986; Jenkins and Maier-Katkin 1988; Hicks 1991; Richardson et al. 1991). It is disputed whether small children lie about outrageous sexual abuse, and most authorities suggest that they cannot have the knowledge needed to invent the stories they present. In contrast, skeptics charge that these stories only emerge after lengthy periods, perhaps months, of active interrogation involving the use of leading questions. In order to understand the outcome of such an inquiry, it is necessary to appreciate both the nature of the investigation and the beliefs of the interrogators.

ROCHDALE

The Rochdale case may be taken as representative of this problem. It began when teachers and social workers became concerned about a deeply troubled six-year-old boy, who began telling fantastic tales about ghosts and the living dead. This had a particular impact because some members of the local social services department had recently attended a seminar on ritual criminality. Advice given by Reachout appeared to confirm an occult interpretation of the case. The boy and his siblings were soon taken into care by authorities, and in June 1990 a series of dawn raids claimed twelve more children from the same housing estate. The children—twenty in all, from a total of six families—were judged to be in urgent need of care and protection from (presumably) homicidal satanic gangs.

The local environment might have encouraged belief. Early modern Lancashire had been the scene of some of the largest witch trials in British history, while in the 1960s "witch-king" Alex Sanders had been based in the Greater Manchester area. Pendle Hill was considered a sacred site by genuine witch covens, of which there were said to be thirty in the northeast of the county alone, "plus an unknown number of other occult groups" (Logan 1988:7–8). And there were still more evocative memories: As the *Sunday Telegraph* observed, "The road that brings you into the district from the west runs along the desolate moorland where Ian Brady and Myra Hindley buried their child victims" (Hall 1990). Kevin Logan's parish at Great Harwood was conveniently close, and local Charismatics and fundamentalists were well organized in groups like the Hyndburn Christian Fellowship (Logan 1988).

The Rochdale cases proceeded gradually through the courts, but in

March 1991, a court decision freed ten of the children to be reunited with their families. Four more children remained in care, all from one family. The judge, Douglas Brown, was extremely critical of the social service department, and his criticisms of the social workers were to be echoed by numerous official inquiries at about the same time (*Scotsman*, March 8, 1991). According to the judge, the investigation had been badly mishandled at several stages. The social workers seemed to have leaped to the conclusion that ritual abuse was involved and were unwilling to explore alternative explanations.

The boy at the heart of the Rochdale case had apparently been watching highly unsuitable videos such as the *Evil Dead* around the time that he made his claims, and this would more than adequately explain the charges of zombies and ghosts. Among other problems, children had been interviewed jointly, which "breached all the rules of good practice. Joint interviews run a serious risk of contamination and in any event this interview was described by them as chaotic." There were moments of near comedy. Important interviews should have been videotaped, but in some cases the staff had been unable to operate the camera, and in others the quality of reproduction made the tapes almost unusable.

The judge remarked that there had been a failure to do anything to balance or undermine the ritual interpretations. "This is a classic illustration of a little learning being a dangerous thing and a telling illustration of the obvious need at the outset for an expert overview." The social services authority had not sought an "independent over-view," which might well have prevented the raids and the draconian seizure of the children from their homes, while a consultant child psychiatrist had not been asked for an opinion. Among other criticisms, affidavits from social workers were "inaccurate and in places seriously misleading." In all, "the local authority have tried, particularly during cross-examination, to make the literature fit a few flimsy pieces of evidence. . . . They were not minor, trivial or infrequent breaches [of procedure], but were substantial ones which rendered the information from the children valueless and unreliable."

This critique was damning enough, and the director of Rochdale social services resigned shortly afterwards. However, the media soon began to explore in detail many other flaws in the investigation. They were especially scathing about the rich significance attached to childish fantasies and about the failure to understand children's modes of communication. In one widely quoted instance, a boy was said to have confessed to eating a cat and proceeded to draw satanic emblems. It proved that the cat was a pasta shape in a lunch item, while the sinister shapes reflected two popular rides at the Alton Towers amusement park in Staffordshire, one of several British imitations of Disneyland. The *People* headlined, "Boy Said He Ate Cats . . . And They Believed Him" (March 10, 1991).

OTHER CASES

For the popular press, the Rochdale incident suggested a picture of social workers obsessed with finding evidence of satanic abuse, even where this involved giving quite exaggerated significance to relatively minor pieces of evidence, and with seeking testimony by browbeating children in custody. This was only one incident of several. On Merseyside, ten children were seized in June 1990 by a task force of over one hundred police and social workers. Seventeen adults were arrested and questioned, but by September, the authorities stated that (as in Rochdale) no criminal charges would be brought (*Mail on Sunday*, September 16, 1990).

Nor were charges brought in a similar case in Ayrshire, in the Scottish county of Strathclyde, in which five families were said to be involved in organized ritualistic activity. In a Humberside case, activist Diane Core not only made claims of ritual abuse, but also argued that this provided the context for the unexplained death in 1984 of Christopher Laverack, one of the names on the Operation Stranger list of child murders. Charges of abuse were made in this case, but convictions were not obtained because of problems with interrogating alleged victims (Eaton et al. 1991).

Another celebrated case involved alleged satanic rites in Epping Forest, near London, with parents abusing their daughters of ten and fourteen. The newspapers presented a barrage of sensational headlines, from "Babies sacrificed in black magic orgies" (*Daily Mirror*, November 14, 1991) to the *Times'* "Parents assaulted daughter in black magic sex rituals" (November 14, 1991). This case actually came to court ("the black magic trial"), but charges were dismissed because the younger girl's evidence was "so uncertain, inconsistent and improbable" (L. Jenkins 1991; compare MacIntyre 1991). The family asserted that the girls had "got it all from video," while the charges had originated at the same time that the Rochdale scandal was at its height.

In Manchester, as in Rochdale, social services had for years cooperated closely with a NSPCC child protection team, and a joint Child Sexual Assault Unit had been involved in important research. Here, the ritual charges originated with two girls taken into care in late 1989: After three months of questioning in custody, allegations of satanic abuse began to be recorded. Thirteen children were seized in this case, but the proceedings ended similarly to those in Rochdale, with a damning review by a judge, Mr. Justice Hollings. He did find "abuse of a sadistic nature in bogus ritual circumstances in two cases," but proceeded to release eight of the remaining children immediately, noting that the social workers were "obsessed with the belief" that they had uncovered a satanic ring. He reported a number of procedural flaws, this time including "grossly inadequate reporting" of interviews (*Guardian*, December 18, 1990; *Daily Mail*, December 23, 1990). Once again, it appeared that children had suffered the traumatic experience of being forcibly removed from their homes for lengthy periods on thoroughly inadequate evidence.

NOTTINGHAM REVISITED

By early 1991, the ritual abuse cases appeared to have peaked in importance, and were unraveling in several areas. There was also a serious reexamination of the key Nottingham case, and of the means by which the satanic charges had been uncovered. As early as 1988, the police had vehemently denied the presence of any occult component in the cases, and the local chief constable had pledged to "kill off once and for all" these tales. A joint inquiry team that reported in December 1989 failed to confirm ritual or satanic elements. A report leaked to the press suggested that the children had indeed told tales of blood, snakes, witches, and monsters. However, it charged that these bizarre interests reflected not real abuse, but the toys and therapeutic aids used by social workers. These were said to have included witches' costumes, plastic syringes, and rubber snakes.

The case remains controversial, and there were continuing conflicts within the social services agency between the director and the ritual abuse "task force" led by Judith Dawson: Legal charges and official complaints were pursued for several years. However, the critique of the whole ritual framework was devastating (*Independent*, April 6, 1991; *Community Care*, 10 October, 1991).

THE ORKNEY AFFAIR

Another notorious case occurred on South Ronaldsay in the remote Orkney islands in February 1991, when police and social workers undertook the by then traditional dawn raids, taking nine children into custody. The events were especially controversial in a remote rural community, where children from four families suddenly found their lives interrupted without even the opportunity to take a few toys with them. Action was justified by the authorities on the grounds of the extreme danger present on the island, where large satanic cult gatherings were said to occur at a local quarry, and where an elderly Church of Scotland minister played the role of chief wizard or coven leader. Goods seized by police as potentially satanic included graduate hoods, a shepherd's crook, cloaks, and a book with a goat on the cover (*Scotsman*, March 3–14, 1991; *Observer*, March 10, 1991).

The charges were all the more preposterous in that such offenses were said to have taken place in a close-knit society, where secrets of this sort would appear hard to keep. The parents swiftly organized an effective support group, the South Ronaldsay Parents Action Committee, led by a local doctor, Helen Martini, who acted as a spokeswoman to the media. They were assisted by PAIN leaders like Sue Amphlett. The group collected petitions of support that showed overwhelming skepticism about the charges and attracted publicity by a poster campaign that asked for information about observations or recollections of ritual music or dancing: No response was forthcoming. The social service agencies were thus confronting a united and well-mobilized community (Thompson 1991).

Fortunately, the Scottish system provides for swift proceedings where the custody of children is concerned, and a sheriff named David Kelbie was able to render a judgment in the case in early April. If anything, Kelbie's findings were even more damaging than the recent English precedents. He found in summary "that these proceedings are so fatally flawed as to be incompetent." The children had been separated and subjected to repeated cross-examination, almost as if the aim was to force confessions rather than to assist in therapy. Where two children had made similar statements about abuse, this appeared to be the result of "repeated coaching" (*Times*, April 5, 1991).

He was particularly scathing about charges that children had been abused to the sound of "ritual music." As the sheriff confessed, he did not know what this might be, "anything from Kylie Minogue to Andrew Lloyd Webber." The charges were all the more outrageous in that they appeared to have so little support, even in terms of popular suspicion. In the words of the *Times*, "Almost no one except the social work department could believe that ritual sexual abuse was taking place on South Ronaldsay" (April 5, 1991).

The media offered a more detailed explanation of what had occurred to produce such a bizarre turn of events, and they found the origins of the case in the internal politics of local social service agencies. During

1989, a group of children from one family had been seized in a nonritual abuse case. In mid-1990, the "reporter" of the local social services permitted them to return to their mother, against the strenuous opposition of the social workers (*Independent on Sunday*, April 7, 1991). This allegedly led to retaliation against the reporter, and her replacement was viewed by parents as a prime mover in the later investigations. Meanwhile, some of the children taken into care were the source of the allegations against the other four families, who had joined together to support the mother in the original case. Another element had been provided by a religious summer camp the previous year, where several island children had had "exorcisms" performed, spreading notions of demons and supernatural ceremonies (*Times*, April 5, 1991; Thompson 1991).

Kelbie's verdict did not mark the end of the Orkney affair, as the social services department continued to argue that he had rushed to judgment without taking account of some of the most damaging testimony. The agency was supported in this by a senior Scottish judge, Lord Hope, the lord president, who berated Kelbie for his haste. However, this did little to quell public perceptions that the case had collapsed.

After Rochdale, Orkney, Manchester, and Nottingham, ritual abuse was left without a single plausible case in Britain. In March 1991, the Home Office's chief inspector of constabulary remarked that "Police have no evidence of rituals or Satanic abuse inflicted on children anywhere in England and Wales. A lot of well-intentioned hype has got out of control" (Waterhouse 1991b).

MEDIA REACTIONS

The child abuse issue had often led to hostility against social workers, but comments were usually inhibited by a reluctance to appear unsympathetic toward children's interests. Even in Cleveland, the argument was that some agencies might have gone too far in combating a genuine problem, but false charges were dangerous because they harmed the real victims of sexual abuse. The ritual affair marked an important departure, as it could be argued that a panic had been manipulated into existence out of literally nothing.

In the autumn of 1990, the press with few exceptions launched an uncompromising attack against the ritual theorists, and the police and social workers who had accepted their views. Sub judice restraints diminished the campaign for some months, but the decisions in the Orkney and Rochdale cases in the spring of 1991 permitted the media to renew a strident campaign against the social work profession in general. The press consistently treated the ritual abuse cases as a major story: In fact, the Rochdale verdicts of March 1991 were one of the first non-Gulf-related stories to receive headline attention in the immediate aftermath of the war with Iraq.

Among the most enthusiastic debunkers were the *Independent* and the *Daily Mail*—an interesting juxtaposition of a liberal quality and a highly conservative popular paper. Both papers undertook some impressive investigative reporting. The *Independent* published information about the internal inquiry into the Nottingham cases, suggesting that children might have been "primed" to give evidence by the use of toys that acted as props. On the Manchester affair too, the paper emphasized the lengthy period of interrogation that had preceded the earliest accusations of ritual activity on the part of any children, while studies in September 1990 suggested serious contradictions in the claims made by various authorities involved in the Rochdale case.

The *Independent* emphasized that the occult interpretations were in essence the work of a handful of theorists, most of whom were either American cult experts or domestic fundamentalists. In March 1991, further articles explored the activities of Maureen Davies, Pamela Klein, and Kevin Logan, who were depicted as prime movers in the Rochdale affair and the network of ritual charges. A lengthy article attacked the myth of Hannah, the alleged brood mare and martyr to the cause of antisatanism (Hebditch and Anning 1990).

The theorists found their harshest critic in the *Mail*, which dogged the social service department throughout the Rochdale affair. In the latter part of 1990, the paper kept the story on the front page, and regularly produced headlines such as "They Stole Their Children and Then They Took Away Their Rights" (September 9, 1990), "Satan Council Condemned" (November 10, 1990), and "Where the Devil Is the Evidence?" In September, a report headlined "Sixteen Youngsters Snatched by Social Workers after a Six Year Old Tells of Satan Fantasy" (September 9, 1990). When the affair broke in March 1991, the paper offered a front-page photograph of a reunited family with the caption, "Happy Family—The Finest Mothers Day Picture of All."

Inside pages presented a serious and powerful account of the roots of "the British Inquisition," which ranks among the best media studies of the construction of a panic. From September 1990, the *Mail* had consistently laid the ritual abuse charges firmly at the door of religious fundamentalists with a strong influence from American therapists and cult "experts": It was a "US theory imported with evangelical zeal": more succinctly, "gobbledegook." Simandl, Davies, Dawson, and Core were repeatedly blamed as the instigators. The paper remarked, "Nowhere in the world where allegations of Satanic abuse have been made has there been a single incident where the slightest piece of physical or forensic evidence was uncovered." The panic must be traced to the "true believers," who read and accepted material like "Facing the Unbelievable."

The successive *Mail* articles offered a detailed analysis of the Reachout Trust and its origins, its fundamentalist affiliations, and the often bizarre religious notions expressed by some adherents. It also explored the dissemination of the satanic indicators composed in this environment, and the role of the series of conferences and workshops like that held at Reading in 1989. Both the *Mail* and the *Independent* were especially hostile toward the NSPCC, one of the most active early claims-makers, and it was with a certain relish that they reported attempts by the organization to withdraw from these initial charges of vast clandestine networks. The *Sunday Times* alleged that the NSPCC had played up the menaces of organized and ritual abuse in order to increase its potential funding.

"SOCIAL WORKER BASHING"

But these investigative accounts were only the most conspicuous part of an almost universal hostility to the whole concept of ritual abuse, and even more to the way that social workers had undertaken their investigations in the various cases. The images were of innocent families persecuted by incompetent, heartless, and ignorant social workers, who knew so little of children that they could wrench such sinister meanings out of their fantasies. Conversely, the papers depicted the delight of the reunited families, so improbable if in fact the children were indeed being returned to a hell of ritualistic abuse and blood drinking. In late 1990, the *Express* had headlined "Satan Children Stay Put—Let Me See My Little Girl, Pleads Mother." When the courts ordered the children released, the *Daily Telegraph* offered a report about a proposed appeal against the decision, but on the same page was a story headed "Hip Hooray, I'm Going Home Today Sang a Little Boy" (April 6, 1991).

This *Telegraph* report also mentioned a theme common to several papers, that the children taken into care had in fact suffered considerably from the institutional environment, where they had learned criminal behavior such as taking drugs and breaking into cars. This depicted social workers as not only hostile to normal families, but unwilling or unable to protect them themselves. As the *Daily Mirror* headline remarked, the Orkney children "Left Here Unharmed, They're Coming Home Abused . . . Mum's Anguish as Sex Abuse Case Is Ditched . . . Cruel Legacy of Orkney Kids Taken from Their Families" (April 5, 1991).

The sense that institutions were by no means safe environments was reinforced about this time by a series of unrelated stories that received very wide press coverage. One theme concerned repeated reports that a majority of arrested child prostitutes were residents of local authority homes (Hugill et al. 1991). A related scandal about brutality in publicly run children's homes in Staffordshire suggested that the inmates might have been systematically abused by a local pedophile ring (Ivory 1991b). In Leicestershire, another well-publicized trial during 1991 presented a picture of children's homes being run by a clique of social workers who for more than a decade employed sexual abuse, torture, and brutality under the guise of therapy. This case—the Frank Beck affair—offered accounts of young male prostitutes operating out of homes, with clients allegedly including a Member of Parliament (Katz 1991).

Also at issue in Orkney were the images of dawn raids, for which the papers drew extensively on the popular British imagery of Nazi Germany and later totalitarian states. As the Reverend Morris McKenzie of Orkney (the alleged wizard of the cult) was quoted as saying in the *Mirror*, "The social workers here were power mad. Children must be protected, but these gestapo tactics must stop" (April 5, 1991). He compared the Orkney social workers to the Ceausescu regime in Rumania. For the *Scotsman*, the Orkney raids had represented "the bureaucratic rape of a community."

Consistently, social workers were depicted as gullible victims of propaganda by religious theorists, who employed ritual abuse to establish their social and sectarian agenda. The *Mirror* commented, "Like their counterparts in Rochdale, the Orkney social workers became obsessed with horror stories told by children." The *Express*s said of the Orkney cases that "This seems to have been a case of people finding what they set out to find in the first place." The *Scotsman* was one of many papers that remarked, "Social workers had been freshly primed on satanic ritual indicators at a seminar." In addition, it seemed that "the allegations of ritual abuse on Orkney stem from the influence of extreme Charismatic Christian groups on British social work departments" (March 14, 1991). Social workers were bigots and witch-hunters, in addition to their traditional role as busybodies.

In summary, the *Mirror* remarked of the Orkney affair that there was "Just no excuse":

Every parent knows that children often dream up fanciful tales. Experience tells them how to distinguish between a fertile imagination and the facts. The social workers who stole the children of Orkney in a dawn raid which would have disgraced a police state

apparently do not. It was their heads which were filled with horror
stories of ritual abuse. (April 5, 1991)

The *Daily Express* stressed, "It must never happen again," and perhaps
confirmed the fears of feminist critics by seeing the verdicts as proof that
family life was not quite as bad as it had been painted: "It is also a relief
to know that the vile events alleged did not take place, that child abuse
is not so widespread that it should be spreading its evil tentacles into
even the remotest part of the United Kingdom" (April 5, 1991).

But the cases not only revealed failings in the particular agencies
concerned: They were a damning indictment of the whole social work
profession, which needed immediate reform. In addition, most papers
called for the dismissal of the social workers and administrators involved. The *Sunday Telegraph* remarked on the "twilight of the social
worker" (March 10, 1991); the *Times* found "a battered profession" after
Rochdale and Orkney, a group "discredited in the public eye by child
abuse cases" (April 5, 1991). The *Mail* offered "In the Dock Again—The
Care Staff Who Go Too Far." One *Mail* story by right-wing sociologist
David Marsland bore the colorful headline, "After the Latest Shameful
Indictment of Our Arrogant, Incompetent Social Workers, *Sack the Lot
and Start Again*" (April 5, 1991, emphasis in original).

Such extreme denunciations led to calls for moderation, not least from
the *Independent*, which had played so central a role in the earlier
campaign:

Cases such as Cleveland, Rochdale and now Orkney do not merely
damage the children involved and their families. They undermine
the credibility of social service departments, thus making it more
difficult for the very many genuine cases of child abuse to be dealt
with vigorously. Aside from the horrors the children suffer, the
harsh truth is that today's undetected victim of abuse is often
tomorrow's abuser. They deserve all the support society can offer
and social workers are on the front line. (April 5, 1991)

DEFENDING THE CASES?

In the face of this storm of indignation, there were still a few who
defended the actions of the social service authorities and the ritual
character of the cases. Tim Tate's book *Children for the Devil* appeared that
fall, while Beatrix Campbell also continued to assert the reality of a
menace (B. Campbell 1991a). In September 1991, a national ritual abuse

conference in Manchester featured speakers like Tate, Campbell, and Ray Wyre. (Other social workers from Nottingham and Rochdale were scheduled to attend, including Judith Dawson, but their agencies forbade their appearance in an official capacity.) At the conference,

> A stunned audience watched a self-confessed Satanist and child sexual abuser explain in detail, on video, how he terrorized his stepdaughters into secrecy with weapons, violently killed animals and Satanic beliefs (*sic*). He was a recent client of Ray Wyre at the Gracewell Clinic, Birmingham. . . . The existence of ritual abuse was not in question at the conference. (*Community Care*, September 26, 1991)

However, these advocates were definitely in a minority. Both the ritual abuse theories and the actions of the agencies involved were criticized by groups and individuals with a long record of children's advocacy and support for the abuse "crusade." Esther Rantzen had traveled to Orkney at the height of the crisis, but to show support for the parents rather than the social workers. The Childwatch agency was divided, with Manchester representative Judith Parry attacking the ritual interpretations emanating from Diane Core.

Many of those who did defend the investigations adopted a rather defensive tone, while leading advocates backtracked. Evangelical groups denied ever having supplied satanic indicators to social work professionals (*Community Care*, April 11, 1991). The NSPCC defended its original charges of *organized* abuse, but denied that it had ever claimed this was occult or satanic in nature. One common defense was that of director Chris Brown, who attempted to portray the total skepticism of the media as a position quite as extreme as that of the ritual zealots: "The current debate swings from wanting to rubbish the whole evidence to the other extreme of Christian sects which want us to believe there are witches' covens in every graveyard" (*Social Work Today*, October 25, 1990). Even so, the society apparently paid a price for its campaign. In September 1990, the government terminated the NSPCC's control over child abuse registers, and funding cuts over the next few months led to the closure of some child protection teams. The society now faced "an immense crisis" (*Community Care*, May 16, 1991).

Growing skepticism was also apparent in the social work press, which anticipated a public backlash even worse than Cleveland. Some papers defended the social workers involved and reasserted the competence of the profession: *Scottish Child* saw the media reaction as an attempt to silence the child victims of "regular" abuse (Rodgers 1991), while *Social Work Today* denounced media "mass hysteria." But even in such journals, there were clearly doubts about the ritual abuse cases. *Community Care* tried to salvage something of the Orkney charges, and noted that Sheriff Kelbie had not paid sufficient attention to the copious testimony (Neate and Hackett 1991; Neate and Sone 1991), but the magazine's leader on the Orkney case was frankly entitled "A Ritual Farce." This accepted that "the reputation of the social work profession is at an all-time low," and several articles emphasized the criticisms of the whole ritual abuse concept (April 11, 1991). Henceforward, *Community Care* and *Social Work Today* both adopted a far more balanced and critical stance toward ritual abuse charges than before (Eaton et al. 1991; though see Nelson 1991; B. Campbell 1991b).

Even the *New Statesman and Society*, which had published work by Dawson and Campbell, now suggested, however tentatively, that social workers might on occasion go too far in removing children from families (Laurance 1991). In such a context, this was a significant retraction. There is no serious doubt here that ritual abuse had caused a fiasco, but it remained to be seen how deep the damage would run: "What is most worrying about the events in Cleveland, Rochdale and the Orkneys is that they risk turning the clock back."

The government responded to the controversy by promptly issuing new guidelines for social service agencies, prohibiting dawn raids of the sort that had become notorious in Rochdale and Orkney, and warning of the dangers of leading questions in child interrogations. There were also a number of official inquiries. In the Orkneys, Lord Clyde began an official judicial inquiry in July 1991, while a more general investigation into ritual abuse was directed by child abuse authority Jean LaFontaine (see, for example, LaFontaine 1990). These investigations are still in progress at the time of writing, but there is little doubt that the whole notion of ritual abuse has been thoroughly undermined.

Of the several panics outlined in this book, ritual abuse is the only one that can be said to have effectively ceased and to have been almost wholly discredited among media and policy-makers. However, this does not mean that the concept itself has perished entirely. Some of the original claims-makers remain active, and the essential ideas of a ritualistic threat have been sufficiently publicized that they may well survive in the public consciousness until they re-emerge in some form as components of a future problem.

*Claims and
Claims-Makers*

— 9 —

Broad social trends encouraged a greater sense of the vulnerability of women and children, while the political context of the 1980s ensured that moral issues would be a symbolic vehicle for attacking partisan rivals. Together, these elements created an environment receptive to claims made by groups or individuals engaged in the pursuit of moral enterprise. This chapter attempts to answer some of the central questions of the whole constructionist endeavor: Who made claims, and how? And who benefited?

ENTREPRENEURS

Successive studies of panics have identified a variety of different types of moral entrepreneur. The British experience offers evidence of all these types, from the lone activist to the organized pressure group and the bureaucratic agency. Several striking examples emerge in the first category, but perhaps the most remarkable is Mary Whitehouse, who was at the center of a series of controversies from the late 1960s into the Thatcher era. In some cases, like the *Gay News* affair, the decency protests would not have occurred without her personal intervention, and it is improbable that the successful child pornography campaign would have attained such rapid influence. Despite her nominal leadership of NVALA, there has never been any doubt that the organization was a pallid reflection of her personal influence.

She benefited greatly from her long-established fame (or notoriety). By the 1970s, she was well-known throughout the media as an articulate speaker, available to provide comment on a broad range of issues. She also had close friends and allies in Parliament, which they could use as a forum to present her views in a widely reported environment. When

195

she began to make claims about a particular issue, enormous resources for publicity and action were thus available to her with minimal delay.

The decade produced other individual entrepreneurs, who like White-house would be active in several areas of concern. Beatrix Campbell is one such, a tireless writer on child abuse and ritual abuse, whose leftist and feminist credentials dated back two decades. This gave her many contacts in the various journals and newspapers, and she was able to present her views in outlets of quite diverse persuasions, including television's Channel Four.

In a slightly different mold, Judith Dawson emerged as an entrepreneur who had nothing like the public visibility of Mary Whitehouse, because she concentrated her efforts within the narrow but important realm of those directly affected by the perceived problem. In exposing ritual abuse, Dawson found her outlets in the social work literature (*Community Care*) and the left-liberal media (*New Statesman and Society*), while she was personally active as a speaker at conferences and professional seminars and as a consultant to various agencies. This was a highly focused approach in terms of claims-making, but it was effective.

Many other individuals might be cited here, including several members of Parliament. The British Parliament differs substantially from the U.S. Congress in that there has not traditionally been the same system of powerful standing committees able to draw attention to an issue by launching a series of hearings. A member who wants to raise public awareness might do so by asking questions of ministers, including the prime minister, or by introducing a member's private bill. While this would have little chance of becoming law, it would at least permit the issue to be placed on the record together with speeches and debates.

Stuart Bell serves as a valuable parliamentary example, as he used the Cleveland case to great effect, to draw attention to what he felt were widespread abuses in child protection procedures. However, perhaps the most active and consistent members in the moralist cause has been Geoffrey Dickens, who has often addressed issues of child abuse, pedophilia, sexual perversion, and diabolism. When he wrote the foreword for Audrey Harper's 1990 book *Dance with the Devil*, he signed himself grandly as "M.P., Child Protection Campaigner." Politically, his parliamentary interventions did much to typify the various problems as a huge menace protected and even sponsored by a corrupt political elite.

In addition, there were medical professionals whose opinions were valued because of their claims to unique expertise. Despite some judicial criticisms, Arnon Bentovim was probably the most important of this group, and he was largely responsible for making the Great Ormond Street Hospital for Sick Children a key institution in the study and treatment of child abuse, and in pressure for legal reform. Local pediatric activists were instrumental in making communities like Tyneside, Leeds, and Cleveland, each in its own way, centers for new policies and techniques.

PRESSURE GROUPS

Other important activists are groups or societies. These enjoy a particular importance in the British political system because of the meager resources available to members of Parliament in terms of support staff, budget, and research facilities. M.P.s can profit from the information and research supplied by a friendly pressure group, whose interests they inevitably tend to represent. Among the active in recent years have been the Society for the Protection of the Unborn Child, Shelter (advocates for the homeless), and the Child Poverty Action Group (Field 1982).

The NSPCC has been critical in child welfare issues, and has long provided a clear institutional base for the child protection movement. This well-known and popular charity was uniquely well-placed to present its cause, as a classic "inside" claims-maker. It was chaired from the 1940s to the 1970s by the familiar and paternalistic Arthur Morton, and this encouraged the image of a conservative establishment group. This promoted public acceptance of its claims, even if these involved the far-reaching ritual abuse statements of 1990. It was also politically difficult to attack an institution with such credibility.

When the NSPCC adopted a more forthright and dynamic model of child protection in the late 1970s, it was therefore likely to gain wide media coverage and general public belief in its statements. This was crucial for the media, which were able to present startling claims about the scale of a social problem, automatically validated by the authority of the NSPCC. In addition, the NSPCC had close ties with both government and the other child protection organizations.

At the same time, the creation of local child protection teams meant that claims were increasingly likely to be generated at local level by relatively autonomous bodies, and extreme statements could well result. Significantly, at the height of the ritual abuse controversy, these criticisms were presented by the otherwise sympathetic *Social Work Today*:

> Some would argue that the NSPCC has had this populist tendency in the past to try and grab the headlines in order to keep its succesful fund-raising activities in the public eye. But there have

been other criticisms that the society has become too bureaucratic
at the center in trying to control everything its 66 local child
protection teams do. (October 25, 1990)

Other claims-making groups were more recent phenomena, arising
from the abuse controversies of the late 1970s, but they too presented
claims about dangers to children. The Children's Legal Centre (founded
in 1979) campaigned for children's rights, while Justice for Children
tried to improve protections for families confronting the social services
(Cohen 1988). The Family Rights Group (founded in 1974) attempted to
protect families whose children had been taken into care, but it differed
from PAIN in placing less emphasis on the dangers of false or malicious
charges, and advocated the reality of the child abuse problem (Family
Rights Group 1988).

The various groups differed considerably in their methods and tactics,
depending largely on the individual leaders involved. Some eschewed
public visibility, while others actively sought publicity and headlines.
The National Association for Young People in Care (NAYPIC), for
example, tended toward an investigative and exposé approach to draw
attention to the problems of young people in care or on the streets. It did
this by using allegations about snuff and sex rings during 1990, while the
following year, NAYPIC-sponsored whistle-blowing led to a national
scandal about brutality and sex in children's homes (Hugill et al. 1991;
Ivory 1991b).

Perhaps the most visible example of such groups is the newest group
of all, ChildLine. This owes its celebrity to the media fanfare surrounding its launching in 1986, and its association with Esther Rantzen, who
had for over a decade been one of the best-known media personalities in
Britain. Whatever the administrative problems, the mere existence of
ChildLine was a fact of great importance for publicizing the child abuse
cause. In addition, acceptance of the issue was enhanced by is identification in the public mind with a known and named individual, in the
same way that Mary Whitehouse was the media personification of
decency. For ChildLine, this role was performed by Esther Rantzen and
later Valerie Howarth, neither of whom was as controversial as Whitehouse, or as deeply unpopular with sections of public opinion.

PAIN, which spoke for falsely accused parents, is another notable
example of a new group that enjoyed rapid success, chiefly by filling a
media need. During an abuse "crisis" like Rochdale or Orkney, the
media wished to let representatives of every point of view speak, and
the parents' perspective would obviously be important. On the other
hand, it was a matter of chance whether an accused parent might be
both articulate and truthful; and there was the danger that a particular

case might be presented as an example of official injustice, only to find later that the individual had been correctly accused. For a newspaper or a news program, PAIN offered immediate access to a network of well-chosen speakers who were validated as innocent victims. The group's leader, Sue Amphlett, also became a well-known media person who served as an effective figurehead instantly identifiable with her cause, a counterweight to Esther Rantzen or Alan Gilmour. It was important that the group be represented by a woman, in order to defuse the issue of gender conflict in debates with advocates of the reality of child abuse.

Some claims-making organizations were linked to wider movements, and two political currents in particular spawned specialized groups: the feminist movement, and the Evangelical-moralist cause. The two operated in remarkably similar ways, with similar structures of organization and propaganda, indeed whole subcultures: networks of publishers, bookstores, magazines and journals, conferences, seminars, and discussion groups. The moralists perhaps had better overall coordination, in the Festival of Light and the Evangelical Alliance, but the feminists also had national and regional women's conferences, and also had better ties to government in the form of the urban local authorities.

In both cases, specific issues resulted in the formation of ad hoc activist organizations, often with overlapping membership and direction. The Evangelicals had special groups for Christian teachers and Christian social workers, for campaigners against obscenity and abortion. The feminists had groups to oppose rape, to fight incest, to aid battered women. Both movements similarly had members who were able to present opinion in mainstream publications and media outlets.

COALITIONS

The comparison between the feminist and moralist causes also raises the issue of the nature of alliances between pressure groups. The agenda of a given group might conflict radically with the views of other members in a coalition or a particular issue. We find, for example, in the attack on pornography, an alliance that includes (but is not confined to) left-wing feminists and morality campaigners anxious to reassert traditional moral values and family roles. The two groups might be diametrically opposed on women's rights or abortion, but they form tactical alliances with some ease (compare Downs 1990). Ritual abuse was denounced by a de facto coalition of feminists and religious fundamentalists.

These associations often involved real tension. For instance, the *Sun* newspaper was strongly conservative in politics and keen to popularize horror stories about pedophiles, homosexuals, snuff films, child pronography, and other aspects of the related panics of these years. On the other hand, it was itself a target of feminist pressure, with its "page three girls" widely denounced by activists as a commonly available form of soft pornography.

It was often difficult to predict exactly what line a particular group or individual would follow on a given issue. To take a specific case, Richard West is a conservative journalist with long-standing connections to moral traditionalist movements, specifically those opposed to pornography and abortion. Yet he wrote a devastating critique of the Cleveland investigation, which he compared to the Jordan farrago in the United States (R. West 1987). The political setting of the panic thus involved contradictions and paradoxes in the rhetoric of the activist groups. The panics regularly transcended the left-right political boundaries, which are normally much sharper in Britain than in the United States.

THE POLICE

Other key interest groups are bureaucratic agencies, especially the police and social service agencies. It has been argued that police needs and attitudes did much to shape new views of serial murder, while some panics assisted the police in the development of special squads and task forces. In both cases, new public fears helped overcome potential opposition to greater centralization, though it is quite uncertain if the police had any conscious policy in this direction.

Of course, "the police" is a large and highly stratified organization, within which we find many divisions of opinion. On the child abuse issue, however, there was unanimity about the need for urgent action. It is instructive here to study the issue in the pages of *Police* magazine, the organ of the Police Federation, which faithfully reflects the views of the police rank and file, and which in the mid-1980s reported regularly and emotionally on the continuing victimization and murder of the young. One 1985 report noted an arrest in the "horrific murder of toddler Leoni Keating" in Bedfordshire. The journal campaigned strongly for proposed changes in the laws of evidence, even more radical reforms like allowing second hand testimony based on expert interview. As with the NSPCC, the police were well placed to make authoritative claims that would automatically receive wide and respectful attention in the media.

Women police officers played a significant role in this. The separate administrative structure for policewomen had been abolished in 1975, ostensibly as a move toward great equality. In practice, it was widely felt that women suffered from this change in that promotion opportunities diminished. The abuse issue of the 1980s permitted the emergence of policewomen as a distinct and vocal pressure group, with forthright demands for reform in the interests of the child. Successful demands in this area helped reaffirm the importance of women as a caucus within the police structure.

SOCIAL WORKERS

Social workers are the other professional group most directly affected by any issue involving children, and the wave of concern during the 1980s led to a major expansion of the profession, at a time when most public spending was ruthlessly cut. In this sense, the profession benefited overall, and there was particular growth in those sections specializing in children's issues. This is easily explained in terms of the priorities of the radical councils that began to dominate many of the cities in the early 1980s, while the child deaths inquiries made it inevitable that the emphasis would shift toward more proactive intervention. A child abuse crisis like Cleveland led to perceptions of a major problem requiring the urgent allocation of new resources: A larger and more specialized child protection establishment would mean more investigation and detection, and thus more concern. This spiral effect goes far toward explaining the overall growth during the decade. As of 1991, "22 percent of newly qualified social workers work mainly with child abuse victims, and two in every three social workers are actively engaged in the child care field" ("Child Abuse Workers Lack Full Training," *Guardian*, June 19, 1991).

Social workers also stood to gain from the panic in terms of status. Though ostensibly professionals, they had little of the respect accorded to the traditional professions, and a large national opinion poll taken in 1986 indicated real hostility. On a six-point scale, only 5 percent of those questioned placed social workers in the top two categories of estimated value to the community which suggested that they were esteemed less than doctors, police officers, teachers, nurses, and clergy. 62 percent placed them in the bottom two categories, a degree of perceived worthlessness exceeded only by clergy (Philpot 1987). By the 1980s there was also a rich tradition of scapegoating social workers as blundering amateurs motivated chiefly by extremist political dogma (Hill 1990).

It is significant here that when a blunder occurred, as in the Beckford case, the problem was investigated not by a supreme professional body like the British Medical Association or the Law Society, but by an inquiry chaired by a judge or barrister: in other words, a lawyer, representing a "real" profession. This naturally created resentment within social work. In the words of a recent text, "The question arises as to why we have allowed lawyers to define our work in this way" (Blagg et all. 1989: 65).

There has been a sense of crisis in social work since the late 1970s, indicated by the title of a much discussed text, *Can Social Work Survive?* (Brewer and Lait 1980; see also *Barclay Committee* 1982). During the 1980s, there was a strong trend toward an even more clearly ideological and activist justification for social work, which seemed likely to intensify public criticism still further. The only way to reaffirm the value of the profession was to show that social workers were dealing with truly menacing problems, which they were uniquely qualified to investigate and combat. Exposing a vast and unsuspected prevalence of child abuse thus fulfilled both ideological and professional needs, and fully justified the need for specialized social service agencies.

"WORKING TOGETHER": INTERAGENCY COOPERATION

Successive government documents repeatedly emphasized the need for agencies to cooperate in the face of this menace. Cooperation was valuable for the social work profession, as it got the opportunity to work on equal terms with other groups that commanded far greater public esteem, specifically doctors and police. The alliance with pediatricians was especially important, and the new diagnostic evidence for child abuse offered objective scientific validation for earlier assertions. In turn, the development of pediatric teams specializing in abuse referrals made positive diagnoses more likely. Unlike family doctors, the consultant pediatricians had little or no direct connection with the parents of the child they were examining, and therefore less compunction about giving diagnoses that might cause untold damage (compare Pfohl 1977).

Also critical were the joint investigations with police, which could be presented as clear evidence that the police unassisted could never assess the true scale of a problem like abuse or pedophilia, still less control it. Proposals for joint task forces suggested the value of social work expertise, while responding to mainstream political demands for effective crime control.

At first sight, the relatively friendly attitude of the police seems surprising, as these joint investigations permitted a civilian intrusion into areas where the police had traditionally enjoyed a monopoly of authority and expertise. There were also political considerations. Throughout the 1980s, relationships with the community were under increasing strain in most urban areas, with riots and conflicts over alleged police brutality. A more intrusive police role appeared to exacerbate this still farther. It is perhaps surprising that the hostile attitudes of the Cleveland police were not more widely shared, and that there were not scandals and conflicts of this sort in Leeds, Newcastle, or several other centers.

On the other hand, the police stood to benefit in many ways from the apparent surrender of their professional monopoly. During the 1970s, relations between police and social workers had often been appalling (see the discussion by Punch in Holdaway 1979:102–117). By cooperating with social and medical services, police defused criticism about their unsympathetic attitudes and coopted agencies that had been among their harshest critics (Thomas 1986). By generating numerous arrests and prosecutions, the police focused attention on their successful efforts against "true" criminals who preyed on children.

The emphasis on child protection helped reaffirm the police's ideological position as impartial defenders of the community, an image tarnished since the mid-1970s by unprecedented criticism over corruption, brutality, and repressive political activities (Holdaway, 1979, 1983; Hain et al. 1980; Coulter et al. 1984; Young 1991). Within the Metropolitan Police, the groups that benefited most from the new directions were often departments or agencies that had been most heavily criticized in the 1970s, like C11—Criminal Intelligence—which acted as a focus for Operation Stranger, or the Obscene Publications Squad, which spawned the Child Pornography unit. And in each case, it was a Metropolitan Police unit that effectively acquired ownership of an issue throughout the nation.

The child abuse concerns therefore offered rewards for both police and social workers, though in the latter case the ritual abuse affair exposed a significant contradiction between the ideology of professionalism and theories of ideological commitment. Ideological assumptions demanded a suspension of skepticism in these cases, but the resulting debacle raised public concerns about social workers to a new height. It remains to be seen whether this conflict will have destroyed the gains in status that resulted from the earlier campaigns.

CUI BONO?

The multifaceted panics of the 1980s involved activism and propaganda by a wide range of groups and individuals, some of which benefited greatly while others achieved little. The consequences might be in the form of a reallocation of resources, but several groups profited ideologically. For example, feminists benefited in this way from the cultivation of the successive panics. Emphasizing the threat of sexual violence was a powerful ideological justification for the whole framework of feminist thought. It provided a degree of urgency, by showing that enacting the feminist agenda was not merely a matter of salary or employment opportunities: It was literally a matter of life and death for thousands of women from all social classes.

For religious groups similarly, the scale and immediacy of the diabolical threat offered ideological confirmation of the limitations of liberal theology. Since the 1960s, the dominant factions in British churches had emphasized social and political activism with a left/liberal slant, with racism and apartheid often seen as the world's most pressing evils. For Evangelicals and Charismatics, this was a lethal distraction from the crucial issues of personal holiness and spiritual warfare. During the 1980s, the point was reasserted by the new focus on black magic cults, ancestral demons, and ritual abusers. As with the feminists, countering perceived threats provided a focus for the efforts of activists and community groups.

THE IMPACT ON SOCIAL POLICY

Of course, the degree of benefit that a group received from these events did not necessarily bear any direct relationship to its original role in creating an issue. This is worth emphasizing because one of the major ideological beneficiaries of the movements described here was the Thatcher administration; and not even the most conspiratorially minded could claim a direct government role in the original agitation.

The redefinition of problems like pedophilia and mass child abuse helped serve the social and ideological agenda of the Conservative government that came to power in 1979. In earlier decades, there had been an emphasis on therapeutic and psychiatric solutions to deviance, with a hope that improved economic conditions might remove the underlying causes of violence and family abuse. In the 1980s, there was a redistribution of resources away from health and welfare spending toward the police, and a concurrent shift toward purely moralistic explanations of problems and abuses.

Often, the various claims-makers were unwittingly supporting such a transformation of priorities and were pursuing policies that were self-defeating within this particular political environment. In order to raise concern about a problem, it was useful to typify it in terms of real harm or danger, and thus as a criminal issue. However, doing this implied solutions that were oriented to criminal justice rather than social welfare or economic reform.

One virtue of alleged threats to children is that they make it easy for governments to act as if they are doing something effective, instead of confronting genuine problems. It is easier to express moral outrage than to mobilize social intervention, to treat symptoms rather than causes. As Best (1990:188) comments on the United States, "Public opinion and social policy depend upon how such issues are defined. A society which is mobilized to keep child molesters, kidnappers and satanists away from innocent children is not necessarily prepared to protect children from ignorance, poverty and ill health." In fact, the emphasis on protecting children from moral dangers may actually detract from the struggle for adequate health and welfare provision. This was nicely illustrated by a *Guardian* cartoon that appeared in October 1990, after the government proposed freezing the level of child benefit payments. The cartoon depicted two smirking politicians, one of whom comments, "They'd just spend it on Aleister Crowley books" (October 23, 1990).

The British panics provide many apposite examples of moral panics causing a diversion from underlying economic problems, but one of the best concerns the issue of rent boys. These should be seen as one component of the larger issue of the homeless young, who have attracted so much attention during the last twenty years; and while statistics are controversial, there is no doubt that the scale of homelessness has increased dramatically, above all in the London area. In 1975, the Roger Gleaves case gave rise to journalistic investigations of the scale of the problem, which presumably has its roots in economic crisis and family decay (see Chapter 4, note 1). Critics of Thatcher policies often adduce the young homeless as the dark side of economic progress.

In the 1980s, the issue of rent boys was commonly typified as part of the wider problem of pedophilia rather than poverty (but compare Lloyd 1979). Rent boys were seen as the product of exploitation by evil pedophiles, who initiated them, preyed on them, and—following the example of Jason Swift—ultimately victimized and killed them. Both NCH and NAYPIC stressed the role of abuse in initiating future prostitutes. The problem was thus seen as one of effective policing and moral enforcement, while broader social failings were ignored or exonerated.

This can be observed from the area in which Swift was killed, the London borough of Hackney, said also to be the setting for the secret grave sites used by the notorious pedophile ring. The story is horrendous enough, but eliminating every pedophile in the area would go only a little way to helping the community or striking at the problems of homelessness, poverty, and family breakdown that cause the existence of so large a population of potential victims.

It happens that Hackney is the subject of one of the classic modern case studies of inner-city poverty and multiple deprivation, written by Paul Harrison in 1983, only two years before the Jason Swift murder. The study notes that the borough already had the second highest proportion of overcrowded households in Inner London, the second highest proportion of children in care, the second highest incidence of violent street crime, and a male unemployment rate of 22 percent (compare Cotterill 1988). Hackney had "by far the highest proportion of dwellings unfit for human habitation . . . the highest proportion of registered disabled in London . . . the highest level of smoke pollution" (Harrison 1983: 31). Harrison addresses the problems of children in the borough in a chapter entitled "Growing Up Nasty," which notes features like "the collapse of social control" and "the disintegration of cultural control." Each year, "between 1000 and 1200 families—five or six percent of all families with children—present themselves as statutorily homeless." (p. 183).

It is difficult to imagine any future government devising a policy of social intervention adequate to these challenges, and the Thatcher administration had less sympathy than most for welfare spending in any form. On the other hand, a draconian policy against local criminals and sexual offenders was ideologically acceptable, and could be portrayed as reflecting concern for the area and its young people.

PRESENTING CLAIMS

Social problems must be understood in terms of those attempting to define them, but we must also address the means by which claims are made, the language in which they are framed. Modes of argument and claims-making have been a theme throughout this book, and major themes might be summarized. In order to make and establish a claim about a problem, it is necessary to show several things: First, the problem must be shown to exist in some form. This is not an issue in most of the concerns discussed here, as nobody seriously doubts the occurrence of serial murder or incest, but we will see below that ritual abuse posed significant difficulties in this regard. It must be shown that the problem is widespread, that it is growing worse, and that it causes real harm. Ideally, it should also be something that affects or could affect everyone in the society to some extent (Best 1990:29–32). All these themes are epitomized by Alan Gilmour:

Child abuse can happen in any kind of home, at any time and at any level of society. Every week children die in their own homes at the hands of those responsible for their care. Year by year, we see an increase in the thousands who suffer lesser levels of physical, mental or sexual assault, or neglect. (Gilmour 1988:1)

Statistics and Authority

The issue of prevalence is especially important, as quantification lends an aura of scientific certainty to a subject. In the area of rape, several polls suggested astronomically high rates of sexual victimization, both by strangers and husbands, though these surveys can be criticized for the phrasing of their questions. The most celebrated example of "statistics abuse" was the MORI one-in-ten figure, which was repeatedly cited in a very inaccurate way. The corollary of this interpretation was the equally memorable figure of one million children at risk in contemporary Britain (extrapolated to particular localities, the figures suggested were in the tens of thousands). In addition, it was often believed that the poll showed that abuse involved serious or repeated sexual assault, and moreover that this usually occurred within the family.

Beatrix Campbell's use of this data is noteworthy. She cites the poll to present sexual abuse as "martyrdom *en masse*—the possibility of more than a million little girls and perhaps almost a million little boys too, being sexually exploited in their own families and neighborhoods, by respectable, ordinary men" (Campbell 1987). First, she casually doubles the alleged number of sufferers: one million children have become "a million little girls," to which one must in fairness add the boys. Second, the emphasis has shifted entirely to children being seriously victimized and repeatedly raped within the family. The floating definition of sexual abuse thus offered rich opportunities for claims-makers.

Criticizing the poll (or its popular misinterpretations) came to be seen not solely as a denial of children's sufferings, but a willful neglect of objective science. In1987, the *Daily Mail* attacked the Cleveland investigators for dogmatically acting on"a belief—namely that sex abuse was rampant and that one in ten children at least were victims of it." Campbell responded that the *Mail* thus "dismisses the *only* substantial, random sample survey of child sex abuse in modern Britain" (Campbell 1987: 9). However maltreated, the poll gave real substance to an argument, and it is worth contrasting the acceptance of its figures with the neglect of other quantitative claims that lacked even this support, such as Diane Core's allegations about four thousand human sacrifices.

Claims were supported by authorities, and language again played a role in validating their opinions as opposed to those of their critics. Advocates with whom one agreed would be referred to in terms indicating experience, expertise, objectivity (e.g., as "professional" or "a quiet-spoken Christian"). Opponents are characterized as intemperate, ideologically motivated, or simply incompetent. In Cleveland, for example, Stuart Bell is described as "the histrionic Labour MP" (Campbell 1988b); Marietta Higgs is "controversial." Later on, Robert Simandl becomes "a self-proclaimed expert on ritual child abuse." On a collective scale, opposition that appears widespread or organized can be dismissed with a term such as "hysteria," "witch-hunt," or "moral panic." When a national NSPCC poll showed that over half the adults surveyed believed that children made up fictitious stories about abuse, *Community Care* headlined its report "Survey Shows Up Public Ignorance on Child Abuse" (September 26, 1991).

Another way of disarming opponents or critics was to employ the language of psychology. In a controversial area like child abuse, a person who refused to accept claims could be described as suffering from the psychological problem of denial, an irrational failure to face unpleasant facts. This device was much used against the critics of the Cleveland investigation and later of ritual abuse. As Phil Cohen commented in *Social Work Today*, "as with physical abuse and then sexual abuse, there is the same pattern with ritual and organized abuse—of initial denial and disbelief that it exists. Once that is overcome the overriding need is to draw together data" (Cohen 1990:3). This approach implies a sense of conviction that one is in the right, while critics have not yet advanced to a comparable stage of enlightenment. It can also be argued that the more strenuous the opposition, the more deeply rooted is the taboo that is being upset, and consequently the greater the degree of denial. In this paradoxical view, intense opposition is a proof of correctness almost as convincing as overwhelming public support.

Establishing Harm

The issue of harm was sometimes controversial. In the area of child sexual abuse, medical opinion had traditionally been divided over the degree of real or lasting harm, and there was genuine skepticism about the effects of a sole incident of fondling or exhibitionism. One authoritative text argued in 1978, "A single molestation by a stranger, particularly of a nonviolent kind, appears to do little harm to normal children living with secure and reassuring parents" (Kempe and Kempe 1978: 55).

During the 1980s, such views were regularly denounced as unfeeling and callous, and it became orthodoxy that abuse resulted in lasting damage. This idea was promoted through the use of emotive language and selective definition. *Abuse* was vague in the extreme, and did not necessarily imply serious harm: In older and more reticent dictionaries, for example, masturbation is simply defined as "self-abuse." For many writers, the term *abuse* was often accompanied or replaced by a phrase that indicated more damaging and intrusive sexual behavior, notably "father-daughter rape" (Ward 1984).

The problem was also commonly described by the term *incest*, which was reconceptualized very broadly to include most sexual contact between adults and children. The Incest Survivors Campaign defined incest as "the sexual molestation of a child by any person whom that child sees as a figure of trust or authority—parents, relatives (whether natural or adoptive), family friends, babysitters, youth leaders, social workers, teachers, church officials, priests etc. . . . Incest is the sexual abuse of power." Incest would be taken by the general public as specifically requiring two things: actual intercourse, and sex within the family. By conflating abuse with rape and incest, advocates were promoting the idea that these were the specific manifestations of the abuse suffered by "one in ten" of the population. The term *incest survivors* further suggests the extent of the physical and psychological harm implied (this had its roots in the earlier *rape survivors*).

Other potent words reinforced this theme. In the aftermath of the "Leeds discovery" about the anal dilatation test, supporters of the mass abuse theory often took to using the word *buggery* to describe anal assault upon children. The usage was somewhat exceptional, as the word chiefly survives in indecent slang, and in archaic legislation. By using such a stark and nearly obscene term in this context, the claims-makers were deliberately seeking shock value, in order to suggest the real harm done by an act of violent rape, usually upon a very young victim. Again, Campbell makes frequent use of the term.

Danger and harm could also be emphasized by reference to the organized and conspiratorial nature of the abuse, and the participation of people of high social status. This enhanced still further the helplessness of the children, the innocent victims so often mentioned, and the difficulty of their finding help or protection. Both the mass media and the professional literature commonly used the term *web* or *spider's web* to describe organized abuse and sex rings (for example, Bibby 1991). This was an effective metaphor as it suggested a variety of powerful images, including predation, entrapment, helplessness, and even violent death.

Actions as well as words could present a claim as to the harm caused by a problem, as when surprise dawn raids became the standard means of proceeding against suspected ritual abuse rings. These tactics are well known, but they automatically imply that the targets of the operation present a serious threat, and they are usually felt appropriate for a group such as terrorists or gangsters. The timing is specifically arranged in order to prevent some dire consequence: Either the group will "go underground," organize resistance, or harm witnesses. This impression was reinforced by the presence in large numbers of police in addition to social workers, almost one hundred in the case of the Liverpool raids. The element of harm is actually strengthened by the refusal of official agencies to explain their actions, as this suggests that sensitive and dangerous operations are still in progress. It also encourages the development of rumor in the local community, which speculates freely about the supposed crimes involved in the case. Whatever the intent of those responsible, the raids were a powerful claim in their own right.

Exemplars

A claim can usually be presented most effectively if it is related to a specific individual or known case, with whom the reader or viewer can identify or sympathize. Of course, the example chosen will follow the pattern the writer wishes to emphasize in presenting a particular interpretation of the problem. Exemplars were much used by the NSPCC, whose annual reports provided a miscellany of case studies, each illustrating one aspect of the charity's work. *Illustrated* should be taken literally here, as each story is accompanied by photographs of sad-eyed children.

An instance from the NSPCC's 1989 report: "When seven year old Karen Jones told her teacher that she didn't like her brother Steven playing 'touching games', the NSPCC was contacted immediately and Karen was interviewed in the presence of a policewoman and her teacher." Finding evidence of sexual abuse by the father, both children were removed under a PSO. The story then concludes: "Mr. Jones denied all the allegations and the subsequent prosecution failed for lack of evidence. However, successful care proceedings were taken to protect the children who now live safely with foster parents." The story is intended to show the vigor of the NSPCC, while there is the suggestion that the agency would not allow itself to be thwarted by the failures of the law and its archaic procedures (the court case actually resulted in acquittal, but the children were removed nevertheless).

In controversies like the Cleveland affair, both sides employed "horror tales" as examples to support their cause. Characteristically, one side would describe a small girl systematically abused for years by a brutal father, until rescued by determined pediatricians and social workers. A lengthy study by Campbell begins: "In the grounds of Middlesbrough General Hospital a tear-stained seven year old is galloping around. She's reaching for the sky. And she's laughing. She feels liberated." After therapy, "the child finally spilled out who it was who's been buggering her." (B. Campbell 1989).

In contrast, the majority of press reports used case studies of individual families to present an Orwellian image of the triumph of feminist dogma over reason and common sense. They told of families who took their children to a doctor for a minor complaint, only to have an intimate medical examination surreptitiously performed. Finding alleged evidence of abuse, the doctor would then ruthlessly plunge the family into the bureaucratic morass of false charges and innuendo, until all children were removed to Dickensian homes or hospitals.

The rival approaches are indicated by two of the lengthiest case studies to emerge from Cleveland. The *Sunday Times Magazine* devoted ten thousand words to the case of one family victimized by social services until it was "torn apart in Cleveland." *New Statesman and Society* answered this with an equally substantial account by the mother of a two-year-old girl raped by a relative, and "torn apart at home" (July 1, 1988).

THE PROCESS OF ACCEPTANCE

When a group or individual makes claims about a specific topic, a number of facts will decide whether that will be taken up by a significant section of the mass media and presented as factual. These might be listed as follows:

Newsworthiness

Different newspapers and television programs have very different ideas about what constitutes worthwhile news. A bizarre story of an occult survivor or an alleged confession of human sacrifice might well provide sensational copy for one or two papers for a day or two, but it is unlikely by itself to provide the basis for a sustained campaign. It is rather like accounts of a UFO contact, which are published (and usually recognized) as "fluff," intended for entertainment value rather than news. To become recognized as part of a real problem, the story should ideally feature one or more of a number of elements (Soothill and Walby 1991; Cohen and Young 1973; Hall et al. 1978).

Like great drama, it should evoke an emotional response such as outrage or pity, which is why innocent victims like children or animals feature so regularly. The story should also suggest a phenomenon that appears to be a real threat, which affects or could affect a large number of the readers or viewers of that particular item. It might concern well-known people, perhaps of high social status, in which there is a good deal of established public interest. It might offer excitement or shock value in the form of unusual sexual activity or violence. The exposure of some hitherto clandestine practice is also useful, in that it shows the diligence and courage of that particular news source. The story might similarly expose a particular individual or group ("we name the guilty men"). Ideally, it would also offer a platform for social action ("something must be done"), perhaps indicated by the demands of politicians, police, or bureaucrats.

The Brighton pedophile attack of 1983 illustrates several aspects of this. It involved a shocking and bizarre act of sexual violence, which was frightening in a number of ways. Because it was wholly random, a similar crime might without warning befall the family of any reader. The coverage of the story was interesting in that it appeared to locate readers within the investigation, as every clue and lead were followed. Analytical articles used the affair as a peg on which to hang speculations about the existence of clandestine networks of pedophiles, possibly in high society. And it provided a foundation for action, in the form of improved child protection, suppression of sex rings and child pornography, or general moral reform.

The timing of a news story is also crucial. One is reluctant to trivialize so heinous a crime as the Brighton attack, but one must ask whether media coverage would have been so intense if it had not occurred in the politically quiet dog days of August. At least since the 1930s, the time when Parliament is out of session has been marked by a dearth of serious political news, and the papers have turned to sensationalistic and more outré topics. This "silly season" has frequently been characterized, for example, by new reports of the Loch Ness monster. The intention here is not to compare the child abuse scandals with these fictions, but to note that the heaviest coverage of abuse stories in the 1980s often occurred in July or August: the Brighton case of 1983, the Cleveland affair of 1987, and the alleged snuff/murder ring of 1990.

Brighton was a genuine event, rather than a claim by a specific group, but it indicates the sort of values that should be presented in order to reach the widest audience. This might be compared with the claims that followed the 1985 MORI poll. Most of the media concentrated on the simple one-in-ten figure without further detail, and the story thus suggested a massive and unsuspected threat to innocent children, and not merely in a few poor or remote areas. It offered several possible directions in which action should and must be taken, and numerous comments by politicians and social service agencies indicated that such a movement was indeed beginning.

The NSPCC's statements in 1990 were another example, which permitted even the qualities to present headlines such as the *Telegraph's* "Children Forced to Kill Animals in Satanic Rites" (March 13, 1990). This was a vast problem, which although in the early stages of recognition had already been described by a full one third of the society's child protection teams, and it was so dangerous that the specific teams could not be identified for fear of their lives. It is difficult to imagine a more successful combination of headline-grabbing themes, from sexual perversion and endangered children to homicidal devil worshippers and heroic investigators.

Sources

The source of the claim is also central. Extravagant claims by lone entrepreneurs often find their way into some stories in a few newspapers; but they rarely provide the basis for widespread interest or action. Sources have varying degrees of credibility, depending in part on their social status and position, and their previous track record. This does not necessarily reflect the media's perception of what is believed to be factually accurate, but what can be presented as plausible. Also important in this regard will be any known associations with extreme ideologies or political movements; so that (for example) a claim about black extremists seeking to carry out random murders of whites would presumably be discounted if it derived solely from a known front organization of a fascist party.

Thus the most respectable claims-makers in the 1980s included the NSPCC and the police, while child protection groups like ChildLine soon came to occupy a similar position. Police claims were treated as perhaps the most valuable of all, in that they had a long record of skepticism about extravagant claims concerning cults or sex rings. It was a deadly blow to the ritual abuse charges in Manchester when they were skeptically received by James Anderton, the conservative and Evangelical police chief. Conversely, it was significant when police appeared to take seriously the existence of a serial child killer in 1986 or snuff allegations in 1990.

There were other reasons why the media tended to attach the highest importance to interpretations offered by police. British crime stories are largely defined and publicized through a select group of veteran London-based newspaper reporters who work closely with police, and who constitute what might be described as a crime lobby, on the analogy of a political lobby. The reporters are fed stories, tipoffs, or photographs, and in turn report favorably on police activities, while some reporters aid or ghostwrite the memoirs of retired officers. "To act without this sort of relationship with the police can mean the drying up of information and the freezing out from the day-to-day blood and guts which sells papers" (Campbell 1986: 7). Police and media exist in a symbiotic relationship, in which the newspapers tend to reflect the concerns of the Metropolitan Police elite at any given time.

Also important were moralist campaigners like Mary Whitehouse. Although strongly right-wing in political disposition. Whitehouse had shown over two decades that she represented the views of a large constituency within Britain and had not made outrageously false factual claims. (Her opinions on matters like the influence of media portrayals of violence on behavior are controversial, but well within the range of normal debate.)

Media assessments of sources can change over time. In 1990, for example, the NSPCC achieved wide acceptance of its original statements about ritual abuse. Within a year, the agency was under serious attack on this issue, and it is unlikely that future claims would receive the same welcome. In other cases, the media initially treated claims-makers as plausible, but later surrounded their comments with qualifiers. When they first came to public attention, Maureen Davies and Diane Core were regarded as knowledgeable authorities whose views on menaces to children were treated with respect. In controversies over ChildLine, for example, Diane Core was quoted as an experienced and authoritative charity worker, usually without mention of her distinctive religious beliefs (Seaton 1987). As 1990 progressed, more investigation was undertaken of the religious origins of some of the ritual abuse claims, and Davies and Core were quoted with more circumspection, and their religious positions were made more explicit.

Plausibility

A successful claim also has to be plausible in the sense of being linked to perceptions of known reality. Those perceptions change over time, depending on changes in public attitudes and the developing amount of information available. To take an extreme example, there are a few activists on the British extreme right who maintain that Jews are murdering Christian children in blood sacrifices and that these cases might in some way be linked to the Jack the Ripper murders (see, for example, Campbell 1991c). However, the social and political circumstances of modern Britain make it impossible for such a charge to gain widespread credence,and any mainstream newspaper presenting such a story would rightly suffer harsh consequences: In other words, the claim is recognized as wholly implausible. On the other hand, the boundaries of acceptability might shift. If, for example, a significant antisemitic political movement emerged, and if there were a well publicized case where a Jewish serial killer murdered children, then a "blood libel" could theoretically reemerge. Once published, the story could then evolve as each new telling suggested further variants.

For a claims-maker, it is essential to root a story in accepted reality. To take the example of satanic cults and human sacrifices, the story has existed as a rumor in Britain for decades, accepted by fringe religious groups. Except as sensational fluff, the tale made no headway in the media, because it was too far removed from known patterns of behavior. By 1989, however, there were enough related precedents to permit a reframing of the story in terms acceptable to win widespread acceptance. Religious groups argued for the existence in Britain of satanic groups that abused children. The Nottingham case appeared to prove the reality of one such group, and American accounts told of cults that both abused children and subsequently sacrificed them.

Ritual abuse was ultimately authenticated by placing it within the known framework of organized abuse, an example of what Hall *et al.* (1978) describe as "convergence" (see Chapter 1). In *Social Work Today*, for example, an article entitled "Networks of Fear" argued "organized sexual abuse of children—in sex rings and satanic cults—exists in various parts of the country" (October 26, 1989). The story thus begins with a known phenomenon, the pedophile ring (proven in several recent trials), and almost in the same breath mentions what had hitherto been rejected as an extravagant fiction. The remainder of the article was predominantly concerned with the satanic aspects of organized abuse.

This effective rhetorical device was widely followed in early reporting on ritual abuse, where there was so clear a need to defuse incredulity. In the *Sunday Times*, for instance, a lengthy story in 1990 studied "Elizabeth . . . the reality behind the newspaper headlines and warnings from the child protection agencies that young children are more at risk than ever from gangs of paedophiles" (*Sunday Times*, April 1, 1990). Once again, the reference here appears to address sex rings, but later in the paragraph, we learn that the abuse derived from "a satanic ring." A large cartoon on the same page depicted blank-faced children following a satanic pied piper, armed with horns and pentacle, into a dungeon. The bulk of the article focuses on the satanic threat, with comments from Maureen Davies, but then returns at the end to "secular" dangers, in this case the alleged threat from pedophiles disguised as social workers.

Panics thus build upon each other, and a claim must be timely in order to be effective. Made without the necessary support, it will fall unnoticed. It is unlikely that the ritual abuse idea would have attained any credence whatever if not for the earlier "discovery" of mass incest, while acceptance of sexual abuse would have been impossible without the prior debate over battering.

Snuff provides a telling example. In 1977, the British media reported heavily on the issue of child pornography, and there were also numerous reports about the American phenomenon of snuff movies. However, not even the most vigorous activist suggested that such movies were or could be made in Britain, because this was too far outside known reality. It suggested a degree of organization and homicidal intent far from anything suggested of British pedophiles (the Moors murders precedent was not noted or recalled). As with ritual abuse, snuff claims could only be made plausibly when an adequate foundation had been laid in other panics. This required several stages in public awareness: acceptance of, respectively, multiple child murder, pedophile rings, and pedophile murder rings.

Established Stereotypes

Hall et al. emphasize the role of the media in placing events in a context that will be familiar to the assumed audience:

> If the world is not to be represented as a jumble of random and chaotic events, then they must be identified (i.e., named, defined, related to other events known to the audience), and assigned to a social context (i.e., placed within a frame of meanings familiar to the audience). This process—identification and contextualization—is one of the most important through which events are "made to mean" by the media. (Hall et al. 1978:54)

Often this process involves the use of existing stereotypes of folk-devils, which provide a ready-made context into which the new facts can be fitted. These images may be based on a specific individual, or in some cases they arose as composite figures during previous panics. In either case, the power and resonance of a story will be augmented by the degree to which it is assimilated to an existing stereotype.

Cohen (1972:28) remarked that while some panics affect public policy, others are "forgotten except in folklore and collective memory," but this collective memory can surface with little provocation. Memories of the real phenomenon of the Moors murders did much to shape attitudes to the child murder threat of the 1980s, but other enduring stereotypes were also drawn on repeatedly. When the press wished to attack the social workers in the ritual abuse affair, they did little more than reproduce stories and themes first elaborated a decade earlier, and subsequently recycled through the Beckford and Cleveland controversies (Franklin and Parton 1991). Only the names and places had changed.

Other successful panics drew on existing stereotypes of threatening foreigners, an idea that gained force as issues like European unity and the Channel Tunnel occupied so central a role in political debate. This theme was cited in the debates over ritual abuse, pedophile rings, serial murder, and (most extensively) child pornography. Xenophobia also played a part in the counterattack against child abuse in general and ritual abuse in particular, in that critics of the respective panics denounced the ideas as American importations. The demon figures of the Beckford and Cleveland cases both included prominent foreigners, respectively Gun Wahlstrom and Marietta Higgs.

This counterattack over ritual abuse raises an issue that has not been extensively addressed in the literature on constructionism, the means by which a panic can be defeated or derailed (though see Best 1990:48–50). It is certainly possible to expose the creators of a panic by detailed investigative journalism that reveals their ideological agenda, or attacks their misuse of statistics or evidence. The debunking of ritual abuse in the *Mail* and *Independent* are notable examples here.

On the other hand, one lesson of this affair appears to be that a panic is most effectively destroyed by counterattack, by generating a new panic that focuses on the original claims-makers. By this standard, the attack on social workers in 1990 and 1991 was a model movement, all the more effective for its relationship to established stereotypes. This even drew on the "loony left" tradition, by exposing the homosexual conviction of a Labour councillor and preacher prominent in the Rochdale case (the *Star* headlined "Sex Secret of Satan Hunt Rev," November 13, 1990).

JUST THE FACTS: ASSESSING CLAIMS

A claim thus had to be plausible in the sense of believable within the current context of established ideas: Of course, this does not necessarily imply that it was based on fact. Panics are diverse phenomena, which differ in the degree to which they reflect objective reality. In some, like serial murder, there is an unquestionable core of real phenomena, in that such crimes may account for perhaps perhaps 1 or 2 percent of

British homicides annually. It is thus depicted as a more serious problem than it actually is. The evidence of courtroom convictions would also seem to validate the existence of quite sizable and complex pedophile rings, and perhaps a handful of murders during the decade can plausibly be associated with this activity.

By contrast, other panics appear to have had no substance whatever, in so far as it is possible to prove a negative. During 1990, the three main panics concerning children involved, respectively, allegations of widespread ritual or satanic child abuse in half a dozen regions, bogus social workers attempting to molest or abduct children, and snuff films made by pedophile murder gangs. At the time of writing, all seem to be false, in that no evidence has been produced to affirm the existence of ritual abuse, the bogus social workers, or a snuff video (though none of these is theoretically impossible).

It is interesting that all three ideas emerged after years of scares based on more substantial evidence, such as the child murders affair of 1986. Perhaps the cumulative, dynamic nature of problem building is significant here. Such wholly fictitious panics are more likely to be found in the later stages of a perceived crisis, when the public and law enforcement agencies have already come to accept the broad outlines of a problem, and are prepared to accept the more elaborate and tendentious views derived from popular folklore, or from the more extreme claims-makers. Studying the construction of social problems must take account of the evolutionary processes at work.

The American Dimension

— 10 —

The British events and conditions noted here were superficially very similar to many of those identified by contemporary American researchers in the area of social problems. In the last two decades, the United States too has experienced scares about child abuse and abduction, serial murder, satanism, and ritual abuse, in addition to social menaces as diverse as drug abuse and explicit sex and violence in rock and roll music. There are obvious parallels between British problems and American incidents such as the Jordan or McMartin child abuse cases, or the satanism scare (Best 1990; Richardson et al. 1991).

Imitation certainly played a role here. American media and experts did much to form British perceptions of menaces like child abuse, serial murder, snuff films, pedophiles, and ritual abuse. In each case, the term itself was either an American importation or else was decisively influenced by American usage: part of what has been called "the export-import trade in social labels" (Hall et al. 1978:27). It sometimes seems as if a new American vogue will almost inevitably be copied in Britain within a few months or years.

The literature on American social problems rarely pays heed to foreign influences, usually because the phenomenon does not exist or is of minimal importance. Researchers in other countries must, however, take account of this dimension, if only to rebut the simple view that problems are a direct imitation of American concerns, disseminated by way of U.S. cultural and political hegemony. The remarks made here about Britain apply with equal force to most advanced English-speaking countries, especially Canada and Australia, both of which have been strongly influenced by American concerns about issues like sexual violence and child abuse (compare *Report on Child Witnesses* 1991).[1]

This chapter examines the similarities and contrasts between British and American conditions, noting the means by which American influences were mediated and the factors permitting reproduction of the original experience. We must ask whether similarities resulted from imitation or whether factors of parallel social and cultural development might play a role. Finally, we will note the rather different outcomes that cases had in the British environment, suggesting the ways in which influences of undoubted force might be limited or modified in a different political context.

AMERICAN INFLUENCES

The power of American social influences is perhaps natural in view of the hegemony of American mass media and consumer culture. Music idols like Madonna and Vanilla Ice are perhaps as popular in Britain as in the United States, and new fashions like disco or rap music very quickly find British imitators (Marwick 1991). American politicians and claims-makers visit Britain in quest of new "markets," i.e., new bases of support and publicity. From the late 1980s, for example, Britain was successively visited by Black activists Jesse Jackson and Al Sharpton, and the pressure groups Guardian Angels and Operation Rescue (the radical prolife movement). All created controversy in their respective ways, and the latter two attempted to establish British chapters.

One of the more surprising illustrations of the extent of Americanization is the infiltration of popular vulgarisms and expletives, which are so deeply based in any culture. Prior to 1980, for example, a common and old-established insult was the V-sign, the waving of two fingers in a gesture that signified "fuck off." Since that time, this has been all but replaced by the American use of the middle finger. Sex crime units with British police forces are sometimes dismissively termed "pussy squads," employing a sexual usage that was rare in Britain before the 1980s. If we consider a comparative list of British and American slang from the 1950s or 1960s, we will be struck by the almost total replacement of the British words by what were then regarded as Americanisms. Even customs like Halloween were adopted during the 1980s [and the practice also brought with it familiar American legends of Halloween sadism (*Times*, October 24, 1986)]

In terms of the construction of social problems, American influences are mediated through both high channels (official and professional contacts) and low channels (the mass media and popular culture). These influences permeate the "public arenas in which social problems are framed and grow" (Best 1990:16). Among low channels, all major news sources maintain American correspondents and receive American wire services, so that British newspapers report on all sorts of sensational U.S. stories. In 1977, for example, British media reported on alleged

American snuff films; in 1986, the papers reproduced American allegations that teenage satanist rings were responsible for instances of human sacrifice; in 1989, the Matamoros drug sacrifice ring attained wide coverage.

Originally, these items might simply be cited as something bizarre and outlandish, but they expand public awareness of events that are believed to be possible and can thus lay a foundation for future claims about social threats within Great Britain. They can also create an expectation that certain events will occur in Britain or, if they do, what form they will take. Since the late 1980s, for example, British media and law enforcement have moved quickly on any suggestion that the cocaine derivative crack might be making a major impact in Britain, to create a crack crisis like that discussed in the United States. Despite the attention, the British crack problem currently appears to be minuscule.

Low channels also include popular culture. Mass market novels and magazines in Britain are often American, as is much of the content of television and the cinema (Marwick 1991). Authors like Stephen King, Peter Straub, and Jonathan Kellerman are all well known, as are films like *The Exorcist, The Believers, Silence of the Lambs, Dances with Wolves, The Evil Dead*—in short, any major Hollywood production—as well as many TV movies and drama series.

The traffic is by no means one-way, and British writers or filmmakers are often successful in the United States. Images of diabolism, serial homicide, or threats to children are much covered in the work of British fantasy-horror writers like Clive Barker, James Herbert, and Ramsey Campbell, all best-sellers in the United States. But all to some degree work within a "midatlantic" context, in part through commercial considerations, and all to varying degrees take account of American concerns and interests. British popular films and television drama are increasingly likely to be the outcome of international cooperative effort, perhaps produced in conjunction with European, U.S., and Australian financing. Accordingly they, too, have to consider the tastes of the international market.

In rock music also, there is a similar pattern of exchange and cross-fertilization. Occult ideas within rock were pioneered by British groups like Black Sabbath and Led Zeppelin, which were then imitated by the American groups, which came to be known as "heavy metal." In turn, this music became popular in Britain, where it serves to disseminate ideas about satanism and to attract moralist wrath.

HIGH CHANNELS

However, there are also high channels. When an issue or problem is identified in Britain, officials and experts tend to interpret it through the literature available in books and specialist journals, which may well be dominated by American research and writing. There is no language barrier, and often the publications are marketed in both countries by multinational conglomerates like Springer or Pergamon. In consequence, and almost unconsciously, the American experience frequently comes to be regarded as normative.

American dominance is especially marked in areas such as criminology, criminal justice, or individual and family development, where recognition as an academic discipline came much earlier in the United States than in Britain. In all these areas, it is common to find a published British case study buttressed by abundant references to the theoretical work of American authorities. Inevitably, this does much to shape the academic agenda of British researchers, and the questions they seek to ask. High channels may include professional journals, in addition to academic conferences and seminars, and the personal visits of researchers or officials to the other country, perhaps as formal delegations or individual sabbaticals. Personal links are facilitated by the presence of many thousands of Americans residing in Britain, and vice versa. Within Britain, Americans constitute one of the largest (if least noticed) immigrant communities.

The moral panics studied here offer many examples of these influences. When child abuse was at issue, the most prestigious figures were Americans like David Finkelhor, Ann Burgess, and Lucy Berliner. American "emissaries" were a powerful influence on the Leeds pediatricians working on reflex anal dilatation; and the whole ritual abuse controversy revolved around the work of American theorists like Simandl and Gallant. American moral entrepreneurs might take the initiative in visiting Britain, but it more often appears that they are invited by like-minded groups to provide the benefit of their expertise. Certain organizations in particular have acted as conduits for American influence over many years, most strikingly the NSPCC, through its decades-long association with Henry Kempe (the name Denver House symbolizes this link).

The police have also been extremely receptive, and due to the nature of intergovernmental contacts, inevitably they have been in the closest contact with federal law enforcement agencies in the United States, above all the FBI. British police have often adopted American terminology and methods over the decades, so that there are now British parallels to VICAP, as well as to recording practices like the Uniform

Crime Reports and the victimization data of the National Crime Survey. Within the last decade, some British police have even started referring to the crime of "auto theft," though *automobile* otherwise remains a purely American usage. It is not surprising that American practices and definitions have shaped official British responses to issues like organized crime, narcotics, serial murder, child pornography, and pedophile rings. In the case of serial murder, British law enforcement agencies and media borrowed the American interpretation of the problem more or less intact, even though this involved a great departure from local precedents (Deer 1986).

Other institutional channels are provided by the religious or political movements that were influenced in their formation by American models and that have since drawn heavily on transatlantic resources. Evangelical and fundamentalist movements were discussed in Chapter 7. These owe their recent success in large measure to the Billy Graham crusades of the 1960s and afterwards, while British Christian bookstores offer literally hundreds of American book titles and albums. Publishers like Word and Kingsway reprint the titles of American counterparts like Huntington House, sometimes with a new introduction by a British religious figure like Kevin Logan (Miller 1990). Popular American authors like Josh McDowell and Frank Peretti find a substantial market in these British fundamentalist circles, and Christian radio stations carry the syndicated shows of James Dobson and Mike Warnke. American speakers, activists, and preachers are naturally sought after for conferences and revival meetings and are well received.

Many of the same points also emerge from the British feminist movement, which modeled its network of Rape Crisis Centers and Women's Aid on American precedents of the early 1970s. Here too, American theorists and speakers are popular, and American research and theory plays an important role in shaping debate. British magazines like *Trouble and Strife* carry advertisments for radical U.S. counterparts like *Hag Rag, Off Our Backs*, and the lesbian *Sinister Wisdom*. In the homosexual movement, American influences are suggested by the British use of the name *Stonewall* for a group and a newspaper.

OBSTACLES

Claims can originate in the United States and easily find their way to Britain. On the other hand, the chance that a given problem will be perceived in a similar way in Britain will depend on a number of factors, and the process is by no means one of simple absorption. One key obstacle is xenophobia, and the continuing power of anti-Americanism. Britain has long demonstrated an ambiguous attitude to America and its culture, and the admiration is tempered by fears of being "swamped" by this alien presence.

Hostility perhaps reached a height during the early and mid-1980s with the controversies over NATO nuclear weapons in Europe, and charges of American militarism and extremism. These themes appeared to be personified by Ronald Reagan, who was deeply unpopular among large sections of British opinion, by no means all on the radical left. British opinion polls regularly asked respondents how much confidence they had in the U.S. government's ability to deal wisely with world problems. The proportion expressing very little or no confidence was about one quarter through the late 1970s, but rose to almost one half of those questioned by 1984 (Heald and Wybrow 1986:187). Throughout the 1980s, a savage caricature of Reagan was one of the most popular features of the successful British television comedy show, "Spitting Image."

There is a continuing hostile stereotype of the United States and its population, which includes elements such as a lack of political sophistication and an obsession with communism, broadly construed to include much left and liberal thought; gullibility; excessive and unhealthy religiosity; extreme violence; and gross commercial materialism. There is a sense that American trends will inevitably find their way to Britain, but the influence is not always desirable. In the debates over rising violence in the early 1970s, the fear of "ending up like America" was frequently expressed: "Britain seems to be edging too close for comfort to the American pattern of urban violence" (quoted by Hall et al. 1978:26). In a more recent study of serial murder, a British police officer was quoted as saying, "We are about fifteen years behind America in all sorts of things, like drugs and race riots, and now we are getting this" (Deer 1986).

Anti-Americanism provides a ready and powerful basis on which one could oppose a particular idea. The *Times* commented damningly that "The spectre of ritual abuse stems from America," while the *Daily Mail* found the origins of ritual abuse in "the fevered atmosphere of American evangelical revivalism." These were evocative statements, likely in themselves to mobilize opposition to the theory. Denouncing a panic as American in origin might therefore carry connotations of gullible fanaticism and witch-hunting, and it is significant that so much literature on the Cleveland crisis discussed whether it could appropriately be described as a "Salem witch-hunt." In reality, witch persecutions claimed many more victims in Britain than in the American colonies, but memories of McCarthyism and Arthur Miller's play *The Crucible* had unfairly tended to give such actions a peculiarly American flavor. In the *Mail on Sunday*, a cartoon depicted two American tourists watching the familiar British folk custom of morris dancing. The Americans are readily identifiable by their "NY" baseball caps: the man is saying "Don't watch, Mary-Lou. I think it's one of their damn ritual sex things" (April 7, 1991).

The example of ritual abuse reminds us that despite apparent resemblances, there remain critical differences between the two societies. We are after all comparing the most religious society in the advanced world with one of the least. It is ironic that America had traditionally been so much more concerned with the threat of satanism, when far more authentic satanist believers and practitioners existed in Britain, and many more crimes could plausibly be associated with their beliefs. The British attitude was less sympathetic to concepts of religious crime, if only because of greater skepticism that satanists could really do any significant material harm. In popular music, similarly, there have long been attempts in Britain to ban records for reasons of obscenity, violence, or sedition, but only the most extreme religious groups attempted to regulate occult, pagan, or outright satanic lyrics.

PARALLEL DEVELOPMENTS

This example suggests that American concerns would be accepted and "naturalized" in Britain only if they struck a chord among a significant sector of British society. In most cases, there had to be some British interest group already organized over a particular issue (such as child pornography) before it sought out an American "expert" to shape its campaign. The American influence might be found in the rhetoric and emphases of a British movement, but it could rarely initiate them altogether. For example, domestic social and political trends in the 1970s would have stimulated a movement demanding greater rights for women and more recognition of their distinctive social interests. The role of the already existing American feminism was to provide theoretical and tactical concepts, and perhaps a range of examples and concerns which affected the emphases of the British movement; but it did not create it.

To take a more extreme example, there was great controversy in 1991 about Al Sharpton's visit to Britain to address sections of the black community. In the weeks following his speeches, there was said to be an upsurge of racial tension and some incidents of violence. Even if the visit did cause a deterioration of race relations, there is no question that the underlying feelings of resentment and hostility long predated Sharpton's arrival, and arose from British circumstances and events.

Parallels between British and American movements can be seen in part as common responses to similar underlying social and economic trends, which have affected the entire Western world to differing degrees. One example might be the concern over pedophilia, which became so prominent in both countries about 1977 and which entered debates about censorship, homosexual rights, and sex education in schools. Certainly, there was American influence, suggested by the appearance of Judianne Densen-Gerber speaking in Britain on the hazards of child pornography. On the other hand, the underlying issues had common origins in the previous decade.

During the 1960s, demographic and economic trends encouraged the emergence in most Western countries of idealist movements mainly composed of young people, with wide-ranging agendas for social reform. The inclusion of sexual liberation among these demands was in part a natural consequence of new reproductive technologies. In several countries, these ideas moved toward an emphasis on gender politics, on feminism, and on the promotion of homosexual equality and rights. Activists might have found a political voice in a new organization, like the German Green party, but others adhered to an established reformist party, such as the Democrats in the United States, Labour in Britain, or the Communists and Radicals in Italy.

However, these libertarian ideas conflicted significantly with traditional moralist perceptions about sexuality and the family, and there was especially opposition to gay rights issues. This provided a platform for conservative political activists, who could use the link with homosexuality as a smear against their partisan opponents and liberalism in general. In Britain and the United States, attacking homosexuals directly was less effective than suggesting the dangers that they posed to children, and thus the issue of pedophilia became prominent. The North American Man-Boy Love Association (NAMBLA, founded in 1979) proved as effective a propaganda weapon in the United States as PIE was in Great Britain (Jeffreys 1990:189–206).

In the United States, the pedophile theme played a role in celebrated gay rights referendums in Florida, California, and other states in 1977 and 1978, and in Texas a few years later. (A typical slogan suggested, "Homosexuals aren't born—they recruit.") In Britain, the issue became a mainstay of the attack on the radical Greater London Council, and on Labour in general. Pedophilia was central to antigay rhetoric until the mid-1980s, when it was largely replaced by the still more effective terror weapon of AIDS. In the two countries, the rhetoric was similar because activists were responding to parallel, but ultimately unconnected developments. Even the chronology was likely to be generally similar, as a common outcome of like events.

THE POLITICAL DIMENSION

American ideas and claims had to be acceptable in the local context before they could be accepted, but even if this occurred, there was no guarantee that the newly identified problem would be treated in the same fashion as in the United States, or that a panic would follow anything like the same course. Panics of the sort discussed in this book were usually felt to require a policy response in terms of legislation, policing, and prosecution; and in every detail, the British system is structured in fundamentally different ways.

The area of policing is suggestive here. British police forces are far more centralized than those of the United States: A "large" American department might have twenty-five to fifty members, while the average British force outside London has over two thousand officers. There are only fifty-two forces in the whole United Kingdom, forty-four of which are found in England; and the Home Office exercises a significant role in coordination through a centralized inspectorate. One consequence of this is the promotion of homogeneity in outlook and policy. Of course, an individual police chief can impose his personal views, from interventionist moralism to liberal community-oriented policies, but any action or policy perceived as grossly deviant will soon be sanctioned and prevented. In addition, the national character of the British media means that no incident can remain purely local for any period of time.

In contrast, decentralized American policing permits much greater room for local entrepreneurial activities that might appear eccentric or even dangerous to agencies elsewhere in the country. This is suggested by the recent example of concern over satanic crimes. Individual officers in several departments became convinced that there was a danger, and sought to respond by disseminating information and undertaking investigations. Individual officers and chiefs became embroiled in notorious incidents where extravagant claims were made about the scale of the satanic danger, and even when these were not substantiated, the ideas lingered in the mythology of anticult groups (Hicks 1991; Richardson et al. 1991). Speculation and extravagant quantitative claims were encouraged by the rival statements of competing agencies with overlapping jurisdiction.

Such local activities—and frequent interjurisdictional conflicts— would be inconceivable in a British context. British police forces tend to be conservative about accepting highly speculative claims and to play a conservative role in moderating the claims of other groups such as doctors or social workers.

Differences in electoral structure and party politics are also significant. There are far fewer electoral offices in Britain, a unitary state that lacks the numerous state positions of the United States. Together with the more homogeneous and centralized structure of the parties, it is more difficult for a claims-maker or entrepreneur to use notoriety as a basis for seeking political office. This is suggested by the fact that even Mary Whitehouse never sought election, despite her high public visibility.

Nor does Britain have elected positions in the judiciary or law enforcement, so that judges, prosecutors, and police officers all tend to be professionals without the aspiration of moving into legislative careers. Many members of Parliament are barristers, or courtroom advocates, and some have undertaken important prosecutions, but until 1986 the decision to prosecute in most cases rested with the police, and thereafter with a government agency, the Crown Prosecution Service (Rozenberg 1988). There are no British parallels to the common American phenomenon of the crusading district attorney who proceeds to electoral office on the basis of a highly visible investigation into corruption or racketeering. As in the case of the police, Britain therefore lacks another significant avenue for official entrepreneurship. Responsibility to the central government and the Home Office discourages local heterodoxy.

COMPARING MASS ABUSE CASES

These differences can be illustrated by comparing the experience of British mass abuse cases like Cleveland and Nottingham with the McMartin and Jordan affairs in the United States. In the latter, activist district attorneys played a crucial role in keeping the cases alive, and in promoting the image of a serious and extensive conspiracy. Charges of bizarre rituals surfaced from therapists' interviews with children and were widely publicized by the prosecution and large sectors of the media. Once the cases were launched, their direction was affected by the powerful electoral pressures on the respective prosecutors. In the Jordan case, only after several prosecutions and long and intense public controversy was the state of Minnesota induced to step in to control the investigation.

In Britain, by contrast, the social workers and doctors who initiated the Cleveland investigation soon found themselves confronted with a skeptical police, who could not be dragooned by a powerful prosecutor with an electorate to consider or a governorship in prospect. Judges also served as a moderating force, and were soon returning seized children to their families. Moreover, the affair swiftly gained national prominence, calling a halt to the affair, and requiring a public inquiry.

The Nottingham case is also suggestive. Therapists and social workers cooperated closely with police in the original investigation of a genuine conspiracy. When, however, some social workers began making claims of ritual activity, the police took the lead in combating these ideas, and the prosecution "filtered them out" of the case. The media tended to give respectful attention to police counterclaims, which thus limited speculation.

Another contrast is that the American judicial process takes much longer from the time of arrest to sentencing, though the McMartin cases were unusual in lasting nearly seven years. In Britain, with fewer procedural niceties, even a major and controversial case like the Yorkshire Ripper prosecution only took a matter of a few weeks. Meanwhile, British newspapers are limited in their comments by strict laws about matters sub judice, and draconian libel restrictions. Unless an individual has been convicted or is named under parliamentary privilege, it becomes a matter of real danger to name him or to attribute criminal actions to him; so strict limits are set to investigative journalism. American media are far freer to comment and to postulate crimes and conspiracies not suggested in the actual charges, and they have more time in which to do it. If the Nottingham case had occurred in the United States, it would probably have been portrayed as a far bigger and more authentically satanic incident than even McMartin.

There are also professional differences at work. In Britain, professional groups like lawyers, psychiatrists, and psychologists are much smaller than in the United States. Allowing for population differences, Britain has less than one quarter as many lawyers as the United States. The mental health professions are also smaller, and they possess less status and visibility than their American counterparts. There are also real differences of substance. British psychiatry lacks the essentially Freudian foundations of the American profession, and there is less acceptance of symbolic and psychodynamic approaches to behavior. In the courts, this is indicated by the skepticism about the play therapy and anatomically correct dolls employed by Arnon Bentovim.

Unlike those in America, fewer British trials involve testimony by batteries of psychiatric expert witnesses, and in general, British courts, police, and lawyers are fare less likely to sympathize with what appear to be speculative claims by therapists and psychiatrists. This is suggested by the Yorkshire Ripper case, where both prosecution and defense essentially agreed on a finding of insanity, based on Sutcliffe's paranoid schizophrenia; but even in so egregious a case, the judge ordered that Sutcliffe be found fit to plead, and a guilty verdict ensued (Burn 1984). It remains to be seen how these attitudes will be affected by the changes in child testimony laws in the last few years.

Complaints about the Americanization of British life and culture have been frequent for much of this century, but the extent of cultural penetration has accelerated in the last ten to twenty years. These changes have been assisted by the movement of British society away from traditional patterns of class polarization, in the direction of a pluralist multiethnic community. A society with an ever stronger resemblance to the United States is thus increasingly exposed to American influences, and it is certain that American perceptions of problems will continue to affect Britain, as well as other advanced European nations. The experience of Britain during the last decade indicates that panics will become even more international and cross-cultural in nature, though they will be adapted to the local environment. For researchers in social problems, comparative study therefore becomes an urgent necessity.

NOTE

1.   The discovery of child sexual abuse in Australia bears a particularly close resemblance to events in contemporary Britain. In 1984, the Women Against Incest movement persuaded the New South Wales government to make one of its major priorities a crusade against child abuse (Roberts 1988a). A Child Protection Council was established, new resources were provided to social service departments, and strict mandatory reporting laws were passed. A major public information campaign was also undertaken. Reported cases of sexual abuse rose from sixty-three in 1980 to four thousand in 1985. American formulations of a serial murder problem were likewise spreading rapidly at the end of the decade.

Conclusion

The Next Menace?

— 11 —

Any attempt at explaining the wave of related panics in modern Britain must take account of a wide range of factors, political and economic no less than social and cultural, and this very complexity makes it exceedingly difficult to predict the future course of problem construction. For example, in the last fifteen years or so there appears to have been a decisive shift in the focus of perceived problems in the direction of threats to women and children, often in the family context. Does this reflect circumstances peculiar to the late 1970s and 1980s, or may we assume that this represents a lasting trend?

Perhaps the ritual abuse case provides the most telling instance of the difficulties that can be encountered in any such predictive endeavor. A social scientist in the mid-1980s would have noted both the intensity of concern about child abuse and the simultaneous growth of antisatanism among certain religious groups. The hypothetical researcher might also have noted the appearance of the ritual abuse concept in the United States, and speculated that these ideas might penetrate the United Kingdom at some point. However, the ritual abuse panic that did arise also appears to have owed much to the exchange of ideas and materials among a tiny handful of well-placed activists. This suggests that the essential context of a problem is defined by broad social trends, but the specific manifestation and impact of that issue can in large measure be determined by a relatively small number of activists, either acting in small groups and even as individuals.

With this caveat in mind, certain tentative statements can be made about the problems that may be encountered in Great Britain in the near future. First, the social trends of the last decade are unlikely to be reversed, in the sense that traditional nuclear family roles appear damaged beyond repair. This makes it probable that the focus on women and children as victims will endure, even if the emphasis moves

231

away from the sexual threat. Also, the perception of soaring crime rates makes it likely that violence, broadly defined, will play a central role in public concerns.

One specific type of violence is certain to increase, at least according to official statistics. In 1990, the Home Office became aware of growing concern about the threat of domestic violence and wife-beating: in response, it issued a circular calling on police forces to establish specialized domestic violence units, and urged that the reporting rates be improved for this type of crime. The Home Office minister announcing the reforms recognized that they would automatically lead to sharp increases in recorded violence, but hoped that the public would not be deceived into misunderstanding this as an actual growth of the criminal behavior itself. Recent precedents suggest that his hopes will prove optimistic, and the battering issue seems likely to reach crisis proportions within a few years.

The general themes of recent problems—sexual violence and "male predators"—have attracted so much attention that they are likely to continue at least for several years to come, either in the form that we have already encountered or else in some closely related manifestation. This is especially true when there now exist significant bureaucratic and political bodies with a vested interest in topics such as child protection. There is also an academic industry of some magnitude working in these areas, and momentous statistics are likely to be generated and widely reported. In a sense, these issues have acquired an impressive social momentum. The precise form of the next "menace" cannot be predicted, as much would depend on the circumstances of a particular case; and it has already been remarked that a case involving child abuse might lead to very different definitions of a social threat. Depending on the circumstances, the media might either choose to make a massive denunciation of an abuse threat, or else depict an attack on the family by radical social workers. In either case, the "believe the children" ideology is now so firmly established that it will continue to play a crucial role in future controversies.

But future crises might well involve perceived victims other than to children. We might hypothesize that emerging demographic trends will have a significant impact on the conceptualization of problems, and prominent among these is the aging of the British population. The social service literature has already begun to present occasional accounts of the problem of "elder abuse" (the phrase represents yet another American importation). Related themes that might be addressed include "medical murderers," homicidal nurses, and abuses within nursing homes or geriatric hospitals. As an arena of so much ethical and political conflict, it is also possible that the euthanasia issue would provide the basis for a perceived crisis or panic.

It is also likely that British problems will draw heavily on American models, *if* those images strike a resonance within local conditions. As a general rule, we might speculate that current U.S. concerns will become major issues in Europe within a year or two, and this will almost certainly include issues such as sexual harassment. The continuing American interest in multiple homicide is also powerfully reflected in the mass media, and this will continue to reinforce the concept in other countries.

One interesting example concerns the image of the satanic serial killer or sacrificial ring, and there is a growing American literature on "cult killers" (see, for example, Mandelsberg 1991; Linedecker 1990; Raschke 1990; Kahaner 1988). We might easily imagine that this stereotype will gain credence in Britain, where it would draw on the powerful memories of several of the problems described above, especially the pedophile murder ring and the whole concept of ritual abuse and sacrifice. The sensationalist appeal to the media will be apparent. Once established with one potential case, the notion would presumably find advocates among groups whose interests it appeared to reflect, especially in feminist and religious circles.

It is also reasonable to expect that xenophobia will continue to play a role in future problem formulation. While nonwhite immigration has faded as an issue, issues of European unification and national sovereignty continue to stand at the center of political debate. Anxiety over national identity and the assertion of national frontiers may well be reflected in issues involving international or cross-national threats, perhaps involving violent or organized criminality emanating from Western Europe. Meanwhile, concern about Americanization is unlikely to diminish.

The themes suggested here are exemplified by a media panic over "killer dogs" in 1991, which denounced the public danger caused by the proliferation of fighting breeds such as Rottweilers or pitbulls. The debate had an anti-American subtext, in that the dogs were generally American-bred animals that had been acquired to defend the owners against rising crime. As in Hall's classic study of mugging, the essential danger was that growing violence was "turning London into New York." In addition, the victims of the much-publicized dog attacks came from all age groups, but almost all the rhetoric of the activism by media and politicians focused on the specific danger to children.

In summary, the panics of the 1980s appear to have established general patterns that will probably be reproduced in British problems over the next decade or so, though no more precise predictions can or should be attempted. It is fair to assume that child protection will remain a central concern of public debate, though with the greatest threats seen as arising from sexual violence and exploitation rather than economic or educational failings. The cast of perceived victims will probably remain more or less constant though, as Best remarks, "whether the most significant issues come to the fore is another question" (Best 1990:188).

References

Ackroyd, Carol, Karen Margolis, Jonathan Rosenhead, and Tim Shallice (1980). *The Technology of Political Control*, 2nd ed. London: Pluto.

Adler, Zsuzsanna (1987). *Rape on Trial*. London: Routledge and Kegan Paul.

Alderson, Andrew, John Furbisher, and Jasper Gerard (1991). "Killing of Women Soars Towards Ten Year Record." *Sunday Times*, September 29.

Allen, A., and A. Morton (1961). *This Is Your Child: The Story of the NSPCC*. London: Routledge and Kegan Paul.

Armstrong, Louise (1991). "Surviving the Incest Industry." *Trouble and Strife* 21:29–32.

Ashworth, Georgina, and Lucy Bonnerjea (1985). *The Invisible Decade: UK Women and the UN Decade 1976–1985*. Aldershot: Gower.

Aubrey, Crispin (1981). *Who's Watching You?* London: Penguin.

BSSRS (1985). *TechnoCop*. London: Free Association Books.

Baher, Edwina, C. Hyman, C. Jones, R. Jones, A Kerr, and R. Mitchell (1976). *At Risk: An Account of the Work of the Battered Child Research Department, NSPCC*. London: Routledge and Kegan Paul.

Bainbridge, William Sims (1978). *Satan's Power: A Deviant Psychotherapy Cult*. Berkeley: University of California Press.

Baker, Anthony W., and Sylvia P. Duncan (1985). "Child Sexual Abuse: A Study of Prevalence in Great Britain." *Child Abuse and Neglect* 9:457–467.

————(1986). "Child Sexual Abuse." Pp. 79–86 in *Recent Advances in Paediatrics*, edited by R. Meadow. London: Churchill Livingstone.

Bamford, James (1983). *The Puzzle Palace*. New York: Penguin.

Bannister, Anne, Kevin Barrett, and Eileen Shearer (1991). *Listening to Children: The Professional Response to Hearing the Abused Child*. London: Longman.

Barclay Committee (1982). *Social Workers: Their Role and Tasks*. London: Bedford Square Press.

Barker, Martin, ed. (1984). *The Video Nasties: Freedom and Censorship in the Media*. London: Pluto.

Bartlett, Nigel (1989). "Facing the Unbelievable." *Community Care*, December 14.

Barwick, Sandra (1990). "Witch Story to Believe?" *Spectator*, March 24.

————(1991). "Not Men Only." *Spectator*, June 1.

Bate, Mary, and Dede Liss (1986). "Plays for Prevention." *Community Care*, October 9.

Beattie, John (1981). *The Yorkshire Ripper Story*. London: Quartet Books.

Becker, Howard (1963). *Outsiders*. New York: Free Press.

Bedell, Geraldine (1992). "Just Like Mummy Wears?" *Independent on Sunday*, January 19.

Beechey, Virginia, and Elizabeth Whitelegg (1986). *Women in Britain Today.* Milton Keynes: Open University Press.

Behlmer, George K. (1982). *Child Abuse and Moral Reform in England 1870–1908.* Stanford, CA: Stanford University Press.

Bell, Stuart (1988). *When Salem Came to the Boro: The True Story of the Cleveland Child Abuse Crisis.* London: Pan.

———, ed. (1990). *The Children Act 1989.* London: Shaw and Sons.

Benn, Melissa (1987). "Adventures in the Soho Skin Trade." *New Statesman* December 11.

Benn, Melissa, Anna Coote, and T. Gill (1986). *The Rape Controversy.* London: National Council for Civil Liberties/Yale University Press.

Benton, Sarah (1991). "Safe Havens." *New Statesman and Society*, May 3.

Bentovim, Arnon (1988). "Who Is to Blame?" *New Statesman and Society*, August 5.

Bentovim, Arnon, Anne Elton, Judy Hildebrand, Marianne Tranter, and Eileen Vizard (1988). *Child Sexual Abuse within the Family.* London: John Wright.

Ben-Yehuda, Nachman (1985). *Deviance and Moral Boundaries.* Chicago: University of Chicago Press.

———(1990). *The Politics and Morality of Deviance.* Albany, NY: State University of New York.

Berridge, D. (1985). *Children's Homes.* Oxford: Blackwell.

Best, Joel, ed. (1989). *Images of Issues.* Hawthorne, NY: Aldine de Gruyter.

———(1990). *Threatened Children.* Chicago: University of Chicago Press.

Bexley [Metropolitan Police and Bexley London Borough] (1987). *Child Sexual Abuse Joint Investigative Project: Final Report.* London: Her Majesty's Stationery Office.

Bibby, Peter (1991). "Breaking the Web." *Social Work Today*, October 3.

Birch, Helen, ed. (1991). *Women Killers.* London: Virago.

Bishop, Mike (1988). "The Most Secret Offence." *Community Care*, July 7.

Blagg, Harry, John A. Hughes, and Corinne Wattam (1989). *Child Sexual Abuse: Listening, Hearing and Validating the Experiences of Children.* London: Longman.

Borders, William (1982). "Britons Outraged over Three Rape Cases." *New York Times*, January 24.

Borland, M., ed. (1976). *Violence in the Family.* Manchester: Manchester University Press.

Boseley, Sarah (1991). "Operation Orchid Chief Promises More Arrests." *Guardian*, June 15.

Bowen, Romi, and Angela Hamblin (1981). "Sexual Abuse of Children." *Spare Rib*, 106.

Box, Steven (1983). *Power, Crime and Mystification.* London: Tavistock.

Box-Grainger, Jill (1986). "Sentencing Rapists." Pp. 31–52 in *Confronting Crime*, edited by R. Matthews and J. Young. Beverly Hills, CA: Sage.

Brake, Michael, and Chris Hale (1992). *Public Order and Private Lives.* London: Routledge.

Bray, Madge (1991). *Poppies on the Rubbish Heap.* London: Cannongate.

Brewer, Colin, and June Lait (1980). *Can Social Work Survive?* London: Temple Smith.

"British Inquisition" (1991). "The British Inquisition." *The Mail on Sunday*, March 10.

Brown, Grodon (1989). *Where There is Greed . . .* Edinburgh: Mainstream Publishing.

Burgess, Ann W., and Marieanne L. Clark, eds. (1984). *Child Pornography and Sex Rings*. Lexington, MA: Heath.

Burn, Gordon (1984). *Somebody's Husband, Somebody's Son*. London: Heinemann.

Butler-Sloss, Lord Justice Elizabeth (1988). *Report of the Inquiry into Child Abuse in Cleveland 1987, Cmnd 412*. London: Her Majesty's Stationery Office.

Byrne, Kath, and Neil Patrick (1990). "Bexley Bounces Back." *Social Work Today*, May 24.

Cameron, Deborah, and Elizabeth Frazer (1987). *The Lust to Kill*. London: Polity.

Campaign for Free Speech on Ireland (1979). *The British Media and Ireland*. London: Campaign for Free Speech on Ireland.

Campbell, Beatrix (1987). "The Skeleton in the Family's Cupboard." *New Statesman*, July 31.

———(1988a). *Unofficial Secrets: Child Sexual Abuse—The Cleveland Case*. London: Virago.

———(1988b). "Champ or Chump?" *New Statesman and Society*, July 15.

———(1989). "Cleveland's Dilemma." *New Statesman and Society*, February 21.

———(1990a). "Children's Stories." *New Statesman and Society*, October 5.

———(1990b). "Hear No Evil." *New Statesman and Society*, October 19.

———(1990c). "Satanic Claims Vindicated." *New Statesman and Society*, November 9.

———(1990d). "Seen But Not Heard." *Marxism Today*, November.

———(1991a). "Satanic Abuse and the Law." *Guardian*, February 20.

Campbell, Beatrix (1991b). "Between the Lines." *Social Work Today*, November 14.

Campbell, Duncan (1986). "Evil Beyond Belief." *New Statesman*, June 6.

———(1991a). "Mercia Police Chief to Head National Unit." *Guardian*, June 4.

———(1991b). "Life for Killer Who Dumped Women's Bodies in Car." *Guardian*, July 4.

———(1991c). "Lady Birdwood Guilty on Race Hate Charges." *Guardian*, October 17.

Campbell, Duncan, and Steve Connor (1986). *On the Record: Surveillance, Computers and Privacy*. London: Michael Joseph.

Campbell, Mark (1991). "Children At Risk: How Different Are Children on Child Abuse Registers?" *British Journal of Social Work*, 21:259–276.

Cant, Bob, and Susan Hemmings (1988). *Radical Records*. London: Routledge.

Caputi, Jane (1987). *The Age of Sex Crime*. London: Women's Press.

Cartledge, S., and J. Ryan (1983). *Sex and Love*. London: Women's Press.

Carver, V., ed. (1978). *Child Abuse: A Study Text*. Milton Keynes: Open University Press.

Castles, Stephen, Heather Booth, and Tina Wallace (1984). *Here For Good*. London: Pluto.

Caudrey, Adrienne (1986). "The Child Protectors." *New Society*, December 19–26.

Chambliss, William, and M. Mankoff (1976). *Whose Law? What Order?* New York: Wiley.

Chant, John (1988). "The Panellist's View." *Community Care*, July 7.

Chester, Gail, and Julienne Dickey (1988). *Feminism and Censorship: The Current Debate*. London: Prism.

Chester, Lewis, Magnus Linklater, and David May (1979). *Jeremy Thorpe: A Secret Life*. London: Fontana.

Chesterman, Mark (1990). *Child Sexual Abuse and Social Work*. Social Work Monograph no. 1, Norwich: University of East Anglia,

Child Abuse (1982). *Child Abuse: A Study of Inquiry Reports 1973–1981*. London: Her Majesty's Stationery Office.

Child Abuse (1988). *Child Abuse—Working Together. A Guide to Arrangements for Interagency Cooperation for the Protection of Children*. London: Her Majesty's Stationery Office.

Child in Trust (1985). *A Child in Trust: The Report of the Panel of Inquiry into the Circumstances Surrounding the Death of Jasmine Beckford*. London: Borough of Brent.

Children's Legal Centre (1988). *Children's Rights after Cleveland*. London: Children's Legal Centre.

Chippindale, Peter, and Chris Horrie (1990). *Stick It up Your Punter!* London: Heinemann.

CIBA Foundation (1984). *Child Sexual Abuse within the Family*, edited by Ruth Porter. London: Tavistock.

Clark, Anna (1986). "Rewriting the History of Rape." *New Society*, August 29.
———(1987). *Women's Silence, Men's Violence: Sexual Abuse in England 1770–1845*. London: Pandora Press.

Clarke, Alan (1987). "Moral Protest, Status Defense and the Anti-Abortion Campaign." *British Journal of Sociology* 38:235–253.

Cohen, Phil (1990). "Organized Child Abuse." *Social Work Today*, May 10.

Cohen, S. (1988). *Child Abuse Procedures: The Child's Viewpoint*. London: Children's Legal Center.

Cohen, Stan (1972). *Folk Devils and Moral Panics: The Creation of the Mods and Rockers*. Oxford: Blackwell.

Cohen, Stan, and Jock Young, eds. (1973). *The Manufacture of News: Social Problems, Deviance and the Mass Media*. London: Constable.

Colegate, Isabel (1991). *The Summer of the Royal Visit*. London: Hamish Hamilton

Coote, Anna, and Beatrix Campbell (1987). *Sweet Freedom: The Struggle for Women's Liberation*, 2nd ed. Oxford: Blackwell.

Corby, Brian (1987). *Working with Child Abuse: Social Work Practice and the Child Abuse System*. Milton Keynes: Open University Press.

Corby, Brian, and Chris Mills (1986). "Child Abuse: Risks and Resources." *British Journal of Social Work* 16:531–542.

Cotterill, Andrew M. (1988). "The Geographic Distribution of Child Abuse in an Inner City Borough." *Child Abuse and Neglect* 12:461–467.

Coulter, Jim, Susan Miller, and Martin Walker (1984). *State of Siege: Miners Strike 1984*. London: Canary Press.

Coward, Mat (1991). "Strange to Tell." *New Statesman and Society*, February 1.

Creighton, S. J. (1984). *Trends in Child Abuse*. London: NSPCC.

———(1985). "An Epidemiological Study of Abused Children and Their Families in the UK between 1977 and 1982." *Child Abuse and Neglect* 9:441–448.

Crewdson, John (1988). *By Silence Betrayed: Sexual Abuse of Children in America*. New York: Little Brown.

Criminal Statistics (1985). *Home Office Criminal Statistics England and Wales 1985*, Cm 10. London: Her Majesty's Stationery Office.

Cross, Roger (1981). *The Yorkshire Ripper*. London: Grafton.

Dale, Peter, Murray Davies, Tony Morrison, and Jim Waters (1986). *Dangerous Families: Assessment and Treatment of Child Abuse*. London: Tavistock.

Dalrymple, James (1991). "Slaughter of the Lambs." *Sunday Times*, June 23.

Davenport, Peter, and Stewart Tendler (1986). "Talks on Child Murders Link." *Times*, April 21.

Davies, Graham, and Jonquil Drinkwater, eds. (1988). *The Child Witness: Do the Courts Abuse Children?* Issues in Criminological and Legal Psychology Series, no. 13. Leicester: British Psychological Society.

Davies, Martin, ed. (1991). *The Sociology of Social Work*. London: Routledge.

Dawson, Judith (1990). "Vortex of Evil." *New Statesman and Society*, October 5.

Dawson, Judith, and Christine Johnston (1989). "When the Truth Hurts," *Community Care*, March 30.

Deeley, Peter (1975). "Sexual Attraction in Exorcist Group." *Observer*, March 30.

Deer, Brian (1986). "Maniacs Who Kill for Pleasure." *Sunday Times*, July 27.

Deer, Brian, and Tim Rayment (1986). "The Kind of Man Who Kills a Child." *Sunday Times*, April 27.

Derbyshire, Ian (1988). *Politics in Britain from Callaghan to Thatcher*. London: Chambers.

"Devil You Know" (1990). "The Devil You Know." *New Statesman and Society*, September 21.

Dibblin, Jane (1987). "The Right of the Father?" *New Statesman*, July 10.

Dillon, Martin (1989). *The Shankill Butchers: A Case Study in Mass Murder*. London: Hutchinson.

Dingwall, R. (1986). "The Jasmine Beckford Affair." *Modern Law Review* 49:489–507.

Dingwall, R., J. Eekelaar, and T. Murray (1983). *The Protection of Children*. Oxford: Blackwell.

Dominelli, Lena (1987). "Father-Daughter Incest." *Critical Social Policy* 16:8–22.

———(1989). "Betrayal of Trust." *British Journal of Social Work* 19:291–307.

Dominelli, Lena, and Eileen McLeod (1989). *Feminist Social Work*. London: Macmillan.

Doney, Richard H. (1990). "The Aftermath of the Yorkshire Ripper." Pp. 95–112 in *Serial Murder*, edited by Steven A. Egger. New York: Praeger.

Dowden, Richard (1985). "Police Hunting Girl, Seven, Fear Double Killing." *Times*, September 20.

Downs, David Alexander (1990). *The New Politics of Pornography*. Chicago: University of Chicago Press.

Doyle, Celia (1990). *Working with Abused Children*. Basingstoke: Macmillan.

Driver, Emily, and Audrey Droisen, eds. (1989). *Child Sexual Abuse: Feminist Perspectives*. London: Macmillan.

Eardley, T (1985). "Violence and Sexuality." Pp. 106–119 in *The Sexuality of Men*, edited by A. Metcalf and M. Humphries.

Eaton, Lynn, et al. (1991). "Ritual Abuse: Fantasy or Reality?" *Social Work Today*, September 26.

Eberle, Paul, and Shirley Eberle (1986). *The Politics of Child Abuse*. Secaucus, NJ: Lyle Stuart.

Edwards, Susan S. M. (1981). *Female Sexuality and the Law*. Edinburgh: Martin Robertson.

———(1989). *Policing Domestic Violence: Women, the Law and the State*. Beverly Hills, CA: Sage.

———(1991). "Review." *British Journal of Criminology* 31(2):209–210.

Elliott, Michelle (1985). *Preventing Child Sexual Assault: A Practical Guide to Talking with Children*. London: NCVO and Bedford Square Press.

Ellis, Mark (1989). "Evil Trade of Child Sex Ring Corrupted 150 Boys." *Times*, February 3.

Ellis, Roger (1990). *The Occult and Young People*. Eastbourne, Sussex: Kingsway.

Ennew, Judith (1986a). "Selling Children's Sexuality." *New Society*, August 22.

———(1986b). *The Sexual Exploitation of Children*. London: Polity.

Enright, S. (1987). "Refuting Allegations of Child Sexual Abuse." *New Law Journal*, July 10–17.

Erikson, Kai (1966). *Wayward Puritans*. New York: Free Press.

Fairclough, Anna (1990). *Responsibility for Incest: A Feminist View*. Social Work Monograph, Norwich: University of East Anglia,

Family Rights Group (1988). *Child Sexual Abuse after Cleveland: Alternative Strategies*. London: Family Rights Group.

Farrar, Stewart (1971). *What Witches Do*. London: Sphere.

Fawcett, Judy (1987). "The Long Road Back to Normality." *Community Care*, October 29.

Feierman, Jay R., ed. (1990). *Pedophilia: Biosocial Dimensions*. New York: Springer-Verlag.

Feminist Anthology Collective (1981). *No Turning Back: Writings from the Women's Liberation Movement 1975–1980*. London: Women's Press.

Field, Frank (1982). *Poverty and Politics*. London: Heinemann.

———(1989). *Losing Out: The Emergence of Britain's Underclass*. Oxford: Blackwell.

Finkelhor, David (1984). *Child Sexual Abuse*. New York: Free Press.

Finkelhor, David, L. M. Williams, and N. Burns (1988). *Nursery Crimes*. London: Sage.

Fletcher, Martin (1985). "Broken Marriages and Unemployment Blamed for Increase in Child Abuse." *Times*, September 19.

Foot, Paul (1989). *Who Framed Colin Wallace?* London: Macmillan.

Foster, Howard (1988). "Yard Officers Seek More Help to Fight Child Pornography." *Times*, April 4.

Fowler, Joan, and Dick Stockford (1979). "Leaving It to the Wife: A Study of

Abused Children and the Parents in Norfolk." *Child Abuse and Neglect* 3:851–856.

Franklin, Alfred White, ed. (1977). *Child Abuse, Prediction, Prevention and Follow-up.* Papers presented by the Tunbridge Wells Study Group on Child Abuse at their Farnham Meeting. Edinburgh: Churchill Livingstone.

————(1981). "British Association for the Study and Prevention of Child Abuse and Neglect." *Child Abuse and Neglect* 5:69–70.

Franklin, Bob, ed. (1986). *The Rights of Children*. Oxford: Blackwell.

Franklin, Bob, and Nigel Parton, eds. (1991). *Social Work, the Media and Public Relations*. London: Routledge.

Frude, N. ed. (1980). *Psychological Approaches to Child Abuse*. London: Batsford.

Fuller, R. C., and R. D. Myers (1941). "The Natural History of a Social Problem." *American Sociological Review* 6.

Furniss, Tilman (1991). *The Multi-Professional Handbook of Child Sexual Abuse: Integrated Management, Therapy and Legal Intervention*. London: Routledge.

Furniss, Tilman, L. Bingley-Miller, and A. Bentovim (1984). "Therapeutic Approach to Sexual Abuse." *Archives of Diseases in Childhood* 59:865–870.

Galloway, Bruce, ed. (1983). *Prejudice and Pride*. London: Routledge.

Geis, Gil, and Ivan Bunn (1991). "And a Child Shall Mislead Them." In *Perspectives on Deviance*, edited by Robert J. Kelly and Donald E. Macnamara. Cincinnati: Anderson.

Gerassi, John (1968). *The Boys of Boise: Furor, Vice and Folly in an American City.* New York: Collier.

Gill, Kerry (1990). "Life Sentence for Sex Offender Who Abducted Girl of Six." *Times*, August 11.

Gilmour, Alan (1988). *Innocent Victims: The Question of Child Abuse*. London: Michael Joseph.

Ginzburg, Carlo (1991). *Ecstasies: Deciphering the Witches' Sabbath*. New York: Pantheon.

Glaser, Danya, and Stephen Frosh (1988). *Child Sexual Abuse*. London: Macmillan Education/British Association of Social Workers.

Glees, Anthony (1987). *The Secrets of the Service*. London: Jonathan Cape.

Golding, P., and S. Middleton (1982). *Images of Welfare: Press and Public Attitudes to Poverty*. London: Martin Robertson.

Gordon, Paul (1983). *White Law*. London: Pluto.

Gould, Catherine (1987). "Satanic Ritual Abuse: Child Victims, Adult Survivors, System Response." *California Psychologist* 22(3):4–7.

Grant, Kenneth (1972). *The Magical Revival*. London: Muller.

Greenland, Cyril (1987). *Preventing CAN Deaths: An International Study of Deaths Due to Child Abuse and Neglect*. London: Tavistock.

Gusfield, Joseph (1963). *Symbolic Crusade*. Urbana, Il: University of Illinois Press.

————(1981). *The Culture of Public Problems*. Chicago: University of Chicago Press.

Hain, Peter (1987). *A Putney Plot?* London: Spokesman.

Hain, Peter, Martin Kettle, Duncan Campbell, and Joanna Rollo (1980). *Policing the Police*. London: John Calder.

Hall, Anthea (1990). "Dark Shadows That Hang over Rochdale's Children." *Sunday Telegraph*, September 16.

Hall, Ruth E. (1985). *Ask Any Woman: A London Inquiry into Rape and Sexual Assault*. Bristol: Falling Wall Press.

Hall, Stuart, with Chas Critcher, Tony Jefferson, John Clarke, and Brian Roberts (1978). *Policing the Crisis: Mugging, the State and Law and Order*. London: Macmillan.

Hanmer, Jalna, Jill Radford, and Elizabeth A. Stanko (1989). *Women, Policing and Male Violence: International Perspectives*. London: Routledge.

Harding, Stephen (1988). "The Decline of Permissiveness." *New Statesman and Society*, November 4.

Harper, Audrey, with Harry Pugh (1990). *Dance with the Devil*. Eastbourne, Sussex: Kingsway.

Harper, Michael (1976). *Spiritual Warfare*. London: Hodder and Stoughton.

Harris, Martyn (1984). "The Strange Saga of the Video Bill." *New Society*, April 26.

Harris, Robert (1991). "The Life and Death of the Care Order (Criminal)." *British Journal of Social Work* 21:1–17.

Harrison, Fred (1987). *Brady and Hindley*, rev. ed. London: Grafton.

Harrison, Paul (1983). *Inside the Inner City*. London: Penguin.

Heald, Gordon, and Robert J. Wybrow (1986). *The Gallup Survey of Britain*. London: Croom Helm.

Hebditch, David, and Nick Anning (1990). "A Ritual Fabrication." *Independent on Sunday*, December 30.

Herbert, Carrie M. H. (1989). *Talking of Silence: The Sexual Harassment of Schoolgirls*. London: Falmer Press.

Hickey, Eric W. (1991). *Serial Murderers and Their Victims*. Pacific Grove, CA: Brooks-Cole.

Hicks, Robert D. (1991). *In Pursuit of Satan: The Police and the Occult*. Buffalo, NY: Prometheus Books.

Hill, Malcolm (1990). "The Manifest and Latent Lessons of Child Abuse Inquiries." *British Journal of Social Work* 20:197–213.

Hillyard, Paddy, and Janie Percy-Smith (1988). *The Coercive State: The Decline of Democracy in Britain*. London: Fontana.

Hobbs, C., and J. Wynne (1986). "Buggery in Childhood—A Common Syndrome of Child Abuse." *Lancet*, 792–796.

———(1987a). "Child Sexual Abuse–An Increasing Rate of Diagnosis." *Lancet*, 837–842.

———(1987b). "Management of Sexual Abuse." *Archives of Diseases in Children* 62:1182–1187.

———(1989). "Sexual Abuse of English Boys and Girls: The Importance of Anal Examination." *Child Abuse and Neglect* 13:195–210.

Hobson, Sarah (1990). "Child Abuse in Great Britain." Pp 112–142 in *Betrayal: A Report on Violence towards Children in Today's World*, edited by Caroline Moorehead. New York: Doubleday.

Hodgkin, Jane (1986). "Parents against Injustice." *New Society*, May 16.

Holdaway, Simon, ed. (1979). *The British Police*. London: Edwin Arnold.

————(1983). *Inside the British Police*. Oxford: Blackwell.

Holloway, Wendy (1984). "'I Just Wanted to Kill a Woman.' Why? The Ripper and Male Sexuality." Pp. 26–46 in *Sweeping Statements: Writings from the Women's Liberation Movement 1981–1983*, edited by H. Kanter et al., London: Women's Press.

Hollows, Anne (1991). "Are We Playing It Too Safe?" *Community Care*, June 27.

Holmes, Ronald M., and James DeBurger (1988). *Serial Murder*. Beverly Hills, CA: Sage.

Hornsby-Smith, Michael P. (1991). *Roman Catholic Beliefs in England*. Cambridge University Press.

Hugill, Barry, (1991). "Child Care in Crisis." *Observer*, June 2.

Inglis, Ruth (1978). *Sins of the Fathers: A Study of the Physical and Emotional Abuse of Children*. London: P. Owen.

Irvine, Doreen (1973). *From Witchcraft to Christ*. London: Concordia Press

Ivory, Mark (1991a). "Unravelling the Moral Knot." *Community Care*, May 9.

————(1991b). "Damning Criticism from Levy Inquiry." *Community Care*, May 30.

Jacobs, Eric, and Robert Worcester (1990). *We British: Britain under the MORIScope*. London: Weidenfeld and Nicholson.

James, P. D. (1989). *Devices and Desires*. New York: Warner.

James, P. D., and T. A. Critchley (1987). *The Maul and the Pear Tree*. New York: Mysterious Press.

Jay, Margaret, and Sally Doganis (1987). *Battered: The Abuse of Children*. New York: St Martin's Press.

Jeffreys, Sheila (1979). "Rape." *Leveller*, no. 25.

————(1982). "The Sexual Abuse of Children in the Home." In *On the Problem of Men*, edited by S. Friedman and E. Sarah. London: Women's Press.

————(1985). *The Spinster and Her Enemies: Feminism and Sexuality 1880–1930*. London: Pandora.

————(1990). *Anticlimax: A Feminist Perspective on the Sexual Revolution*. London: Women's Press.

Jehu, Derek, Marjorie Gazan, and Carole Klassen (1988). *Beyond Sexual Abuse: Therapy with Women Who Were Childhood Victims*. Chichester: Wiley.

Jenkins, Jolyon (1991). "Passions of Crime." *New Statesman and Society*, May 17.

Jenkins, Lin (1991). "Black Magic Case Collapses over Young Girl's Evidence." *Times*, November 20.

Jenkins, Philip (1988a). "Myth and Murder: The Serial Murder Panic of 1983–1985." *Criminal Justice Research Bulletin* 3(11):1–7.

————(1988b). "Serial Murder in England 1940–1985." *Journal of Criminal Justice* 16(1):1–15.

————(1991a). "Sharing Murder: Understanding Group Serial Homicide." *Journal of Crime and Justice* 13(2):125–147.

————(forthcoming). "A Murder Wave: Trends in Serial Homicide in the United States 1940–1990." *Criminal Justice Review* (forthcoming).

————(1991, b). "New Perceptions of Serial Murder in Contemporary England." *Journal of Contemporary Criminal Justice* 7(4):210–231.

Jenkins, Philip, and Daniel Maier-Katkin (1988). "Protecting the Victims of Child Sexual Abuse: A Case for Caution." *Prison Journal* 68(2):25–35.

———(1991). "Occult Survivors: The Making of a Myth." Pp. 127–144 in *Satanism Scare*, edited by James T. Richardson, Joel Best, and David G. Bromley. Hawthorne, NY: Aldine de Gruyter.

———(1992). "Satanism: Myth and Reality in a Contemporary Moral Panic." *Crime, Law and Social Change* 17:53–75.

Jervis, Margaret (1991). "Grey Area." *Social Work Today*, April 11.

Johns, June (1971a). *King of the Witches: The World of Alex Sanders*. London: Pan.

———(1971b). *Black Magic Today*. London: New English Library.

Jones, David P. H. (1991). "Commentary." *Child Abuse and Neglect* 15:163–170.

Jones, David P. H., J. Pickett, M. R. Oates, and P. Barbor (1987). *Understanding Child Abuse*, 2nd ed. London: Macmillan Educational.

Jonker, F., and P. Jonker-Bakker (1991). "Experiences with Ritualistic Child Sexual Abuse." *Child Abuse and Neglect* 15:191–196.

Jowell, Roger, and C. Airey, eds. (1984). *British Social Attitudes: The 1984 Report*. Aldershot: Gower.

Jowell, Roger, Lindsay Brook, and Bridget Taylor (1991). *British Social Attitudes: The Eighth Report*. London: Dartmouth.

Kahaner, Larry (1988). *Cults That Kill*. New York: Warner.

Kanter, Hannah, ed., (1984). *Sweeping Statements: Writings from the Women's Liberation Movement 1981–1983*. London: Women's Press.

Karlsen, Carol (1987). *The Devil in the Shape of a Woman*. New York: Norton.

Katz, Ian (1991). "Greville Janner Named in Court as Child Abuser." *Guardian*, October 31.

Keel, Paul (1988). "Rare Blood Group Gave Detectives Clue in Search for Railway Killer." *Guardian*, February 27.

Kelly, Aidan (1991). *Crafting the Art of Magic: A History of Modern Witchcraft 1939–1964*. St Paul, MN: Llewellyn.

Kelly, Liz (1988). "What's in a Name: Defining Child Sexual Abuse." *Feminist Review* 28:65–73.

———(1991). "Unspeakable Acts: Women Who Abuse." *Trouble and Strife* 21:13–20.

Kelly, Liz, and Linda Regan (1990). "Flawed Protection." *Social Work Today*, April 19.

Kempe, C. Henry, et al. (1962). "The Battered Child Syndrome." *Journal of the American Medical Association* 181:17–24.

Kempe, R. S., and C. Henry Kempe (1978). *Child Abuse*. London: Fontana Books/Open University Press.

Kettle, Martin, and Lucy Hodges (1982). *Uprising*. London: Pan.

Kingdom, John (1991). *Government and Politics in Britain*. Oxford: Blackwell.

Kitsuse, John I., and Joseph W. Schneider (1989). "Preface." Pp. i–iv *Images of Issues*, edited by Joel Best. New York: Aldine de Gruyter.

Kittrie, Nicholas (1973). *The Right to Be Different*. London: Pelican.

Knight, Stephen (1984). *The Brotherhood: The Secret World of the Freemasons*. London: Granada.

Kraemer, William, ed. (1976). *The Forbidden Love*. London: Sheldon.

LaFontaine, Jean (1990). *Child Sexual Abuse*. Oxford: Blackwell.

Lane, Brian (1991). *Murder Update.* New York: Carroll and Graf.

Lanning, Kenneth V. (1991) "Commentary." *Child Abuse and Neglect* 15:171–174.

Laurance, Jeremy (1985). "Tyra: Who Must Take the Rap?" *New Society*, August 2.

———(1986a). "Is the Tyra Henry Inquiry Doomed?" *New Society*, April 4.

———(1986b). "Bentovim's Technique." *New Society*, November 28.

———(1987a). "The Children's Samaritans." *New Society*, July 10.

———(1987b). "Children: Who Cares?" *New Society*, July 17.

———(1988a). "Blaming the Messenger." *New Statesman and Society.* July 1.

———(1988b). "Statistics of a Taboo." *New Statesman and Society.* July 1.

———(1988c). "Verdict on Cleveland." *New Statesman and Society.* July 8.

———(1991). "Abuse of Power." *New Statesman and Society.* March 22.

Lawrence, Peter H. (1990). *The Hot Line.* Eastbourne: Kingsway.

Lees, Sue (1989a). "Trial by Rape." *New Statesman and Society.* November 24.

———(198b). "Blaming the Victim." *New Statesman and Society.* December 1.

Leigh, David (1988). *The Wilson Plot.* New York: Pantheon.

Lelyveld, Joseph (1986). "Devil Did It! A British Man Nets $313,000." *New York Times.* May 4.

Levin, Jack, and James A. Fox (1985) *Mass Murder: America's Growing Menace.* New York: Plenum.

Linedecker, Clifford (1990). *Hell Ranch.* New York: Tor Books.

Lisners, J. (1983). *House of Horrors.* London: Corgi.

Llewelyn, Sue, and Kate Osborne (1990). *Women's Lives.* London: Routledge.

Lloyd, David W. (1991). "Ritual Child Abuse: Where Do We Go from Here?" *Children's Legal Rights Journal* 12(1):12–18.

Lloyd, Robin (1979). *Playland: A Study of Human Exploitation.* London: Quartet.

Logan Kevin (1988). *Paganism and the Occult.* Eastbourne, Sussex: Kingsway.

Longley, Clifford (1975). "Exorcism for Man Who Later Killed Wife Was Unwise, Bishop Says, as Church Bodies Seek Full Report." *Times*, March 27.

Luhrmann, T. M. (1989). *Persuasions of the Witch's Craft: Ritual Magic in Contemporary England.* Cambridge, MA: Harvard University Press.

Lumsden, Andrew (1986). "New Bill, Old Values." *New Statesman*, February 28.

———(1987). "When Grown Men Are Babies." *New Statesman*, February 27.

Lumsden, Andrew, and Denis Campbell (1986). "Anyone for Post-Ptolemaic Sexuality?" *New Statesman*, September 12.

Lund, Jenny, and Rosemary Booth (1991). "Rough Justice." *Social Work Today*, August 8.

Lynch, Margaret A., and Jacqueline Roberts (1982). *Consequences of Child Abuse.* London: Academic Press.

MacGregor, Susanne, ed. (1989). *Drugs and British Society.* London: Routledge.

MacIntyre, Ben (1991). "The Horror Story in Court No. 5." *Sunday Times*, November 17.

MacLeod, Mary, and Esther Saraga (1987a). "How Men Are." *New Statesman*, July 10.

———(1987b). "Abuse of Trust." *Marxism Today*, August.

———(1987c). "Child Sexual Abuse: A Feminist Perspective." *Spare Rib*, July, pp. 22–26.

———(1988a). "Against Orthodoxy." *New Statesman and Society*, July 1.

———(1988b). "Challenging the Orthodoxy." *Feminist Review* 28:16–55.

———, eds. (1988c). *Child Sexual Abuse: Towards a Feminist Professional Practice.* London: PNL Press.

Maher, Peter, ed. (1987). *Child Abuse: the Educational Perspective* (Based on the Stoke Rochford Seminar on Child Abuse Held in the Spring of 1986 and sponsored by the NSPCC). Oxford: Blackwell.

Mandelsberg, Rose G., ed. (1991). *Cult Killers.* New York: Pinnacle.

Mark, Robert (1979). *In the Office of Constable.* London: Fontana.

Marriner, Brian (1990). "Stop the Brutal Beast Who Stalks Young Innocents." Pp. 151–162, in *Serial Murderers,* edited by Art Crockett. New York: Pinnacle.

———(1991). "William (*sic*) Ryan: Horror of the Hungerford Massacre." In *Spree Killers,* edited by Art Crockett. New York: Pinnacle.

Marshall, Kate (1988). "Forum." *Community Care* July 7.

Marwick, Arthur (1991). *Culture in Britain since 1945.* Oxford: Blackwell.

Masson, Jeffery (1988). "Review of books on the Cleveland crisis." *London Review of Books,* November 10.

Masters, Brian (1985). *Killing for Company.* New York: Stein and Day.

———(1991). "The Devil in Us All." *Evening Standards.* March 7.

Matthews, Caitlin, and John Matthews (1985–6). *The Western Way.* London: Arkana. Two Volumes.

Matthews, Roger, and Jock Young, eds. (1986). *Confronting Crime.* Beverly Hills, CA: Sage.

Mayer, Robert S. (1991). *Satan's Children.* New York: Putnam.

McCalman, Iain (1984). "Unrespectable Radicalism: Infidels and Pornography in Early Nineteenth Century London." *Past and Present* 104:74–110.

McFadyean, Melanie (1985). "Sex and the Under-Age Girl." *New Society,* June 14.

———(1986). "I Is for Incest." *New Society,* January 24.

McMillan, Ian (1990). "Sex Rings and Ritual Abuse Information Base Sought." *Community Care,* March 22.

McNeill, Patricia (1987). "Contemporary Witches." *New Society,* October 9.

Meadow, Roy, ed. (1990). *ABC of Child Abuse.* London: British Medical Journal.

Miles, Paul (1986). "Shock! Labour Bans Film." *New Statesman and Society.* July 11.

Miller, Alice (1984). *Thou Shalt Not Be Aware.* London: Pluto.

Miller, Elliott (1990). *A Crash Course on the New Age Movement.* Eastbourne: Monarch.

Molloy, Pat (1988). *Not the Moors Murders.* Llandyssul, Wales: Gomer Press.

Moody, Roger (1980). *Indecent Assault.* London: Word Is Out/Peace News.

Moore, R. I. (1987). *The Formation of a Persecuting Society.* Oxford: Blackwell.

Mrazek, P., and C. H. Kempe, eds. (1981). *Sexually Abused Children and Their Families.* Oxford: Pergamon Press.

Mrazek, P., M. Lynch, and A. Bentovim (1983). "Sexual Abuse of Children in the United Kingdom." *Child Abuse and Neglect* 7:147–153.

Mulhern, Sherill (1991). "Letter." *Child Abuse and Neglect* 15:609–610.

Murray, Kathleen, and David Gough (1991). *Intervening in Child Sexual Abuse.* Edinburgh: Scottish Academic Press.

NSPCC (1989). *Annual Report 1989: Listening to Children.* London: NSPCC.

Nathan, Debbie (1987). "Are These Women Witches? The Making of a Modern Witch Trail." *Village Voice*, September 29.

———(1988). "Child Molester?" *Village Voice*, August 2.

Nava, Mica (1988). "Cleveland and the Press." *Feminist Review* 28:103–121.

Naylor, Bronwyn (1989). "Dealing with Child Sexual Assault: Recent Developments." *British Journal of Criminology* 29(4):395–407.

Neate, Polly, and Will Hatchett (1991). "Children Should Be Seen and Heard." *Community Care*, April 11.

Neat, Polly, and Kendra Sone (1991). "Sex, Lives and Videotape." *Community Care*, April 11.

Nelson, Sarah (1991). "Evidence That Helps No One? *Social Work Today*, October 31.

"Networks of Fear" (1989). "Networks of Fear." *Social Work Today*, October 26.

Newton, Michael (1990). *Hunting Humans*. Port Townsend, WA: Loompanics Unlimited.

Newton, Toyne (1987). *The Demonic Connection: An Investigation into Satanism in England and the International Black Magic Conspiracy*. Poole: Blandford Press.

O'Carroll, Tom (1980a). *Paedophilia: The Radical Case*. London: Peter Owen.

———(1980b). "Age of Consent—Why Children Have the Right to Say Yes." *Leveller* 38:24–25.

O'Hagan, Kieran (1989). *Working with Child Sexual Abuse*. Milton Keynes: Open University Press.

Parker, Russ (1990). *Battling the Occult*. Downers Grove, IL: InterVarsity Press.

Parker, Tony (1969). *The Hidden World of Sex Offenders*. Indianapolis, IN:

Parton, Nigel (1979). "The Natural History of Child Abuse: A Study in Social Problem Definition." *British Journal of Social Work* 9:431–451.

———(1981). "Child Abuse, Social Anxiety and Welfare." *British Journal of Social Work* 11:391–414.

———(1985a). *The Politics of Child Abuse*. London: Macmillan.

———(1985b). "Children in Care." *Critical Social Policy* 13:107–117.

———(1986). "The Beckford Report: A Critical Appraisal." *British Journal of Social Work* 16:511–530.

Peace, D., and R. C. Barrington (1985). "HOLMES: The Development of a Computerized Crime Investigation System." *Police Journal* 58:207–223.

Pearsall, Ronald (1971). *The Worm in the Bud*. London: Pelican.

Pearson, Geoff (1983). *Hooligans: A History of Respectable Fears*. London: Macmillan.

Pearson, Geoff, Mark Gilman, and Shirley McIver (1987). *Young People and Heroin*. Aldershot: Gower.

Peterson, Alan, ed. (1988). *The American Focus on Satanic Crime*, Vol. 1. South Orange, NJ: American Focus.

Pfohl, Stephen (1977). "The Discovery of Child Abuse." *Social Problems* 24:310–323.

Philo, Greg, John Hewitt, Peter Beharrell and Howard Davis (1982). *Really Bad News*. London: Writers and Readers Cooperative.

Philpot, Terry (1987). "Matters of Opinion." *Community Care*, March 5.

Phipps, Alan (1986). "Radical Criminology and Criminal Victimization." Pp.

97–117 in *Confronting Crime*, edited by R. Matthews and J. Young. Beverly Hills, CA: Sage.

Picardie, Justin, and Dorothy Wade (1985). *Heroin: Chasing the Dragon*. London: Penguin.

Pincher, Chapman (1981). *Their Trade Is Treachery*. London: Sidgwick and Jackson.

———(1984). *Too Secret, Too Long*. New York: St Martin Press.

———(1988). *Traitors*. New York: Penguin.

Pithers, David (1988). "Forum." *Community Care*, July 7.

———(1990). "Stranger Than Fiction." *Social Work Today*, October 4.

Pizzey, Erin, and M. Dunne (1980). "Child Sexual Abuse within the Family." *New Society*, November 13.

Porter, Kevin, and Weeks, Jeffrey (1991). *Between the Acts*. London: Routledge.

Porter, Roy (1986). "Plague and panic." *New Society*, December 12.

Priestley, Philip (1980). *Community of Scapegoats: The Segregation of Sex Offenders and Informers in Prison*. Oxford: Pergamon.

Rabinowitz, Dorothy (1990). "From the Mouths of Babes to a Jail Cell: Child Abuse and the Abuse of Justice." *Harpers*, May, pp. 52–63.

Rape Crisis Center, London (1984). *Sexual Violence: the Reality for Women*. Produced by the London Rape Crisis Center. London: Women's Press.

Raschke, Carl A. (1990). *Painted Black: From Drug Killings to Heavy Metal: How Satanism Is Besieging Our Culture and Our Communities*. San Francisco: Harper and Row.

Reade, Brian, ed. (1970). *Sexual Heretics: Male Homosexuality in English Literature from 1850 to 1900*. London: Routledge and Kegan Paul.

Redding, Don (1989). "Smashing a Subculture." *Community Care*,. June 1.

Reed, Dennis (1986). "For Social Worker, Read Scapegoat." *Community Care*, August 14.

Renvoize, Jean (1974). *Children in Danger: The Causes and Prevention of Baby Battering*. London: Routledge and Kegan Paul.

———(1982). *Rape in Marriage*. New York: Macmillan.

Report on Child Witnesses (1991). *Report on Child Witnesses: Ontario Law Reform Commission*. Toronto: Government of Ontario.

Rhodes, Dusty, and Sandra McNeil (1985). *Women against Violence against Women*. London: Onlywomen Press.

Richardson, James, Joel Best, and David Bromley, eds. (1991). *The Satanism Scare*. Hawthorne, NY: Aldine de Gruyter.

Richardson, Sue (1988). "The Practitioner's View." *Community Care*, July 7.

Richardson, Sue, and Heather Bacon, eds. (1991). *Child Sexual Abuse: Whose Problem? Reflections from Cleveland*. London: Venture Press.

Ritchie, Jean (1988). *Myra Hindley: Inside the Mind of a Murderess*. London: Angus and Robertson.

Roberts, Cathy (1989). *Women and Rape*. Brighton: Harvester Wheatsheaf.

Roberts, Gwyneth (1988). "Abstracts: Law." *British Journal of Social Work* 18:325–332.

Roberts, Yvonne (1988a). "It Can Happen Here." *New Statesman and Society*, July 1.

———(1988b). "Unleashed Voice." *New Statesman and Society*, July 22.

————(1989a). "After Cleveland." *New Statesman and Society*, June 2.

————(1989b). "Breaking the Silence: Interview with Marietta Higgs." *New Statesman and Society*, July 14.

————(1989c). "What Went Wrong?" *New Statesman and Society*, July 21.

Rodgers, Derek (1991). "Hands Together for Life." *Scottish Child*, April–May.

Rodwell, Lee (1986). "The Making of a Molester." *Times*, April 23.

Rogers, Wendy Stainton, Denise Hevey and Elizabeth Ash, eds. (1989). *Child Abuse and Neglect: Facing the Challenge*. London: B. T. Batsford Open University Press.

Rolph, C. H. (1980). "The Criminal Mind." *New Statesman*, December 12.

Rose, David (1990). "Murder in Britain." *Guardian*, January 1–2.

————(1991). "Crime—The Facts." *Observer Magazine*, February 17.

Rose, Lionel (1986). *Massacre of the Innocents: Infanticide in Britain 1800–1939*. London: Routledge and Kegan Paul.

Rowbotham, Sheila (1989). *The Past is before Us; Feminism in Action since the 1960s*. London: Pandora.

Rowbotham, Sheila, Lynne Segal, and Hilary Wainwright (1981). *Beyond the Fragments: Feminism and the Making of Socialism*. London: Islington Community Press.

Rozenberg, Joshua (1988). *The Case for the Crown*. Wellingborough, Northants.: Thorson's.

Rutherford, Ward (1973). *The Untimely Silence*. London: Hamish Hamilton.

Schneider, Joseph, and John Kitsuse (1984). *Studies in the Sociology of Social Problems*. Norwood, NJ: Ablex.

Seabrook, Jeremy (1978a). "The Decay of Childhood." *New Statesman*, July 10.

————(1987b). "The Horror of Hungerford." *New Society*, August 28.

Search, Gay (1988). *The Last Taboo: Sexual Abuse of Children*. London: Penguin.

Seaton, Jean (1987). "Odious to the Conscience of the Country." *New Statesman*, May 1.

Seymour-Ure, Colin (1991). *The British Press and Broadcasting since 1945*. Oxford: Blackwell.

Sharron, Howard (1987a). "Parent Abuse." *New Society*, March 13.

————(1987b). "The Hounding of Bell." *New Statesman*, August 14.

Short, Martin (1989). *Inside the Brotherhood: Further Secrets of the Freemasons*. New York: Dorset.

Sinason, Valerie (1990). "Talk of the Devil." *Guardian*, November 3–4.

Sinclair, Ruth (1984). *Decision-Making in Statutory Reviews on Children in Care*. Brookfield, VT: Gower.

Skidelsky, Robert, ed. (1990). *Thatcherism* Oxford: Blackwell.

Smart, Carol (1989). *Feminism and the Power of Law*. London: Routledge.

Smart, Colin (1986). "Wiping the Slate Clean." *Community Care*, April 10.

Smith, Michelle, and Lawrence Pazder (1980). *Michelle Remembers*. New York: Congdon and Lattes.

Snitow, Ann, Christine Stansell, and Sharon Thompson (1984). *Desire: The Politics of Sexuality*. London: Virago.

Social Trends (1991). *Social Trends*, No. 21. London: Her Majesty's Stationery Office.

Social Work Today (1990). "Call for Sex Abuse Probe." *Social Work Today*, May 10.

Sone, Kendra (1990a). "Fact or Fiction." *Community Care*, July 12.

———(1990b). "Strengthening the Resolve." *Community Care*, December 13.

Soothill, Keith (1991). "The Changing Face of Rape," *British Journal of Criminology* 31(4):383—392.

Soothill, Keith and Sylvia Walby (1991). *Sex Crime in the News*. London: Routledge.

Spector, Malcolm, and John Kitsuse (1987). *Constructing Social Problems*. Hawthorne, NY: Aldine de Gruyter.

Spencer, J. R., and R. Flin (1990). *The Evidence of Children: The Law and the Psychology*. London: Blackstone Press.

Spencer, Judith (1989). *Suffer the Child*. New York: Pocket.

Stanko, Elizabeth A. (1985). *Intimate Intrusions: Women's Experience of Male Violence*. London: Pandora.

Stephen, Andrew (1988). *The Suzy Lamplugh Story*. London: Faber.

Strickland, Sarah, and Rosie Waterhouse (1990). "Witch-Hunt Is Launched over Books and TV." *Independent on Sunday*, October 28.

Summit, Roland (1983). "The Child Sexual Abuse Accommodation Syndrome." *Child Abuse and Neglect* 7:177–193.

Sutherland, Ian (1986). "Victims of Crime." *New Society*, June 13.

Symonds, John (1973). *The Great Beast*. London: Mayflower.

Symonds, John, and Kenneth Grant (1972). *The Magical Record of the Beast 666*. London: Duckworth.

Tate, Tim (1991). *Children for the Devil: Ritual Abuse and Satanic Crime*. London: Methuen.

Taylor, Ian (1981). *Law and Order: Arguments for Socialism*. London: Macmillan.

———(1987). "Violence and Video: For a Social Democratic Perspective." *Contemporary Crises* 11:107–128.

Taylor, Ian, Paul Walton, and Jock Young (1973). *The New Criminology*. London: Routledge and Kegan Paul.

———(1975). *Critical Criminology*. London: Routledge and Kegan Paul.

Temkin, Jennifer (1987). *Rape and the Legal Process*. London: Sweet and Maxwell.

Tendler, Stewart (1989). "Four Convicted over Strangling of Teenage Boy Prostitute." *Times*, May 13.

Thomas, T. (1986). *The Police and Social Workers*, Aldershot: Gower.

Thompson, William (1989). "Porn Wars." Paper presented to the annual meeting of the American Society of Criminology, Chicago, IL.

———(1990). "Moral Panics, Pornography and Social Policy." Paper presented to the annual meeting of the American Society of Criminology, Baltimore, MD.

———(1991). "The Cross of Confusion: Social Status and Satanic Panics in Britain 1988–1991." Paper presented to the annual meeting of the American Society of Criminology, San Francisco, CA.

Thompson, William, Alison King, and Jason Annette (1989). "Snuff, Sex and Satan." Unpublished paper.

Tomaselli, S., and R. Porter, eds. (1986) *Rape*. Oxford: Blackwell.

Tomlinson, Martin (1982). *The Pornbrokers: The Rise of the Soho Sex Barons*. London: Virgin Books.

Toner, Barbara (1982). *The Facts of Rape*, rev. ed. London: Arrow Books.

Topping, Peter, and Jean Ritchie (1989). *Topping: The Autobiography of the Police Chief in the Moors Murders Case*. London: Angus and Robertson.

Toynbee, Polly (1983). "The Ultimate Violation." *Guardian Weekly*, November 6.

Tracey, Michael, and David Morrison (1978). *Whitehouse*. London: Macmillan.

Tucker, Nicholas (1985). "A Panic over Child Abuse." *New Society*, October 18.

———(1987). "Sexual Relations." *New Society*, July 10.

Tysoe, Maryon (1984). "The Great British Witch Boom." *New Society*, October 18.

———(1985). "The Porno Effect." *New Society*, March 7.

Vallely, Paul (1986). "How Satanist Conman Persuaded Vicar to Net Him over £200,000." *Times*, April 26.

Vass, Anthony A. (1986). *Aids—A Plague in Us: A Social Perspective*. London: Venus Academica.

Victor, Jeffrey S. (1992, forthcoming), *Rumors of Evil: the Satanic Cult Scare and the Creation of Imaginary Deviance*. Chicago, IL: Open Court Publishing.

Waddington, P. A. J. (1986). "Mugging as a Moral Panic." *British Journal of Sociology* 37:245–259.

———(1991). *The Strong Arm of the Law*. Oxford: Clarendon.

Walkowitz, Judith (1982). "Jack the Ripper and the Myth of Male Violence." *Feminist Studies* 8:543–574.

Wallis, Roy (1976). "Moral Indignation and the Media: An Analysis of NVALA." *Sociology* 10:271–295.

———(1977). "A Critique of the Theory of Moral Crusades as Status Defense." *Scottish Journal of Sociology* 1:195–203.

———(1979). *Salvation and Protest*. London: Frances Pinter.

Wallis, Roy, and Richard Bland (1979). "Purity in Danger: A Survey of Participants in a Moral Crusade Rally." *British Journal of Sociology* 30:189–205.

Wambaugh, Joseph (1989). *The Blooding*. New York: Bantam.

Ward, Elizabeth (1984). *Father-Daughter Rape*. London: Women Press.

Warnock, Mary (1986). "Protecting the Child." *Times Literary Supplement*, October 31.

Waterhouse, Rosie (1990a). "Satanic Cults: How the Hysteria Swept Britain." *Independent on Sunday*, October 14.

———(1990b). "NSPCC Questions Led to Satan Cases." *Independent on Sunday*, September 30.

———(1990c). "Satanic Inquisitors from the Town Hall." *Independent on Sunday*, October 28.

———(1991a). "Therapist's Role in Notts Case." *Independent on Sunday*, April 7.

———(1991b). "Witch Hunt." *New Statesman and Society*, September 6.

Weeks, Jeffrey (1977). *Coming Out*. London: Quartet.

———(1981). *Sex, Politics and Society: The Regulation of Sexuality since 1800*. London: Longman.

———(1985). *Sexuality and Its Discontents: Meanings, Myths and Modern Sexualities*. London: Routledge and Kegan Paul.

———(1986). *Sexuality*. London: Tavistock.

Welsby, Paul A. (1984). *A History of the Church of England 1945–1980*. Oxford: Oxford University Press.

West, D. J. (1985). *Sexual Victimization*. Aldershot: Gower.

———(1987). *Sexual Crimes and Confrontations*. Aldershot: Gower.

West, Richard (1987). "The Abuse of Abuse." *Spectator*, July 4.

Westwood, Philip (1991). "Kenneth Erskine: Seven Victims of the Whispering Strangler." in pp. 181–197, *Spree Killers*, edited by Art Crockett. New York: Pinnacle.

Wheatley, Dennis ([1934] 1966). *The Devil Rides Out*. London: Arrow.

Whitaker, Brian (1981). *News Limited*, London: Minority Press Group.

White, D. (1979). "There's Something Nasty in the Fridge." *New Society*, November 1.

———(1982). "The Phantom Train." *New Society*, July 15.

White, Tom (1990). *The Believer's Guide to Spiritual Warfare*. Eastbourne: Kingsway.

Wild, N. J. (1986). "Sexual Abuse of Children in Leeds." *British Medical Journal* 292:1113–1116.

Williams, Emlyn (1968). *Beyond Belief*. London: Pan.

Wilson, Colin, and Donald Seaman (1983). *Encyclopaedia of Modern Murder*. New York: Perigee.

Wilson, Elizabeth (1990). "Immoral Panics." *New Statesman and Society*, August 31.

Wood, Hazel (1990). "Exposing the Secret." *Social Work Today*, November 15.

Worcester, Robert M. (1991). *British Public Opinion*. Oxford: Blackwell.

Wright, Peter (1987). *Spy Catcher*. New York: Viking.

Wybrow, Robert J. (1989). *Britain Speaks Out 1937–1987: A Social History As Seen through the Gallup Poll*. London: Macmillan.

Wyre, Ray (1989). "Gracewell Clinic." pp. 249–251 in *Child Abuse and Neglect: Facing the Challenge*, edited by W. S. Rogers, D. Hevey, and E. Ash. London: B. T. Batsford/Open University Press.

Young, Malcolm (1991). *An Inside Job: Policing and Police Culture in Britain*. Oxford: Oxford University Press.

Young, Walter C., Roberta G. Sachs, Bennett G. Braun, and Ruth T. Watkins (1991). "Patients Reporting Ritual Abuse in Childhood." *Child Abuse and Neglect* 15:181–190.

Zurcher, L. A., and R. G. Kirkpatrick (1976). *Citizens for Decency: Anti-Pornography Crusades as Status Defense*. Austin TX: University of Texas Press.

Index

Brighton, 42, 46, 63
  sex attack in (1983), 16, 80–1, 212
  see also Bishop, Russell; Colwell,
    Maria; Sussex
Bristol, 32, 62, 135
British Association for the Study and
    Prevention of Child Abuse and
    Neglect, BASPCAN, 113, 135
British Association of Social Workers,
    110, 146
Brittan, Leon, 79–80
Brown, Chris, 192
Brown, Gordon, 60
buggery *see* child sexual abuse: anal
    intercourse
Butler-Sloss, Elizabeth, 26, 140–8

Campbell, Beatrix, 108–9, 117,
    147–8, 175–6, 191–2, 196,
    207–9, 211
Canada, 219
Cannan, John, 62
Castle, Ray, 112–13
Chambliss, William, 4
charismatics, *see* evangelicals and fun-
    damentalists
Chicago, IL., 158–60
child care, 14, 33–4
child physical abuse
  discovery of, 25, 103–7
  statistics of, 122–3
  use of term, 105
child protection system,
  Area Committees, 105–6
  Place of Safety Orders, 105–6, 128–
    130, 138
  Registers of Children at Risk,
    105–6, 122–3, 128–130
  see also Children and Young persons
    Act (1969); National Society for
    the Prevention of Cruelty to
    Children (NSPCC); social work-
    ers

child sexual abuse
  academic study of, 113–4
  anal intercourse, 134–5, 209
  definition of, 120–1
  discovery of, 10, 16, 25, 108–13
  feminism and, 108–10
  legal changes concerning, 55, 124–
    130
  media coverage of, 115–8
  MORI survey, 120–1
  responses to, 117–9
  statistics of, 119–124, 207–8
  see also Cleveland, child sexual
    abuse cases in; incest crisis move-
    ment; medical professions;
    MORI; pedophilia; police; ritual
    child abuse; social workers
childhood, concepts of, 72–3, 102–3,
    114
ChildLine, 25, 97, 117–18, 130, 133,
    137, 180–1, 198
Children and Young persons Act
    (1969), 103–4, 128–30
children, missing, 91–2
  see also murder, child; Operation
    Stranger
Children's Act (1989), 129–130
Children's Institute International,
    CII, 111–12
Children's Legal Centre, 198
Children's Society, 103, 181
ChildWatch, 96–7, 137
  see also Core, Diane
churches
  anglicans, 42–6, 119, 165, 201, 204
  clergy, and sexual abuse, 77, 186,
    209
  religious orthodoxy in, 44–6, 204
  Roman Catholics, 43–5, 165, 167
  see also evangelicals and fundamen-
    talists
Clapton, 94–5, *see also* London.
clergy, *see* churches